WORLD POLITICS AND THE CAUSES OF WAR SINCE 1914

Amos Yoder

University of Idaho

UNIVERSITY
PRESS OF
AMERICA

LANHAM • NEW YORK • LONDON

Copyright © 1986 by

University Press of America,® Inc.

4720 Boston Way
Lanham, MD 20706

3 Henrietta Street
London WC2E 8LU England

All rights reserved

Printed in the United States of America

Library of Congress Cataloging in Publication Data

Yoder, Amos.
  World politics and the causes of war since 1914.

  Bibliography: p.
  Includes index.
  1. War.   2. World politics—20th century.
3. Military history, Modern—20th century. I. Title
U21.2.Y62   1985   355'.00904   85-22759
ISBN 0-8191-5045-2 (alk. paper)
ISBN 0-8191-5046-0 (pbk. : alk. paper)

All University Press of America books are produced on acid-free
paper which exceeds the minimum standards set by the National
Historical Publications and Records Commission.

To my children and my grandchildren
with the hope they will never experience a nuclear war.

ACKNOWLEDGMENTS

Specified quotations from pp. 168-69, 172, 194, 184, and 215 from IN SEARCH OF IDENTITY: An Autobiography by Anwar el-Sadat.

Copyright 1977-1978 by the Village of Mit Abul-Kum. English translation copyright 1977, 1978 by Harper & Row, Publishers, Inc.

Reprinted by permission of Harper & Row, Publishers, Inc. and Collins Publishers, London.

Table of Contents

I.	THE APPROACH TO ANALYSIS	1
	Problems of Traditional Approaches	
	The List of Important Wars	
	The Framework for Analysis	
II.	DEFINING GENERAL AND SPECIFIC CAUSES OF WAR	11
	General Causes	
	More Specific Causes	
III.	WORLD WAR I	27
	The Assassination at Sarajevo	
	The Austrian Reaction	
	Escalation to a European War	
	How the U.S. Entered the War	
	Who Was to Blame?	
IV.	WORLD WAR II	55
	Hitler's Real Aims	
	Hitler's Rise to Power	
	Hitler's War	
	Italy's Attack on Ethiopia	
	The Japanese Conquest of Manchuria	
	How the U.S. Was Drawn into World War II	
	Why the World Went to War Again	
	Causes	
	The Ideas and Ideologies of the Two World Wars	
V.	THE KOREAN WAR	87
	How It Started	
	How the Korean War Became a United Nations' War	
	China Enters The War	
	The Threat of Nuclear War	
	Assigning the Blame	
VI.	THE ARAB-ISRAELI WARS	101
	The Origins	
	The 1956 Suez War	
	The 1967 War	
	The 1973 War	
	The War in Lebanon	
	The Roots of The Wars	

VII.	THE VIETNAM WARS	123
	The First Two Vietnam Wars	
	How The Third Vietnam War Began	
	U.S. Participation in the Vietnam Wars	
	Causes	
VIII.	THE INDIA–PAKISTAN WAR OF 1971	147
	The Spread of the Civil War	
	Religious and Nationalist Causes	
IX.	THE CUBAN MISSILE CRISIS	157
	The Bay of Pigs	
	The Russian Missiles	
	Why We Went to the Brink	
X.	SOVIET INVASIONS OF SATELLITES	167
	The Invasion of Hungary	
	The 1968 Invasion of Czechoslovakia	
	The Soviet Invasion of Afghanistan	
	Why the Empire Strikes Again	
XI.	OTHER RECENT WARS	181
	Vietnam's Attack on Kampuchea and China's Retaliation	
	The Cyprus Wars	
	The Iran-Iraq War	
	The War in the Falkland Islands	
	The Invasion of Grenada	
XII.	THE CAUSES OF WAR SINCE 1914	195
XIII.	THE PREVENTION OF WAR	209
	Alliances as an Instrument to Deter War	
	The U.N. System and Peacemaking	
	The U.N. and Arms Limitation Agreements	
	An Agenda to Eliminate War	

Tables

Table 1	Ideas to Actions as Important Causes of Major Wars	7-8
Table 2	Types of Society and Problems of Aggressors in Major Wars	8
Table 3	International Strategies and Actions	22
Table 4	World War I--Key Names and Places	36
Table 5	Chronology of Events Leading to War, June to August, 1914	37-39

Table 6	The German Depression and the Rise of the Nazi Party	60
Table 7	Middle East Population and Manpower--1967	111
Table 8A	Ideologies, Strategies and Types of Government Helping Cause Major Wars 1914-84	198
Table 8B	Summary Rationale for Markings of Table 8A	199-202
Table 9	Operative Phrases of U.S. Collective Defense Treaties	213

Maps

Map 1	The Balkans in 1914	28
Map 2	Hitler's Conquests 1936-1939	66
Map 3	The Course of the Korean War	89
Map 4	Israel-1967	103
Map 5	Southeast Asia	126
Map 6	India and Pakistan-1971	149
Map 7	Afghanistan and the Strategic Middle East	172
Map 8	Iran and Iraq	187

Figures

Figure 1	Military and Civilian Deaths in Major Wars 1914-1984	4
Figure 2	Total U.S. Military Personnel in Vietnam 1955-1975	139
Figure 3	The U.S. Defense Budget Compared to the Total Budgets of the United Nations and Specialized Agencies (U.N. System)	230

Preface

The aim of this book is to contribute insights that might help to rid the world of the plague of war that in this nuclear age could literally destroy civilization. The reader naturally will wonder why I, as an author, presume to pronounce judgement on this major issue of our time and what I could add to the analyses of political scientists, historians, theologians, officials, and other pundits who have addressed the causes of wars. Following is where I am coming from.

I was studying World War II in a university course as the war engulfed the United States. I then joined the Board of Economic Warfare in Washington, D. C. and later the Army Air Corps. Toward the end of the war I was assigned to the U. S. Strategic Bombing Survey, where I helped evaluate the effects of bombing of Germany and Japan. Later I gained perspective on war as I studied for a Ph.D. under Quincy Wright, who wrote a classic study of war, and under Hans Morgenthau, a famous philosopher of power politics. For the next 25 years I saw wars as a Department of State official affected indirectly by the conflicts. I have spent over 12 years evaluating that experience, while teaching courses about international politics and wars.

When I set out to teach a course on world politics and war, I could find no single text which I considered entirely satisfactory. There are many excellent books analyzing particular wars, but there are relatively few authors who have tried to integrate this material. I, therefore, decided to write my own book. I do not presume to have the final wisdom on this controversial subject, but I challenge readers to come up with better answers if they do not agree with my analysis. This is the essence of the dialectical process of academia and also of democracy. Ideas are presented, evaluated, criticized, and modified as a result.

I first review major studies on the subject and construct a framework of hypotheses about war. I then present what I believe are the most relevant historical facts leading into each of the major wars of our era. Many texts do not include this second step, assuming that the reader knows the background from conventional histories or other sources. I think this is a mistake, because students and readers seldom have the basic facts at hand or fresh in their memory. Also, some authors generalize about wars and draw examples from ancient conflicts to support their theories without addressing unique facts of some wars of our era, which are difficult to fit into a preconceived theoretical framework. Finally, I draw conclusions from the facts and hypotheses as I have presented them. This essentially is the scientific method.

Many observers who have experienced the turmoil of recent wars, particularly the Vietnam War, have been deeply affected by the experience. Also, there are ideologues of democracy and of Communism who tend to blame the other side for wars and exaggerate the virtues of their own system and the evils of the other. Some American observers, offended by exaggerations of their leaders, overcompensate by being too critical of the policies of their democratic system. Some of these Americans fear a revival of the crusading spirit of World War I, World War II, and other wars and fear that our leaders will lead the United States into another war under the banner of a crusade against Communism. Such shying away from self-righteousness can moderate foreign policies, but it clouds analysis. Like a referee, I try to avoid emotion and bias and make the calls as I see them without worrying if the conclusions help one side or the other.

Words are part of crusaders' arsenals and they can distort the truth. I try, therefore, to avoid loaded and ambiguous words and to use key terms as they are defined in the dictionary. To help communicate I use the plain language of the news media and policymakers, rather than scholarly terms with special definitions.

I appreciate the support of the University of Idaho for this project and particularly the patience of Linda Main and the word processing unit for processing the many drafts of this manuscript. I would like to thank Melissa Rockwood for the artwork. As indicated in the footnotes, I draw on the wisdom of many others who have struggled with the problems of war. Comments and questions of students and colleagues have helped tighten up the arguments. I would welcome further critical comments, and particularly constructive criticism with alternative facts and ideas. I plan to use and acknowledge such comments in a future edition, if this book warrants one. I hope the book presents a worthy target for criticism and comments, and that it stimulates others to integrate material on how to prevent nuclear war.

>   Amos Yoder
>   University of Idaho
>   Moscow, Idaho 83843

CHAPTER 1

The Approach To Analysis

Problems of Traditional Approaches

War is the most serious concern in world politics. Reporters, historians, and other observers of the world scene feature the dramas of wars and conflicts. It would be easy to fill a library with their writings. With all their attention, however, they are far from agreement on the causes of war and ways to prevent it. Part of the trouble is that observers have difficulty in generalizing about wars, which tend to arise from unique events. On the other hand, those with simplistic theories often cite events related to a particular war of a previous era that may have little relevance to today's world.

My approach to the problem of war is to present events that led to major wars of our time and provide a framework of ideas, actions, and types of societies to help in analyzing causes. Tracing the actual events and relating them to an array of such factors help readers to test different theories against the historical data. The analytical framework also permits other theories to be tested, and professors and students are invited to insert other factors in the tables and to determine if there are patterns overlooked in my study. My approach permits us to see if certain elements such as Communism or fascism were associated with major wars. On the other hand, the checklists permit us to eliminate certain causes thought to lead to war if they do not show up in the charts.

It is not surprising that historians and political observers often focus on the battles and results of wars rather than on their causes. Wars are much more interesting and dramatic than the duller, non-sensational eras of peace. Wars often change the direction of history. Following conflicts leaders change boundaries, set up new states, and establish new directions of policy. Some conflicts are cataclysmic for the countries concerned and cause losses that last for generations. This can create the desire for revenge among leaders that creates tension and the basis for new wars. Even if wars have little effect on strategic areas, such as the case of the Falklands War, reporters fill the media with stories of the conflicts. In short, our picture of the relative importance of war and peace may be distorted by the human tendency to give attention to the dramatic, bad news rather than the good news of peace. This may be part of a vicious circle that helps cause new wars. In studying the causes of war, therefore, I will try to keep the importance of peace in perspective.

The question remains of why there is a lack of consensus on the causes of war. I would suggest that one reason is that wars resist generalization. Much of the political analysis today depends on a statistical approach, and it is particularly difficult to apply statistical techniques to the relatively small number of major wars. Events surrounding a war tend to be unique, and to get a data base for a sizeable number of wars it is necessary to go back for a century or more. However, at that time the political environment was different, and it is difficult or impossible to get data comparable to today's. Although we have computers to process large amounts of data, it is hard to get meaningful data. At best, the data might point to a few underlying political or psychological causes of wars over the centuries, and these probably have already been suggested by traditional analyses. Often complicated statistical studies contradict other studies. One elaborate statistical study concluded increased alliance formation is related to general international instability or war. Another similar study concluded alliances occur randomly, except that there is a decline in alliance formation before war.[1] The samples of 40 to 50 countries that were used were small, even when working with physical data, and when using war as a unit for analysis, where many political and psychological factors are involved, the small sample was even more unsatisfactory.

Even if correlations are found, this does not mean there is a causal relationship. Elementary texts on statistics stress there is no necessary cause and effect relationship even where there is a high correlation coefficient.[2] In any event, statistical analyses of war data do not lend themselves to textbooks about wars, particularly of the relatively few wars most relevant to today's problems.

My approach is to use conclusions of traditional as well as statistical analyses of major wars since World War I in trying to find certain common denominators as causes. I have prepared charts at the most elementary statistical level which use factors which analysts state have caused wars, and then checked these factors for each war to see what patterns emerge. I use only factors that appear relevant to the outbreak of the wars we are studying. My simple check sheets do not claim the high degree of statistical accuracy implied by the statistical work of some analysts. I do invite, however, students and professors to test other hypotheses by inserting possible additional factors into the charts.

My survey of causes of war in the world system is like a survey of causes of floods in a great river system that periodically overflows its dikes and dams and causes havoc in the societies along its shores. This means I do not examine all the sources of the river and of high water that periodically strain the system but that are successfully contained. However, I do, for example, examine in detail storms such as the one that broke out in the Balkans in 1914 and the failure of leaders to use alliances and diplomacy to contain it. Before World War I such factors as the imperialistic race for colonies, French resentment of the loss of Alsace-Lorraine, the naval arms race, and friction between the Kaiser and English leaders had caused historic tensions in the system, but I do not assign them as the cause of World War I because they had been successfully contained in previous crises. For example, the great powers had kept the Balkan wars of 1912 and 1913 within bounds. I do, however, concentrate on the assassination at Sarajevo and the reaction to this event, because the leaders' failure to control it plunged Europe into World War I.

It is relatively easy to point to the hurricane that arose in Germany in the 1930s as the cause of the European part of World War II. It is more difficult to show the origin of this storm and to show how Hitler was able to take over control of Germany and conceal his true goals from most world leaders. The two world wars shaped world politics for the decades that followed and set the stage for future wars. The world wars, therefore, deserve more attention and should not be statistically submerged in other conflicts. Their importance is reflected in Figure 1 which shows the tremendous casualties of the two wars in comparison with the others.

World War II affects many of today's leaders far more than previous wars, and even distorts their views of previous wars. This impact of ideas, of course, is the major way history affects life today. For example, many American and Russian leaders are convinced Hitler's aggression was encouraged by weakness and that war can best be deterred by strength. This belief of course fuels the arms race. Russian leaders are so influenced by World War II and their Communist doctrine that this colors their view of World War I, and they believe both were caused by imperialistic capitalism. Many Americans, also influenced by World War II, believe World War I was also caused by German imperialism. My analysis takes issue with some of these beliefs.

There are basic factors affecting the outbreak of war that are unique to the eras since World War I and World War II. This

figure 1
Military and Civilian Deaths in Major Wars 1914-1984

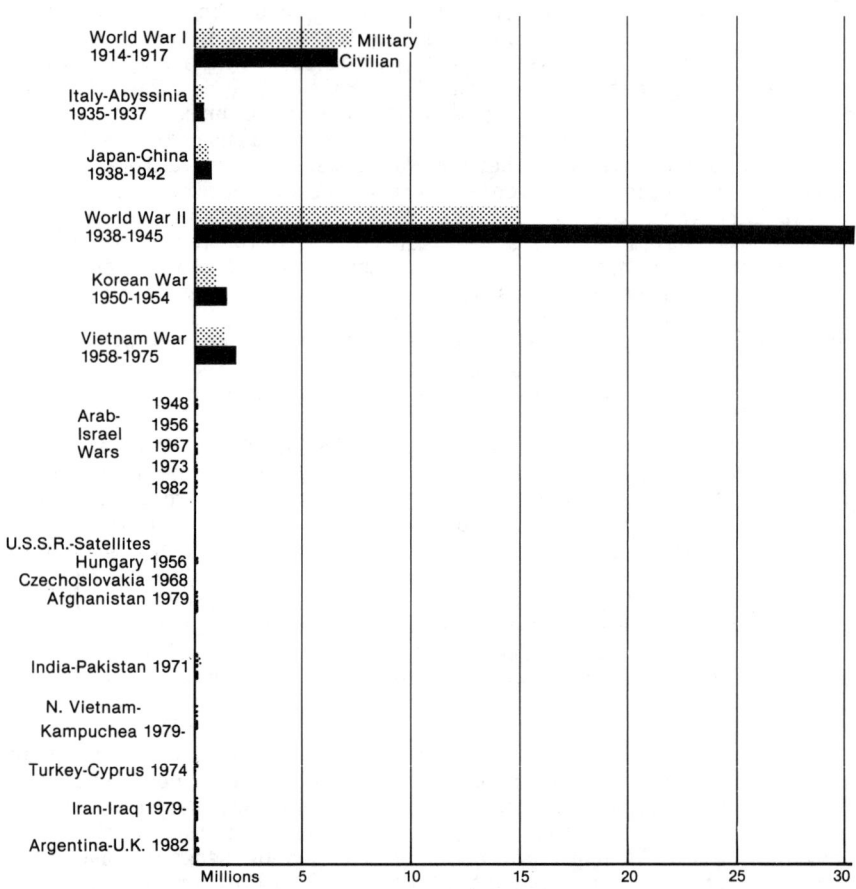

Sources: Ruth Leger Sivard, "World Military and Social Expenditures-1983," (Based on records maintained by William Eckhardt, Peace Research Laboratory, St. Louis, Missouri); R. Ernest Dupuy and Trevor N. Dupuy, The Encyclopedia of Military History (New York: Harper & Row, 1970); David Wood, Conflict in the Twentieth Century (London: Institute for Strategic Studies) Adelphi Papers Number 48, June, 1968, and press reports.

period has seen the growth of ideologies with a world-wide impact, such as fascism and Communism; democracy has also expanded. Religious ideologies, which polarized nations, caused conflicts which threatened to trigger global wars. New technologies of communication have telescoped distance and time and helped nations confront each other almost instantly. Conflicts in formerly remote areas can undermine the world economy and rapidly escalate into world crises. For example the 1973 war between Israel and its neighbors brought about a nuclear alert between the superpowers and brought about a cutback in oil exports which caused a world recession.

Improved technology, of course, has also caused casualties and the costs of war to mushroom, despite medical advances. The deaths of World War I and of World War II each exceeded those in all previous wars. The next world war could wipe out civilization.

Since World War II, new nations formed from old colonial empires have "weighed in" on war and peace issues. This has been helped by the new world organization, the United Nations, where new nations are represented and which has intervened in most international crises since World War II. In previous eras colonial empires dominated the action. All these factors tend to separate out major wars of this century from past wars.

The List of Important Wars

I have selected for analysis 22 major international wars since the World War I era that have had a major impact on international relations. They are deemed to have had a major impact if (1) the superpowers or their close allies were belligerents, (2) if major world powers were belligerents, or (3) if wars were fought in areas such as the Middle East considered vitally important to major powers. All of these conflicts were featured in the world's news media. The statistical universe of 22 wars is not large enough to permit sophisticated statistical analysis, but it is large enough to reveal significant patterns of causes of war in today's world.

I use the accepted definition of war as a "state of usually open and declared armed hostile conflict between states or nations." The major wars I have selected with the above criteria are the wars of World War I and of World War II, wars between the Arab nations and Israel, the Vietnam Wars, the Afghanistan War, the Vietnam-Kampuchean War, the Chinese-Vietnamese War, and the Iraq-Iran War. I also examine the Russian attacks on Hungary (1956) and Czechoslovakia (1968) and the Falkland Islands War. Although the latter wars had few casualties, important lessons can be drawn from them. For the same reason I examine the U.S. intervention against Cuba and the subsequent Cuban Missile Crisis. It was not an international war, but Russia and the United States did come close to war during this confrontation.*

I have excluded civil wars, colonial wars, and relatively minor or short wars that did not involve great powers and did not threaten to escalate into major wars. Thus, I do not include the Chaco war of 1932-35 between Paraguay and Bolivia, and minor wars in Africa which did not involve the direct confrontation of major world powers. I consider the wars between India and Pakistan of 1947-49, 1956, and 1965 as winding down of the Indian civil war even though technically they were international wars.[3] Some of these are "close calls," and I invite readers to include these or other wars of this century that they wish to include. If such wars are weighted according to casualties or their international impact, I doubt they would change conclusions I have drawn based on the wars of my list.

I have broken some of the wars into different conflicts to help in analysis of causes. For example, World War I is divided into the initial war between Austria-Hungary and Serbia, the subsequent escalation by Germany into a European war, and finally the events three years later that brought the United States into the war.

The above list of wars is consistent with the definition of war under international law. Under the U.N. Charter nations agree not to use force against the territorial integrity or political independence of any state. The wars we will consider involve this type of use of force, and they do not include civil wars, which are a matter of domestic jurisdiction and outside the scope of the United Nations Charter unless they threaten international peace.

The United Nations, in fact, has at one time or another placed on its agenda the post World War II conflicts on my list. It has also considered other less important conflicts and crises involving the use of force and has even sent observers to some of these conflicts such as those between India and Pakistan, which originated in the Indian civil war. As indicated above, I have not included these conflicts because of their minor importance in world politics.

The Framework for Analyses

The framework for the analysis of the above wars is set forth in Table 1 and Table 2. At the top of Table 1 are the most abstract levels of generalizations, and at the end of the table we find actual actions that led to major wars in this century. Using this chart for a basis of analysis, I will try to get to generalizations at the lower, concrete levels of the chart.

In the accounts of specific wars I outline the actual events that led to the war, and then give reasons indicated by policy-makers who made the decisions that resulted in armies marching across borders and causing international wars. This could be

TABLE 1

IDEAS TO ACTIONS AS IMPORTANT CAUSES OF MAJOR WARS 1914-1983

		World War I	World War II					Vietnam	Arab-Israeli Wars									
	Aggressors:	Austria-Hungary Germany July 14	Germany Aug 14 1917	Germany '31	Japan '36	Italy '39	Germany '41	Japan	North Korea '50	Hungary '56	Czech. '68	North Vietnam '59-75	Arabs '48	England, France, Israel '56	Egypt '67	Egypt '73	Israel '82	India-Pak. '71	Cuba '62 None	Cyprus '74 Turkey	Afghan- istan '80 Russia	Kampuchea & China '78 '79 Vietnam	Iran '80 Iraq	U.K. '82 Argentina	Grenada '83 United States

I. IDEAS
  A. Human Instincts and Behavior
    1. Aggressiveness of human nature.
    2. Warlike attitudes caused by periodic disease of mind.
    3. Self-preservation which blends into aggression.
    4. Frustration about conditions.
    5. Acceptance of war as an instrument of foreign policy.
    6. Greed and personal profit.

  B. Impressions and Attitudes of Leaders
    1. Misinformation
       a. False Image of hostile intent
       b. Optimism about own strength
       c. False estimate of reactions
       d. Overreaction to perceived threat
       e. Underestimation of suffering
    2. Attitudes of extreme nationalists
       a. Aggressiveness
       b. Enthusiasm for ideals
       c. Determination to maintain right
       d. Desire to protect vital interest
       e. Hatred of another government

  C. Ideologies
    1. Nationalism
       a. Independence
       b. Expansion
       c. Prestige & Power
    2. Fascism
    3. Communism
    4. Anti-Communism
    5. Promote democracy
    6. Religion
    7. Racist

  D. Strategies
    1. Power Politics
       a. Imperialism
          i. Territory
          ii. Economic
          iii. Strategic Areas
       b. World Policeman
       c. Balance of Power—Defensive
    2. Internationalist

7

TABLE 1 (continued)

Aggressors:

	WWI July 14 '14 Austria-Hungary	WWI Aug 14 '14 Germany	'17 Germany	'31 Japan	'36 Italy	WWII '39 Germany	'41 Japan	Korea '50 North Korea	Hungary '56 Russia	Czech '68 Russia	Vietnam '59-75 North Vietnam	Arab-Israel Wars '48 Arabs	'56 England, France, Israel	'67 Egypt	'73 Egypt	'82 Israel	'71 India-Pak.	Cuba '62 None	Cyprus '74 Turkey	Afghan-istan '80 Russia	Kampuchea & China '78 '79 Vietnam	Iran '80 Iraq	U.K. '82 Argentina	U.S. '83 Grenada
II. ACTIONS OF AGGRESSORS																								
A. Precautionary																								
1. Alliances	x	x		x	x	x	x				x	x												
2. War Planning	x	x		x	x	x	x				x													
3. Mobilization Schedules	x	x				x	x				x	x												
4. Arms Race		x	x	x		x	x				x			x										
B. Provocative																								
1. Breaking Relations	x	x	x	x	x	x	x				x	x	x	x	x									
2. Media Incitement	x	x	x	x	x	x					x	x		x	x									
3. Speeches, Rallies, etc.	x	x	x	x	x	x	x				x	x		x	x									
4. Propaganda	x	x	x	x	x	x	x				x	x		x	x									
C. Forceful																								
1. Military Mobilization	x	x		x	x	x	x	x	x	x	x	x	x	x	x	x	x		x	x	x	x	x	x
2. Terrorism											x	x												
3. Probes				x	x	x	x				x	x												
4. Clashes				x	x	x	x				x	x												
5. Attack	x	x		x	x	x	x	x	x	x	x	x	x	x	x	x	x		x	x	x	x	x	x

TABLE 2 (Revised)

TYPE OF SOCIETY AND PROBLEMS OF AGGRESSORS IN MAJOR WARS OF THIS CENTURY

	Austria-Hungary	Germany	Germany	Japan	Italy	Germany	Japan	North Korea	Russia	Russia	North Vietnam	Arabs	England, France, Israel	Egypt	Egypt	Israel	India-Pak.	None	Turkey	Russia	Vietnam	Iraq	Argentina	Grenada
I. FORM OF GOVERNMENT OF AGGRESSOR																								
A. Democratic													x			x	x		x				x	x
B. Authoritarian	x											x		x	x							x	x	
1. Military Dictatorship				x			x							x	x							x	x	
2. Monarchy	x	x		x			x					x												
C. Totalitarian			x		x	x	x	x	x	x	x							x		x	x			
1. Fascist					x	x	x																	
2. Communist								x	x	x	x							x		x	x			
II. LEADERSHIP OF AGGRESSORS																								
A. Military	x	x		x			x							x	x				x			x	x	
B. Political-Civilian			x		x	x		x	x	x	x	x	x			x	x	x		x	x			x
III. FORM OF ECONOMY OF AGGRESSOR																								
A. Capitalist	x	x		x	x	x	x						x			x	x		x			x	x	x
B. Communist or Socialist			x					x	x	x	x	x		x	x			x		x	x			
IV. ECONOMIC PROBLEMS OF AGGRESSORS																								
A. Depression			x	x		x	x															x	x	
B. Population Pressure				x	x		x																	

called a policymakers' approach that avoids the temptation to use only vague generalizations about causes of war.

Some political scientists and social scientists, particularly as wars recede into distant history, express their conclusions in generalizations about foreign policy strategies of various states. For example, observers have asserted the U.S. entered World War I to prevent Germany from upsetting the balance of power in Europe. Hans Morgenthau states President Wilson brought the United States into World War I for this reason even though Wilson himself did not realize it at the time.[4] As we will see, Wilson rather convincingly called for U.S. participation in World War I because of Germany's unrestricted submarine warfare, and this decision made sense as he explained it to his Cabinet and the Congress. Moreover, World War II took place during a period when the balance of power in Europe was perceived as relatively stable; U.S. entry into the war was what changed the balance. I, therefore, do not accept the generalization that the U.S. government acted to restore the balance of power.

However, I do not discard this type of generalization, but I include this in the list of ideas that influenced policymakers and the people they represent. Starting with ideas policymakers use to explain their actions, I classify the ideas into "impressions and attitudes of leaders," "ideologies," and "strategies." I then evaluate the ideas that led to decisions to go to war. We will also then look at actions that led to these conflicts.

After analyzing the events and causes of each war, we will check the charts of Table 1 and Table 2 to see what patterns emerge. The intention is not to obtain precise percentages, ratios, or correlations, because the sample is far too small, and we are dealing with unique events and leaders, not some homogenous statistical mass. However, if certain factors like extreme nationalism or terrorism keep recurring, this is evidence that these factors should be watched if we are looking for causes and danger signals for war.

Toward the end of the book, I evaluate the present international structures for deterrence and for peaceful settlement of disputes. These center on two major systems--the alliance system and the U.N. system. Throughout the book, I will try to evaluate the usefulness and the possible dangers of relying on these different systems to avoid war.

NOTES

[1] Patrick J. McGowan and Robert M. Rood, "Alliance Behavior in Balance of Power Systems: Applying a Poisson Model to Nineteenth-Century Europe," American Political Science Review, September, 1975, pp. 859-870; Francis A Beer, Peace Against War (San Francisco: W.H. Freeman, 1981), pp. 230-232 summarizing a study by Dana Zinnes and John V. Gillespie, Mathematical Models in International Relations.

[2] For example, I once had an argument with a government econometrician who showed a 99 percent correlation between military spending in the Thai economy and overall economic expansion as proof military spending dominated its economy. I disagreed since I had been following the Thai economy for years and was convinced that agriculture, which accounted for more than half of the gross national product, was the major factor causing fluctuations in Thailand's GNP. Finally, to prove my point I took some statistics at random from the World Almanac, put them into the computer with his formula and got a similar 99 percent correlation between horserace betting in New York and the expansion of the Thai economy. The problem with his formula was that any ascending series over a period of five years would show a 99 percent correlation. This illustrates a major problem in using statistical data above for drawing meaningful conclusions on the cause of war.

[3] I also do not include the Russian-Finnish War (1939), the Spanish Civil War of 1936-39, the Chinese invasion of Tibet (1950), the India-China Border War (1962-63), India's invasion of Goa (1961), the Soviet suppression of East German revolts (1953), Honduras versus El Salvador (1969), the Syrian-Jordanian conflict (1970), the Somalian war against Ethiopia (1977-78), Libya's invasion of Chad (1980), and other minor conflicts. For a list of conflicts see J. David Singer and Melvin Small, The Wages of War 1916-1965, A Statistical Handbook (New York: John Wiley, 1972), and Robert Lyle Butterworth, Managing Interstate Conflict, 1945-74: Data with Synopses (Pittsburgh: University of Pittsburgh University Center for International Studies, 1976).

[4] Hans Morgenthau, In Defense of the National Interest (New York: Alfred A. Knopf, 1951), pp. 25-26.

*This paragraph (page 5) has been revised to answer John F. Murphy's question why I included the Cuban Missile Crisis in the list of wars. (John F. Murphy's review of World Politics and War, American Journal of International Law, July, 1987, pp. 822-824.)

CHAPTER 2

Defining General and Specific Causes of War

The fundamental task of political scientists and social scientists is to generalize. Some generalizations at the most abstract level are little more than tautologies. This means they are true because they repeat the same idea in different words, or that they are true by virtue of their logical construction alone. For example, the statement that we have wars because human beings are naturally aggressive is close to being tautological. In other words this would say that nations engage in wars because leaders are human and naturally decide to wage war over serious issues; this throws little light on the problem. Such a statement, however, can raise other questions. For example, some observers would argue that human beings naturally like peace, and this is worth debating with those who say humans are naturally aggressive. My approach is to discuss such abstract levels of generalization at the beginning, and to leave to the last chapters an analysis of more specific ideas and actions that started each of the major wars of our era. Somewhere between these levels of general and specific, I hope to find patterns that indicate where states enter political areas of danger that lead to war.

General Causes

The aggressiveness of human nature is suggested as the first abstract cause of war in Table 1, but this factor has been challenged by many authors including Geoffrey Blainey.[1] He asserts the records of peace are as extensive as those of war, but that they are less obvious. His thesis is that people really prefer peace to war, but they get drawn into conflicts for a variety of reasons not related to any basic characteristic of human nature. He also suggests that the news media, reporters, and historians by highlighting and dramatizing war, not peace, actually help create vicious circles of wars.

This is supported by our personal experience. Rarely, if ever, do we see or read "good news" stories about the peaceful societies--Switzerland, and the Scandinavian countries, or peaceful countries in Latin America, Africa, and Asia. Melvin Small and J. David Singer in their study of wars from 1816 to 1965 point out that more than half the nations were able to escape international war entirely.[2] When these countries do make the headlines, it is probably due to a natural disaster or an internal conflict. Let there be a single bombing or assassination attempt against a public figure in Italy, or Germany, or another country by one terrorist or a small group, and it will probably make the headlines and the six-o'clock news. This is not to imply that the media should be controlled, but merely to point out to the serious analysts of war the distortions toward violence that naturally occur in the news media and other reports of human affairs.

Freud and other psychoanalysts have evaluated human nature as it relates to war. Freud asserts that people are not gentle creatures who want to be loved, but they are endowed with an instinct of aggressiveness. If their neighbor is weak, they are tempted to "satisfy their aggressiveness on him, to exploit his capacity for work without compensation, to use him sexually without his consent, to seize his possessions, to humiliate him, to cause him pain, to torture and to kill him."[3] This is the death instinct. Freud also said there was a more positive side to human nature which he called Eros, the life instinct, and that either of these instincts can dominate a person's actions.

Psychoanalysts have elaborated on his theory by calling attention to the dangers when instinctive drives are repressed. Durbin and Bolby have suggested that adults are just as cruel and destructive as any group of animals. They say that although this aggression has been repressed in children by discipline, group life can permit such aggression to surface and take a social form such as war. In their "Personal Aggressiveness and War" they assert:

> We have suggested that there is no substantial difference in behavior, that adults are just as cruel --or more so--just as destructive, as any groups of animals or monkeys. The only difference in our view is one of psychological and intellectual mechanism. The causes of simple aggression--possessiveness, strangeness, frustration--are common to adults and simpler creatures. But a repressive discipline drives the simple aggression underground--to speak in metaphors--and it appears in disguised forms. These transformations are chiefly those of displacement and projection. These mechanisms have as their immediate motive the reduction of anxiety and the resolution of the conflicts of ambivalence and guilt. They result in the typical form of adult aggressiveness--aggres-

sive personal relations of all kinds--but above all in
group aggression: party conflict, civil war, wars of
religion, and international war. The group life gives
sanction to personal aggressiveness. The mobilization
of transformed aggression gives destructive power to
groups. Aggression takes on its social form. And to
justify it--to explain the group aggression to the
outside world and to the group. . . . --great structures of intellectual reasoning--theories of history
and religion and race--are built up. The impulses are
rationalized. The hatred is justified. And it is
typical of the complexity of human affairs that something in these theories is always true, but most is
false, most of it a mere justification of hatred, a
sickening and hypocritical defense of cruelty. This
is particularly true of the political persecutions of
dictatorships.[4]

Durbin and Bolby do not go on, however, to suggest to the reader that war will be inevitable, and they stress that the forces making for peaceful cooperation are stronger than those making for war.

Most of us have known people who are affable on the surface but who seemed to be repressing an inner hatred of someone or some situation. Psychoanalysts are trained to detect symptoms of repressed aggressiveness and perhaps to release such feelings, which are often not understood by their patients. Repressed resentments can overrule reason and force leaders and people into warlike acts. Freud and others have suggested that emotional situations or crises can bring such feelings to the surface, which, when released, overrule reason and lead nations to war.[5] War certainly unmasks the evil in man, and all of us who have been in war realize how soldiers will commit violent acts they would never do in peacetime, and similarly how civilian populations will enthusiastically support violent acts of their governments against the enemy.

Some scientists have located the internal mechanism for violence in muscles, glands, tissues or in the central nervous system. This is not surprising. All of us who experience anger can readily believe that there are physiological triggers to our glands, muscles, and heart-beats that prepare us for taking violent action.[6]

Louis P. Richardson in a related view, which is my category two, published a book in 1919 stating war resembled a deep disease of the mind. He suggested that a long and severe bout of fighting confers immunity for a decade or two. At first glance, this gives little help in determining the cause of war, but more meaning can be found at a lower level of generalization. This would be that leaders and people tend to forget about the horrors of war, and after 10 or 20 years are more tempted to get into a conflict.

John Stoessinger and others have also suggested that war resembles a disease of the mind. Stoessinger hopes that just as other habits of mankind have been discarded, people will someday discard war. He notes that thousands of years ago, human beings ate each other and drank each others blood as a part of "human nature." Even a hundred years ago, he adds, millions of Americans believed that God had ordained black people to be slaves. "Like slavery and cannibalism, war too can be eliminated from mankind's arsenal of horrors."[7]

Francis Beer makes the idea of war as a disease his central theme in his survey of writings on the causes of war. His first sentence states: "This book aims to provide an epidemiology of peace and war." He goes on to explain that epidemiology is the branch of medicine that investigates the incidence and elements contributing to the occurrence of a disease in a population. He points out that originally gods were thought to be the cause of misfortunes such as disease and wars. He states that with our new scientific perspectives we can relate causes of war to the nature of social systems and of human beings. Many studies that he examines make associations between peace, war, and various aspects of the social environment.[8]

The third generalization about war suggests that concern for self-preservation can blend into aggression. Reinhold Niebuhr, a noted theologian who strongly opposed the policies of Hitler before World War II, has elaborated on this theme.[9] He states that every group, just as every individual, has an instinct of survival that expands beyond simple attempts to survive. The "will-to-live" develops into a "will-to-power." Moreover, means of defense by their very nature can be easily changed into means of aggression. Therefore, he says, there is no possibility of drawing a sharp line between a group's "will-to-live" and a "will-to-power." As man strives to enhance his own and his collective power, the resulting conflicts of groups are conflicts between survival instincts.

He continues with an analysis that jumps through the list of Table 1 to the role of nationalism as an ideology that leads to war. He points out that all governments use coercion against their subjects. Even if the subjects regard this use of power as impartial, this same power can bring about a war when used in disputes among sovereign states; leaders of nations are never impartial when representing their countries' national interests. Niebuhr continues by noting people may become willing tools of the imperial ambitions of their leaders or of their group. People get satisfaction out of the power and aggrandisement of their nation. He states that their love of countryside and familiar scenes of their youth are transmitted into a patriotism, so that in a crisis people have given a blank check to their nation's leaders in the use of power. He adds that as members of a group, people lose their identity in the nation, and they accept much greater violence between nations than they would when it is confined to a personal level. Niebuhr asserts this explains the psychological basis for arms races and the willingness of citizens to go to war under the banners of nationalism. Such nationalistic behavior is prevalent in most nations of our era and have supported the war fighting of this century, including defense as well as aggression.

Related to this instinct of survival is the instinct to protect one's territory. Dr. Konrad Lorenz and other psychologists have studied animal behavior to find analogies between animal and human aggressiveness.[10] Certain scientists have even claimed to link up territoriality to certain genes and to heredity.[11] We all are aware of how our dogs and other pets will instinctively become aggressive to protect what they see as their own territory.

Other writers have drawn analogies between human beings and their societies with animals' struggles for survival over the eons that Darwin describes as the survival of the fittest. Herbert Spencer and others have applied this to struggles between societies and nations, as if they were engaged in a struggle to bring about the survival of the strongest societies.[12] The master race theories of Hitler cited Darwin as support for the claim that Germans had the right and mission to struggle for more lebensraum and to assert themselves as a master race. This perversion of Darwin helped bring Germans enthusiastically into World War II.

The fourth factor of Table 1, which has been suggested by Quincy Wright's classical study of war,[13] is that war is due to frustration about conditions. It is obvious that violence, including war, is often caused when a leader or person strikes out at others in frustration over conditions imposed on that individual or his country. This is closely related to the psychoanalytical approach suggested above, but it also leads us down the chart into Section B which gives more concrete causes of frustration.

The next generalization--support of war as an instrument of foreign policy--seems close to a tautology. There are, however, many implications to this hypothesis. Francis Beer in his encyclopedic study of the causes of war presents as a major conclusion that military values have permeated societies and led to dangerous attitudes of militance and to arms races. He states that war is both a cause and effect of such militance. He notes the influence of the military-industrial complex in society as supporting arms expenditures. He does not accept, however, the argument that munitions makers are the ones that have caused wars.[14]

On the other hand, others have suggested that promoting the ideas of peace can solve the problem of war. Colonel House, who was Woodrow Wilson's principal adviser on foreign policy, in exploring ideas for the League of Nations with Lord Robert Cecil of Great Britain, called for a new moral standard that would not support war under the cover of patriotism. He added:

> I believe the most viable element in bringing about a world wide reign of peace is to have the same stigma rest upon the acts of nations as upon the acts of individuals. When the people of a country are held up to the scorn and condemnation of the world because of the dishonorable acts of their representatives, they will no longer tolerate such acts.[15]

President Wilson picked up this statement in his 1917 inaugural address. The philosophy of that statement is as relevant as the U.S. policy that led to the boycott of the Olympic Games in 1980 in which over 60 nations cooperated. World leaders showed their condemnation of the Soviet Union's invasion of Afghanistan by this boycott and other actions, such as cutting back on sales of wheat and high-technology goods. These leaders may have achieved their aim of discouraging further aggression, at least during the initial Polish crisis a few months later. Russian troops did not move in to break up the strikes of the Solidarity movement, even though the strikers challenged the Communist system.

Colonel House's statement also leads to a consideration of the value of international law, treaties, and agreements creating a climate of opinion that rejects war as an instrument of policy. In the final chapters we will consider these instruments as a deterrent along with the growing consensus among delegates of the United Nations, who routinely condemn war and aggression when the issue is presented in the U.N. forum.

Irving Janis has further developed the idea of the danger of support of war as an instrument of foreign policy in connection with his description of the phenomena of "group think." He describes how strong team spirit develops among those making crisis decisions that persuades persons to go along with a decision that even involves war. He believes this force was at work in the decisions around Pearl Harbor, the Bay of Pigs, and other crises where officials who normally would have disapproved of warlike actions were swept along by the group spirit to join supporting a decision for war.[16]

Related to this is the perception that war is glamorous and exciting. We will see in our description of the events leading up to World War I how at first people demonstrated in support of belligerent decisions of their leaders. The accounts and newsreels of the time show enthusiasm in enlisting for war. Young people in particular were attracted by the glamour of uniforms and the chance for excitement and adventure. In today's world there is the excitement of joining the military to control the high technology for war and its mighty weapons of destruction. If the nation goes to war, this can be even more exciting if one is pressing buttons and controlling the huge engines of destruction, if that person is insulated from the death and devastation they cause.

The sixth general characteristic element of human behavior is listed as that of greed and personal profit. Students, the media, and people of the world would probably list this first and foremost as a general cause of war. In the United States the image of the military-industrial complex supporting the arms industry and the arms race was sanctioned by President Eisenhower in his famous valedictory speech He warned against the "lobbies of the 'military industrial complex' that spring up to argue for even larger munitions expenditures. And the web of special interest grows."[17]

The news media have embedded into the public's mind the image of the "iron triangle" which consists of the Pentagon, defense contractors, and the Congress, all benefiting from large-scale defense contracts. The Communist and socialist ideologies, which are probably the most influential in the world, blame war and war hysteria on munitions makers and capitalists who profit from huge war contracts. These business circles, according to Communist theory, manipulate and control governments from behind the scenes. Keynsian economics, which is respected in the democratic West, points out how armament expenditures can stimulate the economy. Certainly the interests of defense contractors, Congressmen, the powerful defense lobbies, and others benefiting from high defense budgets stimulate the arms race. It is not surprising, therefore, at the beginning of courses when I ask students for reasons for war, that they list private profit and economic causes at the top of their list.

The Communist doctrine has elaborated on the greed factor, pointing their fingers directly at the capitalists:

> All wars in the past and present....were caused by private ownership relations and resultant social and class antagonisms in exploiter formations. Capitalists cannot rest content with the mass of the surplus value being created by the proletariat of their own country. Their appetites are insatiable. They scour the world in search of high profits. Wars are a means of rapid enrichment for the capitalist and, hence, a constant traveling companion of capitalism....War is a means by which the

bourgeoisie obtains new raw material sources and markets, robs foreign countries, and makes easy profits.[18]

The target of our analysis, however, is not what causes arms races but what causes war. I would not argue with the general proposition that arms races can create tensions that could make war more likely, and that private profit and greed help support increases in defense budgets. However, the major question is-- have defense contractors and businessmen from behind the scenes forced or influenced decisions that led nations into war? We will keep this question in mind as we examine the causes of World War I, World War II, the Korean War, the Vietnam War, and Mideast Wars, the India-Pakistan War, the war against Afghanistan and the Cuban Missile Crisis. I maintain that in my studies of these wars and in my long experience in the State Department I have found no evidence of a business elite controlling the decisions of war and peace.[19] It would take a vivid imagination to believe presidents like Wilson, Roosevelt, Truman and Johnson were dictated to by business interests and, therefore, plunged their nation into war. As alternative hypotheses, which are open to challenge by the reader, I would suggest that certain dangerous ideas and ideologies are primarily responsible for leading nations into war, and not the private profit motives of businessmen. I would quickly add that arms races could be dangerous in raising tensions, but that the above major wars were not caused primarily by arms races, although in several cases arms races occurred before the outbreak of hostilities.[20]

However, it must be remembered that wars are unique occurrences and often surprise political observers. I can envisage a future war caused basically by greed and triggered by tensions arising from an arms race. In a nuclear era when decisions of war and peace can be forced in less than 20 minutes, the tensions arising from a nuclear arms race could lead to disaster, even though there is no historical precedent for such a war. The greed of leaders of major powers to take control of the Middle East oil fields could cause a crisis that could escalate into World War III as major powers confront each other in that area. History and political science, however, can only give limited insights into the future, and political scientists by definition should base their analysis on facts and not speculation. This study is limited to an analysis of the causes of important past wars. Although greed and private profit do not emerge as major causes of these wars, such motives could threaten our future, and this study could show danger signs for such a crisis.

The above discussion of human instincts and elements of human behavior as they relate to causes of war has used a number of analogies to animal behavior and disease. One of the first rules of logic is that one can not prove anything by an analogy, although one can use analogies to construct interesting hypotheses. Human behavior is different in fundamental respects from that of warring ant colonies or that of experimental animals. War is not a disease caused by a virus or other agent. If there is any hope at all for mankind to survive, that hope is based on the belief that men and women can reason together and control any bestial instincts. The hope is they will shape their environment rather than be controlled by it.

The above discussion, however, does alert us to the dangers of following our instincts in a crisis and for the need to stay cool and to try to be reasonable. Macho action in a nuclear world could destroy civilization as we know it. This fear of what might happen is, of course, a reason for pursuing the study of the causes of war and how it can be prevented.

More Specific Causes

The second group of ideas of Table 1, which writers have suggested as a cause of war, are impressions and attitudes of leaders or people caused by their experiences. As implied in Table 1 such impressions could set a course toward war. World War I, which involved many false and dangerous impressions of leaders and nations about their opponents, has resulted in shelves of analyses of its causes and, as we will see in the next chapter, conclusions that war was caused primarily by false and dangerous attitudes. The most important of these, in my view, are listed under Part B of the table, which indicates those views also played an important role in other major wars of this century.

Francis Beer sees the hostile impressions of leaders and peoples of different nations resulting in "image races.["][4] Such hostility can be caused by a war, and thus wars can lay the basis for future wars. Hostile perceptions of leaders and of the people react on each other and create mirror images. After a period of time the process obtains a momentum of its own with hostility feeding upon hostility. Such images give political support for arms races. Actions are interpreted in the worst way by an opponent, and conditions are created that could lead to war.[21]

The next and most powerful category of ideas is that of ideologies. The word is made up of Greek and French roots meaning ideas plus doctrine, and it means "integrated assertions, theories and aims that constitute a sociopolitical program." Hundreds of millions of men have marched to war under banners of nationalisms, which are the most powerful ideologies. People have also fought for Communist, democratic, fascist, religious, and other ideologies. Following are the commonly used definitions of these words that I employ:

> nationalism--a sense of national consciousness exalting one nation and its interests above other nations or international organizations.

Communism --with a capital C is a doctrine based on revolutionary Marxian socialism (government ownership of the means of production) and Marxism-Leninism. Marxism-Leninism calls for a single authoritarian party of the workers to control political and economic activities of the state, and it asserts that exploitation and imperialist wars over colonies are a natural result of the capitalist system.

democracy --democracy is a form of government in which supreme power is exercised by the people through a system of representation involving free elections. The democratic process implies that political and civil liberties should be protected, and particularly that an opposition party should have the right to organize and present its views.

fascism --a political philosophy that exalts nation and race above the individual and that stands for a centralized autocratic government that suppresses opposition. Private ownership is permitted under fascism, although the state controls economic and political activities.

There are natural antagonisms among the above doctrines with democracy and its support for political freedom opposing the authoritarian and dictatorial elements of Communism and fascism. On the other hand, the Communists accuse both the democratic and the fascist societies as being dominated by capitalist elites who control governments from behind the scenes. Communists call for workers to unite across national borders to suppress capitalists, and Communists can come into conflict with nationalists. Russia's military domination of Eastern Europe, for example, is explained by Russian leaders as necessary to protect the Communist commonwealth of nations against capitalist attempts to undermine the system. Eastern European nationalists from time to time demonstrate against or even revolt against such Russian Communist domination. On the other hand, we will see that Communism can ally with nationalism, as in the Vietnam Wars, against capitalist and colonial exploitation. Leaders have used the conflicting ideologies to mobilize whole populations for war.

These ideologies are like weapons--they can be used defensively or offensively. Unscrupulous leaders can also shape and distort ideologies to achieve their ends. For example, both leaders of the Western democracies and those of the Communist nations call their systems real "democracy," although the one is based on freedom of expression and political competition among parties and the other is based on a strictly controlled one-party system and suppression of dissenting opinions. A man from outerspace might be confused as to which side owns the word democracy. It is possible to avoid that argument in this book by merely stating that in order to communicate with the reader I will use the Western dictionary. Thus, such controversial words as democracy, fascism, and Communism have the above meanings commonly used by the United States' news media and authors who rely on Western dictionaries.

Part D of Table 1 lists foreign policy strategies that have led to war. The "internationalists" would assert that people need not accept war as a legitimate instrument of national policy except in self-defense. Internationalists promote principles of international law and propose policymakers do likewise in order to establish habits of thought and traditions that reject aggressive war as a policy. "Nationalists" would rely on power politics and their own nation's power for deterrence against war. They would say internationalist policies are weak and utopian and not adequate in today's world for stopping an aggressor. The internationalists would reply that the use of power is necessary, but they would state that promoting a world order respecting international law is the only long-range hope for the survival of civilization in the era of nuclear weapons.

Table 3 puts these strategies into the context of international law beginning with the internationalists on the left side of the table, who consider military operations illegal unless under the framework of the United Nations Charter. Their ideal is a world community banded together which settles disputes by peaceful political methods, or by force if authorized by the U.N. Table 3 shows the peaceful methods at the left side including publicity, resolutions, reports, etc., moving right along the scale through mediation and arbitration, through breaking off diplomatic relations and trade, to police or military operations authorized by the United Nations. With the veto and political processes of the U.N. it is difficult to get U.N. authorization for the forceful measures. The aim of internationalists is to get the world community more oriented toward using all these instruments.

Other observers and policymakers believe the U.N. framework is not adequate for settling disputes in the international arena, and that, realistically, war can be deterred only by methods of power politics such as balance of power methods. These include using trade and economic and military aid as tools of policy. To the right of the balance of power strategy is the world policeman strategy, which can be either defensive or offensive depending on whether it is sanctioned under international law and by the U.N. Often there are conflicting points of view. Many U.S. leaders would consider U.S. efforts under the Monroe Doctrine to help suppress Communist movements in Latin America by force as defen-

TABLE 3

INTERNATIONAL STRATEGIES AND ACTIONS

DEFENSIVE	OFFENSIVE

STRATEGIES

DEFENSIVE		OFFENSIVE
	Balance of Power	
	Power Politics	
	World Policeman	Imperialism
Internationalist		
(Through the United Nations)		
Collective Security	"Peacemaking"	

ACTIONS

Power Politics*

Alliances	Military Visits	Threats	Military Volunteers	Blockade	Covert Operations	Military Operations
Exercises	Joint Command				Terrorism	Sea
Bases						Air
						Land

Police Units	Military Operations
	Sea
	Air
	Land

Publicity   Breaking Off: Supplying:
Propaganda Diplomatic Relations   Economic Aid
            Trade   Advisors
            Communications   Military Aid

Internationalist
(Through the United Nations)

Publicity   Mediation   Breaking Off: Aid
Resolutions Arbitration Diplomatic Relations
Reports   Judicial   Trade
Enquiry   Action   Communications
Observers

*Actions on this side of table are considered "offensive" if done without U.N. approval or if not in self defense in accordance with criteria of international law.

sive, but would consider Soviet forceful intervention in Eastern Europe countries as offensive. The Soviets would have an exact opposite point of view. A panel of international lawyers would probably judge both categories as offensive. However, if sanctioned by the U.N., the world policeman strategy could be defensive, such as in the U.S. action in the Korean War. Imperialism at the extreme right of the table by definition is aggressive since it means extending the control of one nation over the territory and activities of another. I do not include normal trade, aid, and investment as imperialistic, although Marxist writers tend to do this.

The second part of Table 1 lists specific types of actions that could lead to war beginning with alliances and planning for a conflict, going through breaking off of diplomatic relations, gearing up public opinion for war, up to an actual attack. This list is useful in showing danger signals of war. Table 2 is a similar check list showing what types of government, leadership, and economies are associated with war. Such associations do not necessarily indicate causes, as has been pointed out, but they suggest areas for inquiry, which will be pursued in later chapters. For example the fact that aggressors usually are authoritarian governments will be analyzed.

Our study of war will be directed mostly at the immediate causes of war. Traditional historical analyses start with underlying causes of conflict, and with such a perspective the impression has often been given by historians that the wars were inevitable. However, serious differences between nations can exist for decades and never give rise to open warfare. Historians could trace historical causes for a war between the United States and the Soviet Union in a convincing manner, yet the United States has never gone to war with the Soviet Union. A similar type of case could be made for a war between the Soviet Union and China, yet in this century there has been no war, although border clashes have occurred. The point is that it is useful to focus on the direct, immediate causes and events that precipitate wars in order to obtain an understanding of how wars are caused.

We will not attempt a statistical analysis of the precipitating causes of war, but will attempt to fill in the blanks of Tables 1 and 2 to find patterns that may indicate how wars are caused and how they might be prevented. At this point, the X's and patterns are hypotheses, and we will examine them in more detail while we evaluate the events that triggered World War I and other major wars and crises of this century. Readers of this book are invited to make their own checks in the tables and to add categories of causes as they examine these conflicts. In the final chapters we will evaluate the patterns that have appeared in order to work out causes, including the ideas of leaders, the types of society, and other factors that caused wars. We will also evaluate the adequacy of the alliance system and the U.N. system in deterring wars we have studied, and, finally, suggest how the U.N. could be used to prevent wars.

NOTES

[1] Geoffrey Blainey, The Causes of War (New York: Free Press, 1973).

[2] Melvin Small and J. David Singer, "Patterns in International Warfare 1816-1965," The Annals of the American Academy of Political and Social Science, September, 1970, pp. 144-155; Francis A. Beer, Peace Against War, (San Francisco: W.H. Freeman, 1981), Chapter 1.

[3] E.F.M. Durbin, et al., War and Democracy (London: Kegan Paul, Tench, Tribner & Co., Ltd., 1938), pp. 3-31.

[4] Ibid.

[5] Sigmund Freud, Collected Papers (New York: Basic Books, 1959), Vol. 5.

[6] D.D. Thiessen, The Evolution and Chemistry of Aggression (Springfield, IL: Thomas, 1976); S. Fields and W.H. Sweet, Neural Bases for Violence and Aggression (St. Louis: Warren Green, 1975); Beer, op. cit., p. 9.

[7] John G. Stoessinger, Why Nations Go to War (New York: Saint Martin's Press, 1978), p. 222; Norman Alcock, The War Disease (Oakville, Ontario: Canadian Peace Research Institute, 1972).

[8] Francis A. Beer, Peace Against War (San Francisco: W.H. Freeman, 1981), pp. 1-3.

[9] Reinhold Niebuhr, Moral Man and Immoral Society (New York: Charles Scribners Sons, 1952).

[10] Richard A. Falk and Samuel S. Kim, The War System: An Interdisciplinary Approach (Boulder, CO: Westview Press, 1980), Chapter 4.

[11] Eibl and Eibelsfeldt (New York: Viking, 1979); R.E. Leakey and R. Lewin, Origins: What New Discoveries Reveal About the Emergence of Our Species and Its Possible Future (New York: Dutton, 1977); Beer, op. cit., p. 9.

[12] R. Naroll and W.T. Divale, "Natural Selection in Cultural Evolution: Warfare Versus Peaceful Diffusion," *American Ethnologist*, February 3, 1976, pp. 97-130.

[13] Quincy Wright, *A Study of War* (Chicago: University of Chicago Press, 1942).

[14] Beer, *op. cit.*, Chapter 5.

[15] Charles Seymour, *The Intimate Papers of Colonel House* (Boston: Houghton Mifflin, 1938), Vol. 4, p. 18.

[16] Irving Janis, *Victims of Group Think* (New York: Houghton Mifflin, 1972).

[17] Dwight D. Eisenhower, *Waging Peace* (Garden City, N.Y.: Doubleday, 1965), pp. 614-616.

[17] *Marxism-Leninism on War and Army* (A Soviet View), (Moscow: Progress Publishers, 1972) translated by U.S. Air Force (Washington, D.C.: Government Printing Office, 1974), pp. 31-39.

[19] See also Bernard Brodie, pp. 290-296, and Beer, *op. cit.*, pp. 287-288.

[20] See Beer's discussion on the ambiguous relationship between arms races and war. Beer, *op. cit.*, pp. 269-273.

[21] Francis A. Beer, *Peace Against War* (San Francisco: W.H. Freeman, 1981), pp. 239-240, 271, and 275.

CHAPTER 3

World War I

Historians have combed over the hundreds of thousands of documents and memoires about World War I. The causes of that war are complicated, and many historians would agree that the list in Table 1 includes the direct causes. I would agree that many of them played an important part, but I would also like to keep two themes in mind in reviewing the record. One is that the leadership of the countries making the critical decisions was deficient. The other theme is that confusion and delays in communicating to many different centers of power prevented effective action, and that an international forum where the key leaders could have met to discuss the issue might have prevented the tragedy. These elements were painfully evident to the leaders who were personally involved in the decisions, but these conclusions are sometimes lost in the masses of analyses of the causes of World War I.

To save time and focus on the causes of the war rather than the complete background, we will start with the assassination of Archduke Ferdinand and work backward. The usual approach is to build up the background before discussing this critical event, but working backward saves time. Also, I will separate the outbreak of World War I into two conflicts--that between Austria-Hungary and Serbia, and the later events that rapidly brought the other countries into a European war. Finally, I will evaluate the third series of events that brought the United States into World War I.

The Assassination at Sarajevo

The assassination of Archduke Ferdinand and his wife took place in Bosnia-Herzegovina in the extreme south of the Austro-Hungarian Empire. Bosnia-Herzegovina was located next to Serbia and had been given to Austria-Hungary to administer by the Congress of Berlin, which started carving up the old Turkish empire.

**map 1
The Balkans in 1914**

This 1878 congress was in the wake of a Russian war against Turkey, and the European countries gathered to share in the spoils. Bosnia-Herzegovina was not formally annexed until 1908, when the overly clever Austro-Hungarian foreign minister persuaded the Russian foreign minister to permit annexation in return for Austria-Hungary's promise to back the Russian desire to open the straits at Constantinople for Russian warships. The trouble was that Serbia, which had close cultural and political ties with Russia, resented that diplomatic bargain. Serbian leaders had ambitions for Greater Serbia which would include Bosnia-Herzegovina and other areas of the Austro-Hungarian empire. In fact, after World War I, the new country of Yugoslavia was founded on the basis of this Greater Serbia, and Bosnia-Herzegovina was in the center of the new nation. Serbian literature had originated in Bosnia-Herzegovina as well as illustrious figures of the Serb nation. About half of the Bosnia-Herzegovina population were Serbs, that is, Slavs of the Serb-Orthodox faith, which was closely related to the Greek Orthodox religion. Numerous Serbs, including future assassins of Francis Ferdinand, had left Bosnia-Herzegovina to become educated in Serbia.

Although Serbian nationalism was very strong in Bosnia-Herzegovina, about half of the population were non-Serbs and many were loyal to Austria- Hungary. During the fateful visit of Franz Ferdinand, many of them gathered along the roads and streets to welcome him and his wife.

The governor of the Austrian province of Bosnia-Herzegovina had invited Franz Ferdinand, as heir to the throne and as Inspector General of the armed forces, to military maneuvers in Bosnia-Herzegovina. This, of course, had been announced well in advance of the visit and preparations had been made to give him a royal welcome. The invitation appealed to Franz Ferdinand because he favored a policy of trialism which would have given the Serbs an equal voice to that of the Hungarians and the Austrians in the affairs of the empire.[1] He saw this as a chance to improve relations with the Serbs, his future subjects after the old Franz Josef died. Moreover, Franz Ferdinand was an ardent miltary man who appreciated the chance to inspect the forces in that area. Finally, his wife, a commoner, was not accepted as royalty at the court in Vienna, and this gave a chance for her to be received with honors in this part of the Empire.

The possibility of alleviating Austria's problem with its Serbian minority by giving the Serbs a major voice in the Austro-Hungarian empire alarmed the villain of the tragedy, Colonel Dragutin Dimitrijevic (called Apis), who was the guiding spirit of a Serbian terrorist organization and of the plot to assassinate Franz Ferdinand. This organization, the Black Hand, was formed in 1911 and had a membership of 2,500. It was an elite organization, composed mostly of army officers, and its major revolutionary activity was approved by a central committee. Colonel Dimitrijevic was the head of Serbian military intelligence, and he was able secretly to recruit members and terrorists from the Serbian students who were studying in Belgrade. A number of them who had come from Bosnia-Herzegovina were trained in terrorism. Moreover, his military connections allowed him to get officers appointed along key areas of the border between Serbia and Austria and facilitate the movement of terrorists. He did not, however, have the backing of the Serbian government for the plot, or of its prime minister, Nicola Pasic, who was engaged in a political struggle with the Black Hand over military versus civilian control of territories Serbia had annexed during the Balkan Wars.

Apis was an experienced terrorist. He had organized the murder of King Alexander, the former king of Serbia, who was pro-Austria. That king was replaced by a king who was more sympathetic with Russia. Apis had also received money from the Russian military attache to help finance an intelligence network in Austria. The historical evidence seems to indicate, however, that the Russian government was in no way implicated in the planning for the assassination of Franz Ferdinand, and what money did pass to Apis was for intelligence against Austria.

At the beginning of 1914, Dimitrijevic learned of Franz Ferdinand's plan to visit Bosnia, and he decided to assassinate him. Apis left the details of recruiting assassins and arranging the murder to his principal aid, Tankosic. He had no difficulty enlisting three Serbs from Bosnia, including Princip, who was the one that committed the assassination. Prinicip was the son of a poor postman in Bosnia and was studying for his final high school exams in Belgrade. Tankosic had another intermediary, Ciganovic, a native of Bosnia, who had served as a partisan in one of the Balkan wars. By using these two intermediaries, Apis was able to conceal his connections with the crime even during the trials of the assassins that took place after Franz Ferdinand was assassinated.

When Serbian prime minister, Pasic, learned about the plot through a spy in the Black Hand, it was too late to stop the assassins who had already crossed the border into Austria. He transmitted a low-level warning to the Austrian authorities that it would be unwise for the Austrian crown prince to risk a public appearance in Sarajevo. The warning was relayed in Vienna by the Serbian ambassador there, but it was so vague that it was ignored. The point of the visit of the Crown Prince was to generate support in Bosnia-Herzegovina for the Austrian government, and it would have been very unlikely that Franz Ferdinand, who was known for his personal bravery, would have cancelled the visit even if he had received the warning. Another interesting point is that Apis later informed the central committee of the Black Hand of his action, and after a vigorous debate even the central committee of the Black Hand opposed the asassination. Thus, the crime was the personal project of Apis, who, due to his influence in the Black Hand, was able to use the organization for his purposes.

After entering Austria with the aid of underground Serbian military officers at key border points, the assassins were helped on their way by the "underground railroad" organization in Bosnia-Herzegovina. Princip then was able to recruit four residents of Sarajevo for the crime with the aim of making it appear to be a local affair.

The governor of Bosnia-Herzegovina has been criticized for not making better precautions to protect Franz Ferdinand. He did make 28 precautionary arrests of known radicals, but there were no soldiers lining the streets. One reason for this was that during the 1910 visit of Emperor Franz Josef he had been plainly displeased by the excessive security arrangements. Moreover, as already noted, Franz Ferdinand was known for his personal bravery, or even recklessness, and his dislike of being burdened by secret police protection. The purpose of the visit was to give people a glimpse of the future emperor, and Franz Ferdinand would have probably not stood for any extensive security arrangements.

On June 28, 1914, early Sunday morning, Franz Ferdinand was on the way to the city hall for a special reception. One of the seven assassins, by the name of Cabrinovic, hurled a bomb at the Archduke's car. The driver heard the sharp noise of the percussion cap being struck and saw an object coming toward the car, so he stepped on the gas. Franz Ferdinand also saw the object and raised his hand at the bomb, deflecting it, so that it bounced back into the street. It exploded, slightly wounding about a dozen spectators and damaging the car. The car stalled, and Franz Ferdinand and his wife, Sophie, transferred to another auto. Cabrinovic, according to plan, swallowed cyanide and jumped into the river to commit suicide. The cyanide did not work, and four onlookers scrambled into the river and dragged him out, and the police arrested him.

After discussion of the attempted assassination at the city hall, Franz Ferdinand agreed that the parade route would be changed, but unfortunately the driver was not informed. After the driver started back on the original planned route, he was asked to stop in order to change routes. As fate would have it, he stopped right by Princip, who had crossed the street from his original position. Princip at close range fired two fatal shots, killing both Franz Ferdinand and Sophie. The mob closed in on Princip to prevent him from killing himself and he was arrested.

That afternoon, mobs of Croats and Moslims in Sarajevo went on a rampage against Serbian properties, damaging their schools, homes, and shops. It took troops to clear the streets, and 50 persons were wounded, some severely.

The presiding officer of the Bosnian parliament condemned the deed, and many messages of condolances were sent from Bosnia to Vienna. The Serbian government newspapers and most Belgrade newspapers also condemned the deed, except for one, which was secretly controlled by the Black Hand. Altogether, about half the people in Bosnia-Herzegovina were non-Serbs and, as indicated above, many of them had welcomed Franz Ferdinand. The point of this detail is that many of the citizens of Sarajevo and Serbia were outraged at the crime. Franz Ferdinand was a moderate who wanted to give the Serbs more power in the empire, and thus the crime did not originate as a protest by the people of Bosnia-Herzegovina against oppression. Rather it was a terrorist crime organized by one powerful individual, not even supported by his own terrorist command structure.

Franz Josef, the emperor of Austria-Hungary, according to historical accounts, did not appear to be sincerely grieved at the crime. He did not like Franz Ferdinand, particularly because he had married a commoner, and even seemed somewhat relieved that another, favorite nephew would be next in line for the throne. Franz Ferdinand did not even get a proper, regal burial, and although foreign royalty were interested in attending, they were not encouraged to do so. The time for mourning was limited to four hours. Sophie was put in her place, even in death, by white gloves being placed on her coffin, symbolizing her former commoner position as a lady-in-waiting. The funeral procession, nevertheless, was an impressive affair because the officers of the Austrian cavalry, loyal to the Crown Prince, spontaneously accompanied the cortege as a guard of honor.

One of the plotters, who was rounded up by the police, made a bargain with the judge to tell all to save him from death. Thus, all the assassins, save one, were eventually rounded up. During the trial, however, Princip was successfully able to conceal the connections to Apis, the head of Serbia's intelligence, so that Serbia as a nation was not then implicated.[2]

The news made the front pages in Europe, but there was no hint from reporters that the assassination threatened the peace of Europe. In the United States, the event was hardly noticed. This lack of concern was caused by a perception that there was a stable military equilibrium in Europe. For example, the periodical Fortnightly Review of England, in an analytical article, before the crime, stated "The main peace-keeping factor is that Europe is nearer than in any past time to a stable military equilibrium, and that there is a salutary knowledge on both sides there can be no certainty of victory." The title of the article was "The End of Weltpolitik" with the theme that Germany, because of this equilibrium, was recoiling from any adventurous world policy. The same article gave a perceptive report on German strategy in the event of war. The periodical correctly reported that the strategy involved attacking France first, and then turning to take care of the Russian army. This same fortnightly saw no threat to the peace of Europe even a few week later and was completely taken off balance by the onset of the war.[3] An edition dated August 1, 1914 stated that it was "unlikely murder of the Archduke would lead to war with Serbia." How then, and why, did Austria declare war on Serbia?

The Austrian Reaction

Conrad Hotzendorf, the chief of staff of the Austro-Hungarian military forces, came back to Vienna after the assassination convinced that this was the time to settle accounts with Serbia or else the empire would be broken up. Emperor Franz Josef and the prime minister of Hungary, Tisza, counselled patience, wanting to see the results of an inquiry into the crime and the reaction of the public. Most of the press was calling for war. In the previous five years Austria had been on the verge of war with Serbia several times.

The cabinet decided first to check with their German ally to see if they could receive Germany's support. At that time Europe was balanced by the triple alliance of Germany, Austria-Hungary, and Italy, opposed by the Franco-Russian alliance plus the French Entente, or understanding with the United Kingdom. This latter understanding concerned mostly colonial matters and was not a formal alliance. Moreover, the triple alliance and the alliance between France and Russia were defensive in nature. They would come into effect only if one country were attacked by another, not if one of the countries committed aggression.

Tisza, the Prime Minister of Hungary, learned from the Austro-Hungarian foreign minister, Berchtold, on June 29 that he intended to make the Sarajevo outrage the occasion for settling accounts with Serbia. War was abhorrent to Tisza and besides, if it succeeded, it would mean absorbing more Slavs and decreasing Hungary's role in the empire. A peaceful message, mostly drafted by Tisza, was sent to Berlin with an inquiry about Berlin's reaction. But Foreign Minister Berchtold managed to get his emperor to add a letter blaming Serbia for the Sarajevo crime. The concluding sentence of Franz Josef's letter said that Serbia should be eliminated as a political power factor and that the peace policy of all European monarchs would be menaced as long as the focus of criminal agitation in Belgrade was unpunished.[4] Tisza, when he learned of this additional sentence, was outraged and tried to get it removed before it was presented to the German Kaiser, but it was too late.

The letter, probably as planned, provoked Kaiser Wilhelm. The Kaiser had been a personal friend of Franz Ferdinand and had seen him only a few weeks before at Franz Ferdinand's hunting lodge. Moreover, the call for action by Emperor Franz Josef struck a sympathetic chord with the Kaiser, who wanted to preserve the authority and empires of European monarchs and particularly that of Germany's only close ally, Austria-Hungary. The Kaiser, on July 3, wrote on the margin of the dispatch from Austria, "It is high time a clean sweep was made of the Serbs." He told the Austrian ambassador to Berlin that they could reckon on the full support of Germany.[5] We will come back to this "blank check" again when we discuss how the war against Serbia mushroomed into an all-European war, but we will first address the question of how Austria decided to attack Serbia.

With the assurances of "full support" of Germany and with increasing pressure from his cabinet colleagues, Tisza succumbed to their pressure for an ultimatum to Serbia. His condition, which was accepted, was that there would be no annexation of Serbian territories. The Austro-Hungarian ultimatum to Serbia was timed to come to Russia's attention after President Poincare of France, who was on an official visit, had left Russia by ship.

The ultimatum was delivered to Serbia on July 23 with a demand that an answer be received by July 25. It was a stiff ultimatum, clearly designed not to be accepted by Serbia in all respects. The key sentence that the Serbian government could not accept without undermining its sovereignty was in paragraph 5, which required Serbia "to accept the collaboration in Serbia of organs of the Imperial and Royal Government in the suppression of the subversive movement directed against the territorial integrity of the monarchy." This meant that officials of the Austro-Hungarian empire would be working along with Serbian officials in Serbia to suppress the Serbian subversive movement. The Serbian government, after consideration, accepted almost all the conditions of the ultimatum with the exception of the ones impinging on its sovereignty, and even made a gesture at negotiating these. The Austro-Hungarian Ambassador to Belgrade, acting under strict instructions from Vienna, glanced at the Serbian reply, saw that it did not accept completely all the demands, and announced that Austria-Hungary was rupturing relations with Serbia. At this point, war between Austria-Hungary and Serbia became inevitable.

Escalation to a European War

We will now address the question of how the war between Austria-Hungary and Serbia mushroomed into a European war. At this point, the center of action shifted to Russia and Germany. Berchtold, in proposing the ultimatum to Serbia, informed the Austro-Hungarian cabinet that it was likely to result in war with Russia.[6] The implications of the ultimatum were also apparent to Sazonov, minister for foreign affairs of Russia. After receiving news of the Austro-Hungarian ultimatum on July 23, he said, "This is the European war" and "You are setting fire to Europe."[7] His reaction was to ask for partial mobilization against Austria-Hungary.

There was general confusion in St. Petersburg and later in Berlin about the mobilization question. The mechanics of mobilization both in Russia and Germany were such that within a few days the military was guiding policy and Europe was rushing down the tracks to a European war. As indicated in the Observer article previously cited, it was well known the basic problem for the military was that Russian mobilization took weeks because its forces were so large and its communications relatively slow. German strategy, to offset the slow moving but ominous Russian mobilization, was designed to crush France first in a quick sweep through Belgium and then turn in a few weeks to meet the oncoming Russian forces.

The German Government considered itself committed to assist Austria-Hungary, its only reliable ally, to oppose the strength of the Franco-Russian alliance. Another basic element, common to both Russian and German mobilization, was that once mobilization had started, the military believed it would cause hopeless confusion to change the direction or extent of mobilization. With troops roaring toward certain destinations by train, a change in orders to turn the trains around would have caused, the military asserted, hopeless tie-ups in their transportation network.

When Sazonov was informed of Austria-Hungary's ultimatum to Serbia, he asked for only partial mobilization against Austria-Hungary as a warning and a deterrent not to attack Russia's close friend. General Janushkevich, the new Chief of the General Staff, did not explain to Sazonov that it was not possible for a Russian mobilization against Austria-Hungary only. Even General Janushkevich did not know that plans worked out for mobilization required troops to go through the Warsaw district and mobilize in Russia's western border areas which would threaten Germany as well as Austria-Hungary. Thus, for a crucial few days, Sazonov was under the illusion that Russia could mobilize as a warning to Austria-Hungary only, without threatening Germany.

The situation was further confused by the fact that Sazonov himself did not order mobilization, but had to wait hours to make an appointment for the Czar to get his approval for the actions of the Russian government. On July 25, in response to Sazonov's pleas, the Czar approved partial mobilization. Leaves were cancelled and reserves were called in for "a period preparatory to war." These moves could not be kept secret and became aware to the diplomats in St. Petersburg.

Despite Sazonov's attempts to reassure the German military that the mobilization was not directed against Germany, the mechanics of the process made such assurances meaningless in German eyes. By July 28 Russia had received another assurance of support by France, and it was only at this point that Janushkevich explained to Sazonov the mechanics of mobilization and the impossibility of mobilizing partially against Austria-Hungary. The Czar

TABLE 4

WORLD WAR I -- KEY NAMES AND PLACES

Berchtold, Leopold von - Austro-Hungarian Foreign Minister
Bethmann-Hollweg - German Chancellor
Bosnia-Herzegovina - Slavic province of Austria-Hungary where
  Archduke was assassinated
Conrad von Hotzendorf - Chief of General Staff of Austria-Hungary
Czar Nicholas II - Czar of Russia
Dimitrijevic (Apis) - Head of military intelligence of Serbian
  General Staff and head of Serbian Black Hand terrorist
  organization
Archduke Franz Ferdinand - Nephew of Franz Joseph and heir to
  throne
Franz Joseph - Emperor of Austria and King of Hungary
Grey, Sir Edward - British Secretary of State for Foreign Affairs
Izvolsky - Russian Foreign Minister until 1910 and then Ambassador
  to Paris
Janushkevich - Chief of General Staff of Russia
Kaiser Wilhelm II - German Emperor
Moltke - Chief of the German General Staff
Paleologue - French Ambassador to Russia
Poincare - President of France
Pourtales - German Ambassador to Russia
Princip - Serbian student who killed Archduke Ferdinand
Sarajevo - Bosnian town where assassination of Archduke took
  place
Sazonov - Russian Minister of Foreign Affairs
Schlieffen - German Chief of Staff until 1906 who made Schieffen
  Plan, which was basis for Germany's military strategy
Tisza - Hungarian Prime Minister
Zimmerman - German Under Secretary of State for Foreign Affairs

TABLE 5

CHRONOLOGY OF EVENTS LEADING TO WAR - JUNE-AUGUST, 1914

June 28	Archduke Ferdinand assassinated by Serbian terrorist.
July 5	Germany sends "Blank Check" to Austria. Zimmerman and Bethmann urging quick action against Serbia.
July 7	Berchtold says war will probably result with Russia if Austria enters Serbia.
July 13	Wiesner report (Austrian)--Serbia not to blame for assassination.
July 14	Berchtold gets Tisza consent for ultimatum on condition of no annexation of Serbian territory.
July 21	President Poincare of France visits Moscow.
July 23	Tisza insists on no annexation of Serbian territory. Austrian ultimatum to Serbia: answer due 7/25.
July 24	Sir Edward Grey proposes conference--Germany, Italy, Austria and United Kingdom. Janushkevich fails to explain to Tsar and Sazonov why partial mobilization by Russia is almost impossible. Poincare says Austrian ultimatum means European war. He leave Russia by ship. Tisza urging Emperor to mobilize troops.
July 25	Serbian answer to Austrian ultimatum meets most conditions. Austrian Ambassador ruptures relations with Serbia under instruction of Austrian government. Czar gives approval to partial mobilization--leaves cancelled and reservists called in "period preparatory to war."
July 26	British Fleet to remain on station--ordered by Churchill. Grey proposes French, German and Italian ambassadors meet with him.
July 27	Germans refuse to have German Ambassador meet with Grey and other ambassadors. Germans ask Vienna to accept Serbian reply to negotiate.
July 28	Austria declares war on Serbia.

	Kaiser asks Austrians to "Halt in Belgrade." Sazonov tells powers Russia beginning "partial mobilization" against Austria. France tells Sazonov it will fulfill obligations under alliance.
July 29	Kaiser sends personal telegram to Czar saying Kaiser was working on Austrians, and Russian mobilization would end hopes for peace. Belgium calling up reservists. Czar signs orders for both general mobilization and partial mobilization--general mobilization to come into effect 7/30 if necessary. Lord Grey tells Germans England might not stand aside if French are drawn into conflict. Austria-Hungary learns of Russian mobilization of 7/26. Evening--Czar cancels general mobilization and replaces it with partial mobilization. German Ambassador tells Sazonov further Russian mobilization means German mobilization and probable European War.
July 30	Berchtold tells Berlin Austria-Hungary must mobilize against Russia if Russian mobilization not revoked. 2:30 a.m.--Czar revokes general mobilization. Czar telegraphs Kaiser informing him measures "five days ago" were defensive. Conrad pushing for mobilization against Russia. Berchtold decides to ask Emperor's approval for general mobilization. Czar, urged by Sazonov, approves general mobilization. Bethmann urges restraint on Austrians. Berchtold and Emperor decide on general mobilization. Conrad tells Moltke Austria-Hungary is mobilizing on 7/30 but does it on 7/31. Tisza supporting action against Serbia. Bethmann states Germans have proclaimed "imminent danger of war."
July 31	German ultimatums: (1) to Russia--suspend mobilization in 12 hours or face German mobilization, (2) to France--be neutral; if so hand over Toul and Verdun. Grey asks Germans for neutrality of Belgium. Conrad gets telegram from Moltke to mobilize against Russia. Austria-Hungary orders general mobilization. Czar tells Kaiser Russian forces will not take provocative action.
August 1	French reject ultimatum and order mobilization. Germans follow 15 minutes later.

38

German Ambassador asks Sazonov if mobilization can cease--Sazonov says no.
German Ambassador hands note to Sazonov of declaration of war and breaks into tears.
German troops invade Luxemburg.

August 2 German ultimatum to Belgians--Germany must march through Belgium.
British decide if Belgians resist, British will intervene.

August 3 Belgians reject German ultimatum.
Germans invade Belgium.

August 4 British ultimatum to Germany to cease attack.
Germans reject ultimatum.
British declare war on Germany.

was even more confused, but by July 29 he was persuaded to sign orders in advance both for partial and general mobilization to permit quick decisions by telephone if necessary. By this time Sazonov had received warnings from Germany that further progress of Russian mobilization measures would compel Germany to mobilize and in that event the European war could scarcely be prevented. On July 30, the Czar revoked the general mobilization order as a result of a message from Kaiser Wilhelm that the Germans were trying to get Austria-Hungary to hold back. This was the famous Willie (Kaiser Wilhelm)-Nickie (Czar Nicholas) correspondence, where two emperors tried to stop the rush toward war at the last minute. It was too late because the military and diplomatic leaders under them were acting as if war were inevitable. After confusion on July 29th and 30th of the Czar revoking mobilization and then approving it, Sazonov phoned Janushkevich and told him he could go to full mobilization and smash his telephone to prevent further reversals by the Czar, and disorder in the mobilization.

On July 28 Austria-Hungary declared war against Serbia, and by July 30 three of its ships (monitors) bombarded Belgrade. World War I had begun. On July 31 there was a large scale battle as Austrian troops crossed the Danube and the Save rivers in a pincer movement against Belgrade. By this time Berchtold had informed Berlin that Austria-Hungary must mobilize against Russia if the Russian mobilization was not revoked, and on July 31 Austria-Hungary did mobilize against Russia.

There is some confusion in the historical accounts on how the German mobilization led to war. At first even the Kaiser did not know that German mobilization plans required German forces to cross Belgian and Luxembourg borders.[8] In the exchange of correspondence between the Czar and the Kaiser on July 30, the Kaiser received a letter from the Czar, which among other things, mentioned the measures taken five days ago that were purely defensive because of the Austrian threat. This made the Kaiser furious because he thought that he had been tricked into permitting the Russians to obtain a five day head start on mobilization schedules. He had not realized that the Czar had already approved cancelling leaves and calling up reserves in a "period preparatory to war," which, in effect, was partial mobilization. The Kaiser, therefore, at the urging of Moltke, Chief of the General Staff, approved an ultimatum which was delivered on July 31 to Russia to suspend mobilization in 12 hours or face German mobilization. At the same time he sent an ultimatum to France to be neutral and to demonstrate its neutrality by handing over the French fortresses of Toul and Verdun. This demand was even more impossible for France to accept than the original Austro-Hungarian ultimatum to Serbia, which would have permitted Austria-Hungary to take over governmental responsibilities in Serbia. France did, however, withdraw its troops 10 kilometers from the German borders to demonstrate it had no aggressive intentions. Faced with a French rejection of the ultimatum, the Kaiser authorized full German mobilization at 5 p.m. on August 1.

To most countries, the mobilization meant moving the troops to or toward the borders in preparation for war. In Moltke's mind, mobilization was essentially the same as putting the Schlieffen plan into operation. The Schlieffen plan called for sweeping through Luxembourg and Belgium into western France with the strongest force possible in order to crush the French armed forces and then turn against the Russian forces, which were much slower to mobilize. By July 31, Moltke saw war as inevitable so that he started to implement the Schlieffen plan, called mobilization. It was possible to stop the troops and, in fact, the Kaiser did order them stopped after receiving a message from London indicating that the British would be neutral and guarantee French neutrality in the event of a German war against Russia. However, by August 2, the matter had been clarified that Britain in fact was not making such a commitment.[9]

The Kaiser, on receipt of the first message, ordered Moltke to telephone Trier, the border town, and stop German troops from crossing into Luxembourg. Moltke, who was almost shattered by this order, did not actually implement it. He was taken off the hook by the later clarification of the British message and the Kaiser's subsequently giving authority to proceed with the mobilization- Schlieffen plan as originally decided.

There had been a number of efforts in the last two weeks before the outbreak of the war to halt the plunge into chaos. Sir Edward Grey, on July 24-25, proposed a conference of the powers to settle the dispute. His proposal, however, was overtaken on the same day by the Russian partial mobilization, and Austria-Hungary's rejection of the Serbian reply to its ultimatum. During this period, the Czar proposed submitting the dispute to the international court at the Hague, but Sazonov killed this suggestion and it did not even get off his desk. Lord Grey, again on the 26th, proposed a meeting in London to discuss the matter. The Kaiser impulsively rejected the suggestion, but on the same day, the Kaiser and the German diplomats put pressure on Austria to localize the conflict. By July 28, the Kaiser was suggesting that the Austrians "halt in Belgrade," and that the powers then meet to settle the matter.

On July 29-31, there was an exchange of correspondence between Kaiser Wilhelm (Willie) to Czar Nicholas (Nickie) with Willie saying he was trying to restrain the Austrians, and the Czar assuring Willie that Russian forces would not take provocative action against the Germans.

The above attempts had little impact on the work of the diplomats and generals. By July 28-30, the military staffs and diplomatic staffs were so committed to mobilization schedules and preventing their countries from being put in vulnerable positions by failure to mobilize, that war was probably inevitable.[10]

Although Bethmann was able to restrain German military authorities for a day or two, by July 31 the Germans delivered an ultimatum to Russia that it should suspend mobilization in 12 hours or face German mobilization, and to France to be neutral and to show that neutrality by withdrawing from Toul and Verdun. At 6 o'clock in the evening on August 1, the German ambassador, Pourtales, called on the Russian foreign minister, Sazonov, and asked if there was any hope to a favourable reply to the request that Russian mobilization cease. He obviously was hoping for some sort of qualified answer that would permit grasping at a straw to preserve peace. Sazonov said no. Ambassador Pourtales went to the window, burst into tears, and said, "I am then instructed to hand you this note." He then gave Sazonov a note declaring war on Russia.

That same day German troops invaded Luxembourg, and on Sunday, August 2nd, Germany presented an ultimatum to the Belgian foreign minister. This message was drafted by Moltke, symbolizing how the German military had taken over direction of diplomacy in the last days before the war. The note said Germany must march through Belgium, but at the end of the war it would evacuate all territory and make restitution for any damage. Belgium could not accept such an ultimatum and preserve its sovereignty.

Belgian refusal to accept the ultimatum triggered the final decisions for the war. The Belgian action activated the 1839 treaty by which Britain had guaranteed the defense of Belgium, particularly the channel ports, which Britain considered vital to Britain's defense. Britain issued an ultimatum to Germany to cease its attacks. The Germans refused. The Germans said, later, that they could not understand how Britain would come to war over a "scrap of paper." Britain, however, considered its honor and security at stake, and on August 4, Britain declared war on Germany. The war had engulfed Europe.

How the U.S. Entered the War

In August, 1914, President Wilson proclaimed U.S. neutrality in the European conflict. Wilson viewed neutrality in terms of international law, which, at that time, recognized the right of neutrals to trade with belligerents unless an effective blockade by surface vessels was imposed. Wilson hoped by staying aloof from the conflict that the United States could play the role of an impartial mediator and help negotiate the peace.

The major problem with neutrality during the first two years of the war was with Britain. Great Britain at that time owned 43 percent of the world's merchant marine, and carried about half of its trade. Britain's navy ruled the seas, and Germany never challenged it during the war.

By August, 1915, Britain was starting to tighten the blockade against Germany in a way that went against traditional neutral rights under international law. The British navy mined the North Sea and then requested ships trading with the Continent to check in at British ports to allow British authorities to check cargo for contraband. The United States protested strongly against these actions, which were contrary to international law, but Britain was able to stall and negotiate the issue without precipitating an open break with the United States. U.S. trade with the Central Powers declined from $169 million in 1914 to about $1 million in 1916, while at the same time, U.S. trade with the Allied Powers rose from about $800 million to about 3 billion during the same period.

The German authorities, in frustration, announced unrestricted submarine warfare on February 4th, 1915. On May 7th, 1915, a German submarine attacked the Lusitania off the coast of Ireland. This passenger liner sunk rapidly with a loss of 1,198 lives of whom 128 were U.S. citizens. The American public was outraged at this unprecedented attack on civilian shipping. Despite increasing cries for the United States to retaliate, Wilson refused to be drawn into war on the issue. American demands were negotiated with the German authorities, and by February 16, 1916, the Germans had apologized and agreed to assume liability for the loss of American lives. Later, historians were able to determine that the German claim that the Lusitania carried contraband was correct, in that it had 4,200 cases of rifle cartridges and other contraband on board. By September, 1916, the situation had cooled down and Count Bernstorff, the German ambassador in Washington, D.C., was able to assure that United States passenger liners would not be sunk without warning and without taking measures to insure the safety of lives of passengers, provided the liners did not offer resistance.

However, about six months later, Wilson was requesting the Congress of the United States to recognize a state of war existed with Germany. President Wilson agonized over this decision. He was raised in a Presbyterian parsonage in the South, and was known for his strict moral standards. Many of his speeches and statements reflect his aim to marshal moral and spiritual power behind a just settlement of World War I. In January, 1915, President Wilson sent Colonel House, his chief foreign policy advisor, on a peace mission to Europe. This mission and a similar one in 1916 did not succeed. By November, 1916, Wilson had won a campaign for re-election on the slogan "He kept us out of war." At the end of 1916, Wilson sent a note to the warring powers suggesting a conference on peace and asking them to state their terms. He had had the note under consideration for several months, but had held it up until after the elections. By the time he had finally got around to sending the note, the Germans had sent a similar note. Wilson received a rather forthcoming reply to his note from the Germans, who had been thinking along the same line, but he received a rejection from the British and French leaders. By this time, they were politically and emotionally involved with the war, and they were in no mood to negotiate with the Germans in ascendancy.

While President Wilson was considering renewing his initiative, the German military began pressing Bethmann, the prime minister, for permission to institute unrestricted submarine warfare. Generals Ludendorff and Hindenburg, the top two military leaders, stated they could not take responsibility for military operations if unrestricted submarine warfare were not instituted on February 1st. They claimed that they could bring England to its knees in six months, even if America should come into the war. The Kaiser was strongly in favor of their plan and impatient with Bethmann for trying to stall. Meanwhile, the German ambassador in Washington, D.C., Bernstorff, was pleading with Berlin not to start unrestricted submarine warfare until Wilson was able to implement his peace initiative.

Despite Bernstorff's pleas, Bethmann instructed Bernstorff to inform the U.S. Secretary of State Lansing on January 31st that Germany was instituting unrestricted submarine warfare. Bernstorff, in presenting the note to Lansing, expressed his deep regret and in leaving the State Department told the press that he was finished with politics for the rest of his life.

After consulting his cabinet, Wilson on February 3rd broke diplomatic relations with Germany. At the time Wilson said that he was still hoping for peace, but that he would wait for an overt act before reassessing the situation. About three weeks later, another element entered the picture. When the British received word that the United States was breaking relations with Germany, they had in hand a secret telegram, which they had deciphered, from the German foreign office to its ambassador in Mexico. This German telegram proposed that Mexico attack the United States with German assistance with the aim of Mexico regaining Arizona, New Mexico, and California. By February 24th, the British authorities were able to get another copy through their intelligence in Mexico. This source and version of the message concealed the fact that the British had broken the German code, and they turned over a copy to the United States. Wilson, when he received the message, was furious, and on March 1st he released it to the American press. There was some doubt among the U.S. intelligentsia about its authenticity, but on March 3rd, Zimmermann, of the German foreign office, acknowledged that the message was authentic. He apparently was afraid that he could be proven a liar if he denied it.[11] His statement caused a further uproar in the American press.

A book of Wilson's speeches, published with his approval, entitled In Our First Year of War indicates his thinking during the critical month of March, 1917. In his second inaugural address of March 5, 1917 the President stated it has been impossible to ignore the effects of the war and that the United States was determined to "stand firm" for its rights under armed neutrality. He noted that "we may even be drawn on, by circumstances, not by our own purpose or desire, to a more active assertion of our rights as we see them and a more immediate association with the great struggle itself." He added "We are provincials no longer. The tragical events of the thirty months of vital turmoil through which we have just passed have made us citizens of the world." He then restated a favorite theme that the U.S. should be the leader in establishing a system to maintain peace by saying that all nations are equally responsible for the maintenance of peace of the world and the political stability of free peoples.

Within two weeks the "circumstances" had occurred. On March 12, 1917 the unarmed merchantman "Algonquin" was sunk without warning, and on March 19 the United States Government learned three more merchantmen had been sunk with the loss of 15 of their crew. This was the last straw. Wilson had been under pressure from his foreign policy advisors, Secretary of State Lansing and Colonel House, to join the allied powers in the war against Germany. On March 20 Wilson consulted his cabinet and found it also in favor of war against Germany. On March 21 he issued a call to Congress to convene on April 2 in a special session for a presidential message. The stage was set for his request to Congress for a declaration of war.

In his April address to Congress President Wilson opened by attacking Germany's ruthless policy of attacking vessels without warning. He called it a war against mankind. He said that when he addressed Congress on February 26th, he had thought it would be sufficient to assert our neutral rights with arms, but now he saw that "armed neutrality, it now appears, is impracticable." Because of Germany's denials of neutrals to use arms, and because of its acts, he deemed it his duty to advise the Congress the Imperial German Government was waging war against the United States. Later in the speech, he indicated his object was to set up among the free and self-governed such a "concert of purpose and of action" that will insure the observance of principles of peace and justice. The speech continued with upon the duty of democratic nations to keep the peace through a "league of honour." No autocratic government could be trusted to observe the convenants of such a partnership. The statement about a league of democratic nations was a reference to the fact that on March 19th, scarcely two weeks previous, the Russian revolution, led by Kerensky, a social democrat, had overthrown the Czar's government. This was before the Communists took over, and the President could, with justification claim, it was now a war between the European democracies, including Russia, and autocracy. Only one sentence of his speech to Congress was devoted to the Zimmermann telegram to Mexico, although additional references were made to German spies in the United States.

The official record, together with the action of President Wilson and his cabinet, indicate that the violation of neutral rights on the high seas was the foremost reason for their decision to go to war with Germany. This was an agonizing decision for President Wilson, and he joined it with a higher aim to establish a league of honour, a system of peace for preventing war in the future. It is hard for some historians to accept the maintenance of neutral rights as the main reason for the United States to enter war. It has been pointed out that only 25 American lives had been lost through action against American shipping when he addressed Congress. Norway, Sweden, and Denmark kept out of the war, although they lost more of their nationals from submarines than did the United States. However the reasons presented by Wilson were enough for rapid Congressional action. The Senate passed the war resolution 82-6, and the House 373-50.

Who Was to Blame?

The Versailles Conference set up a Commission on Responsibility of the Authors of the War and on Enforcement of Penalties, which carried out an inquiry on the basis of official documents provided by the Allied Governments. Historians point out that this record was not complete, and that some of the documents were falsified. In the wake of emotions of the war the Commission found that the war was "premeditated" by Germany and Austria-Hungary. The Allies then forced the German representatives to sign the notorious war guilt clause of the Treaty of Versailles asserting the war was imposed on the Allies by "aggression of Germany and her allies."[12] Since then shelves of books have been published distributing the blame among the Central Powers and the Allies in different proportions.

A legalistic look at the issues can help determine who was to blame. During this century the proposition has become generally accepted it is wrong to wage aggressive war, and that nations should try to observe principles first widely endorsed in article one of the 1907 Hague Convention signed by major powers that nations "as far as possible" should not resort to force in relations with other states and "use their best effort to ensure the pacific settlement of international disputes." Assessing the guilt from this standpoint helps to sort out the many charges and counter-charges levied against the officials involved in World War I.

In regard to the first war, the leaders of Austria-Hungary and Serbia bear most of the blame. Despite the explicit investigative report from an Austria-Hungarian diplomat that the Serbian Government was not implicated, Austria-Hungary used the incident as an excuse to launch a war to punish Serbia. The fact that later revelations showed the Serbian Government was implicated and that Prime Minister Pasic knew of the crime and did not act effectively to stop the tragedy somewhat diminishes Austria-Hungary's guilt.

Despite the verdict of many historians, I would not place most of the blame on the German blank check for Austria-Hungary's aggressive action. Austria-Hungary, despite efforts of German authorities and others to restrain them at the end of July, would not agree to stop an attack against Serbia. Moreover, in the Austria-Hungary cabinet meetings officials indicated they realized such an attack could involve Russia and perhaps its other allies in war. Emperor Franz Josef was ultimately responsible for Austria-Hungary's action, and he was welcomed as a hero in Vienna after the war against Serbia began.

Some historians tend to lose sight of the responsibilities of the three emperors for the escalation of this crisis. Perhaps in using their magnifying glasses on the 60 thousand documents and numerous memoires, historians lose perspective and blame the lesser officials because they drafted the instructions. However, the emperors were not figureheads, and although they left the great bulk of work to subordinates, they made critical decisions.

All these emperors were inept. Franz Josef, though most historians say he had a clear mind during this crisis, was long past his prime at the age of 84. Czar Nicholas, who made confusing decisions on mobilization that brought the German forces into the war, was not well informed. The record indicates on the crucial days when decisions of war and peace were being made, he was swimming in the sea with his family. At the end, he seemed to be possessed by a fatalism that events were beyond his control. Kaiser Wilhelm personally made the decisions to give Austria-Hungary all-out support that triggered the war, and at a critical time refused to support Lord Grey's proposal for a meeting to prevent the tragedy.

The responsibility of these monarchs as leaders of their country was clear to observers at the time. The New York Evening Post, in the week following the war, wrote, "Whatever happens in Europe--humanity will not settle back into a position enabling three emperors--one of them senile, another subject to melancholia, and the third often showing signs of disturbed mental balance--to give on their individual choice or whim, the signal for destruction and massacre." The San Francisco Chronicle blamed monarchial cliques and absolutists.[13]

Below Emperor Franz Josef were Foreign Minister Berchtold and Chief of Staff Conrad von Hotzendorf, as leading Austrian hawks, who pushed for war and persuaded those who had doubts.

Some historians assign major blame to French and British leaders. This seems unjustified. The historians seem not to recognize the terrible pressures of time under which these officials worked. The critical decisions were telescoped into a period of two weeks. Although historians have had decades of study for the 60 thousand documents and numerous memoirs, they still cannot reach a consensus on the blame and causes of World War I. How then, could the diplomats of France and Britain on the fringes of the action and faced with incomplete knowledge, with a necessity of drafting messages in minutes and hours, and with the pressures of getting approval for these messages stop the avalanche toward war? They did make commitments to their allies, which may have encouraged a more belligerent stand, but the major aim of the British and French leaders was to strengthen their defensive position and not encourage allies to go to war.

What then are the lessons to be learned from the first part of World War I? Sir Edward Grey, the British foreign minister, in an exchange of letters with Colonel House, on August 10, 1915 said:

> My own mind revolves more and more about the point that the refusal of a conference was the fatal step that decided peace or war last year, and about the moral to be drawn from it; which is that the pearl of great price, if it can be found, would be some league of nations that would be relied on to insist that disputes between any two nations must be settled by arbitration, mediation, or conference of others. International law has hitherto had no sanction. The lesson of this war is that the powers must bind together to give it a sanction.[14]

Sir Edward Grey believed a league of nations would provide a forum that would allow leaders to meet in a crisis and try to arrange a peaceful solution. A month later Lord Grey asked directly if President Wilson would propose a league of nations. On May 27, 1916, Wilson in a speech before the League to Espouse Peace proposed a league, and December 18, 1916, in a note to the belligerent powers, Wilson asked directly if they were able to form such a league. The usefulness of such an instrument is a major issue to be examined later.

Another underlying problem, particularly in the last few days before the war, was the tight mobilization schedules that pressured the military to act before their opponent gained an advantage. German strategy was based on involving France first before the Russians with superior numbers completed their mobilization. Diplomats only too late realized that this interlocking of mobilizations would bring war. Hans Morgenthau, in his classic text on international politics, states as a fundamental principal of diplomacy, that, "Armed forces should be an instrument of foreign policy, not its master." By the end of July and the 1st of August, armed forces were the masters of foreign policy in Central Europe.

In 1914, the nations of the world had weeks, or at least days, to formulate policy and react. Today, leaders of major powers only have minutes to make decisions if they are faced by a threat of nuclear war. The mobilization schedules of World War I may have an alarming lesson for us today. If the view prevails that an enemy has a major advantage in nuclear weapons that could destroy all but a minor part of your own weapons in the first strike, the situation is dangerously unstable. Within a period of 12 months in 1979-80, the Pentagon warning system three times falsely reported a Soviet attack was under way.[15] At that time a number of military experts thought the Russians did have a superiority in nuclear weapons. Fortunately, the Pentagon generals discovered the computer mistake before putting our nuclear forces on full alert. With the paranoia that can develop about nuclear strategy, it is possible that some leaders might have proposed getting our nuclear missiles on the way to the Soviet Union before they would have been presumably destroyed if an attack had been underway. In other words, hair-trigger preparedness and action in a nuclear alert could cause the disaster they are designed to deter, just as mobilization schedules rushed countries into war in World War I.

World War I also revealed fatal weakness in the alliance system. At that time, there was no central military command of either the dual alliance or the triple alliance of Germany, Austria-Hungary, and Italy. Communication was slow between the major powers. Moreover, even military and diplomatic leaders did not realize the provisions of the secret alliances and the dangerous implications of the mobilization plans. Lord Grey, in his speech before Parliament explaining the ultimatum to Germany, admitted that he did not know the provisions of the dual alliance between England's ally, France, and the Soviet Union. The Russian chief of staff and Russian foreign minister did not know until days too late, that their mobilization plans did not permit partial mobilization against Poland and that their mobilization, therefore, threatened Germany. These were fatal gaps in knowledge. The post-World War II alliance system has corrected these weaknesses by publicizing provisions of alliances, providing central military commands with elaborate communications, and arranging for an exchange of military attaches during military exercises so that exercises would not be misinterpreted as mobilization.[16]

As noted above, the deficiencies in leadership by the Czar, Kaiser, and Emperor were a major cause of the conflict. After World War II none of the great powers were ruled by absolute monarchs.

World War I demonstrated a number of danger signals, including the following: terrorism, extreme nationalism, the view that war is a legitimate instrument of power politics, and an assumption of the worst intentions in regard to a rival. Terrorism and such dangerous attitudes are still prevalent today, but at least we can recognize the dangers that they pose.

Other lessons were not so obvious, and depending on their point of view, observers drew dramatically different conclusions. As we will see, the peace settlement laid the ground for the Great Depression and for the disillusionment that followed World War I. By the 1930s, the publication of tens of thousands of documents and extensive historical analyses, supported the conclusion that Germany was not solely to blame for the war. The view, which is still commonly held, was that the war grew out of the over-reaction of Austria-Hungary, Germany, and Russia to the assassination of the archduke. Moreover, a Senate investigation by the Nye committee in the 1930s blamed war profiteers for promoting an overreaction that drew us into war. Historians and political scientists have criticized the use of allied propaganda to exaggerate the German actions and atrocities of World War I. All these factors together helped create a cynicism among the American people and gave support to neutrality legislation of 1936 and 1937, which would prevent the United States from sending goods to or investing in any belligerent country. There was widespread resistance to the idea of being entangled in European conflicts, and the majority of the American people did not see the rise of Hitler to power and his actions as a threat to them.

Hans Morgenthau, whose texts on international politics dominated the field for decades, concluded that only by the proper use of balance of power diplomacy could a nation keep the peace. He was very critical of President Wilson for trying to establish a framework of peace under the League of Nations. In Morgenthau's view, idealism and morality should not determine foreign policy, but strict calculation of the national interest. He agreed with Wilson's decision to enter World War I, which had the effect of preventing Germany from dominating Europe, but he said Wilson did it for the wrong reasons. Morgenthau believed that Wilson's work for the utopian League of Nations was a major factor in causing the American people to become disillusioned with world affairs and to reject not only the League of Nations but to ignore the proper role of diplomacy and the use of power in maintaining the peace.[17] Morgenthau characterized Wilson's policy as "utopianism" or as a moralistic-legalistic policy and called his own policy realism. Of course, just accepting these labels would decide the issue. Few people would want to be called a utopian when they could be called a realist.

President Wilson's view, as expressed in his inaugural address, was that "peace cannot securely or justly rest upon an armed balance of power." His aim was to establish a league of nations to keep the peace based on international law and the cooperation of democratic nations. He saw the war as being caused by the despots and as a conflict between despotism and democracy. He wanted a peace built on international law. Contrary to a popular impression he was enough of a realist to bargain hard and long against the power brokers of the Paris peace conference. He succeeded against their initial opposition in selling the League of Nations and in easing, somewhat, the terms of a peace of revenge. Nevertheless, because his popularity was based on the appeal of the Fourteen Points to the people of Europe and the world and because he failed to sell the League to his own nation after his health broke, historians and political scientists often picture him as an ineffective idealist.

The hardliners at the conference, Clemenceau of France, Lloyd George of England, and others drew the lesson from World War I that Germany should never be allowed to threaten Europe again. They imposed harsh economic terms on Germany as well as limits on its ability to rearm, and they regarded the League of Nations as an instrument to coordinate their strength to prevent Germany from again becoming a threat.

Who were right? Were the realists vindicated when the League failed and Hitler rose to power by ignoring the League of Nations? Or was Wilson right in trying to prevent a peace of revenge and trying to get the United States to participate in the league to maintain peace? It is hard to answer this question even in light of history. Perhaps our task in regard to World War I is not to judge, but just to understand what happened.

As we will see, one important observer named Harry Truman, who at that time was a small businessman, was inspired by Wilson and the debates over the League to believe that a strong international organization was necessary to keep the peace. Truman's first act as president in 1945 was to confirm that the San Francisco Conference would meet after World War II to approve the U.N. charter which was based upon the League. Truman in his memoirs warmly acknowleges Wilson's inspiration for Truman's successful efforts to mobilize congressional and public opinion in favor of the U.N. charter. We will evaluate this organization later.

Finally, another observer, a bitter, partly-mad corporal, drew the conclusion from the tragedy of World War I that Germany must again rise to power and shatter controls imposed by the Versailles Treaty. We will see in the next chapter how Adolph Hitler drew on German resentment of the harsh terms of the treaty to promote his political power. We will also see how Hitler played on the guilt complexes of the victorous nations over their harsh treatment of Germany under the Versailles Treaty, to support his shattering of the Treaty. By cynically promoting self-determination for Germans and an equality for Germany in Europe, which were denied under the Treaty, Hitler divided the other European countries and promoted German strength. By the time they understood what was happening, it was too late to stop Germany from dominating the continent of Europe, and the final result was World War II, a war even more terrible than the first.

NOTES

1 Franz Josef, the emperor of Austria-Hungary, kept his multi-racial domains from boiling over by allowing autonomy to the Hungarians who were the principal minority. The Hungarians were about as numerous as the other nationalities together, and the Austro-Hungarian empire was based on a system of dualism by which the Germans of Austria shared the power equally with the Hungarians.

2 Joachim Remak, The Origins of World War I, (Hinsdale, IL: Dryden, 1967); and Sarajevo (New York: 1959).

3 Fortnightly Review (London), June 1, 1914, pp. 985-996.

4 Luigi Albertini, The Origins of the War of 1914 (London: Oxford University Press, 1952), vol. 2, p. 134.

5 Ibid., p. 140.

6 Albertini, vol. II, p. 166.

7 Ibid., p. 292.

8 Albertini, vol. III, p. 581.

9 Albertini, vol. III, pp. 382-386.

10 O.R. Holsti, Crisis, Escalation, War (Montreal: McGill-Queen's University Press, 1972) in a statistical evaluation of the record shows how leaders saw they had no choices but to act as they did in the crisis. (Cited in Beer, op. cit., pp. 16-18.) Tuchman in Guns of August, op. cit., cites the reply of Chancellor von Bullow to the question of how did it all happen--"Ah, if only we knew."

11 Barbara Tuchman, The Zimmerman Telegram (New York: Ballantine Books, 1958).

12 See German White Book (New York: Oxford University Press, 1924).

[13] The Outlook, August 15, 1914.

[14] Charles Seymour, Intimate Papers of Colonel House, vol. II, p. 87.

[15] Washington Post, May 28, 1981, p. A28.

[16] I believe the nature of alliances, including provisions for publication and measures for reassuring the other side, are more important than the numbers of alliances as a factor affecting the risk of war. See Beer, op. cit., pp. 230-231 and studies that he cites which focus on numbers of alliances.

[17] Hans Morgenthau, In Defense of the National Interest (New York: Alfred A. Knopf, 1951), pp. 26-28.

CHAPTER 4

World War II

World War I set the economic and political stage for World War II, the most cataclysmic war. The heavy reparations levied on Germany, that were later financed temporarily by U.S. loans, together with the United States' insistence on repayment by its allies of their World War I debts, helped undermine the world economy and bring about the economic depression of the 1930s. Political factors arising from that war included a realization by historians that World War I was not caused by an aggressive plot of the Germans but primarily by blunders of diplomacy and military planning of several countries. This helped create a cynicism in the United States and isolationism from European affairs. It also created a bad conscience in some circles in Europe, which Hitler was able to exploit with slogans of self-determination for Germans and demands for living space like other major powers.

The day of reckoning was delayed until the early 30s when loans to Germany and other countries came due and could not be paid. Runs on the banks started in Europe. The United States had helped create the economic problems, but it refused to cooperate after 1932 in efforts to solve the international economic crisis. For example, the U.S. refused British offers to write off reparations from Germany if the U.S. wrote off its war loans to Britain. The U.S. also raised its tariffs in 1931 under the Smoot-Hawley bill, which made it more difficult for European countries to ship goods to the United States to pay off their debts.[1]

Politically, the United States isolated itself from the action when Congress passed the Neutrality Acts of 1936 and 1938, which prevented the United States from trading with belligerents--aggressors or victims. Meanwhile, Hitler by his bluff, bluster, and the use of force, was starting to take over key areas of

Europe. Historians, with their gift of being able to analyze events after the action is over, generally wonder how we could have been so dumb. We will try to determine why we failed to recognize the threat of Hitler, and why it took so long to form a coalition against him. By focusing on the rise of Hitler, we hope to get to the origin of World War II without building up a detailed background of German history. This includes evaluating how the German government permitted Hitler to take power, and how his Nazi Party led Germany into war. An understanding of Hitler's rise to power is still important today because many leaders in political life, in the media, and in academic life were greatly influenced by these events, which still color their thoughts and actions. This, of course, is the major way in which history affects later generations.

Hitler's Real Aims

The fact that Hitler had two or three faces is a major reason that the leaders of the 1930s at first did not see through his propaganda. Some of the wiser leaders read his Mein Kampf and took it seriously, while the less perceptive concentrated on his speeches of the 1930s. The historical record indicates that Mein Kampf gave an insight to his real views that he concealed in his later speeches and propaganda.

Mein Kampf, as his translator explains, was written in "white-hot hatred." Hitler was born in Austria, a beautiful country infected by racial hatred and anti-Semitism. How this beautiful country, that was known for its culture, nurtured the seeds of both World War I and World War II, is a mystery. In any event, Hitler, even before he entered World War I on the side of Germany, was infected by this virulent anti-Semitism. During the war, he was humiliated by the German defeat by the Allies, and he blamed it on some great conspiracy managed by the Jews. At the end of the war he ended up in a hospital gassed and wondering how the "great German race" had been defeated and "stabbed in the back."

After he was released from the hospital, he worked for a while as an undercover agent of the German army attending political meetings. In September, 1919, he went to a rally of the German Workers' Party in Munich. At this meeting he heard speakers blaming the Jews for the German disaster, which was in line with his own convictions. He joined the party and within a few months became a leader. He was particularly skilled in stirring up party members at mass meetings. His party took over the Volkischer Beobachter, a newspaper which disseminated his racism and called for violence. This was a period of great disruption for Germany with Communist groups organizing in the Ruhr trying to take control, and with a former general, Wolfgang Kapp, trying to succeed in a coup against the government. Hitler's party members fought against the Communists and organized storm troopers to battle them.

In 1923, Hitler led the so-called Beer Hall Putsch, an attempt to take over the state government of Bavaria by force. He was arrested, tried, and given a sentence for five years in jail. He served only one year of the sentence before being released, but this one year was enough to write the draft of Mein Kampf. This later became a best-seller, second only to the Bible in Germany.

In the trial, and in Mein Kampf, Hitler gave a warning of what his policies would be. He told the judge that:

> In political life there is no such thing as principles of foreign policy. The programmatic principles of my party are its doctrine on the racial problem and its fight against pacifism and internationalism. But foreign policy, in itself, is merely a means to an end. In questions of foreign policy, I shall never admit that I am tied by anything.

In his chapter on foreign policy, Hitler stated, "Our aim in foreign policy is to secure for the German people the land and soil to which they are entitled on this earth." The new rights, he said, should include the very last German. When it did this, he added, it would be evident that Germany would need additional foreign soil to guarantee its daily bread, and only an adequately large space assures a nation of freedom of existence. He asserted England, the United States, Russia, and China, had ten times the space of the Reich. He said the frontiers of 1914, imposed by the Treaty of Versailles, were a political absurdity. When he spoke of lebensraum, or living space, he made it clear that he spoke of Russia and its vassal states. The major enemy, he claimed, was the "Jewish Hydra." He ranted on how the Jews had corrupted states such as Russia and promoted Bolshevism as a plan for them to achieve world domination.

The book was written in 1923 immediately after the French invasion of the Ruhr, which forced Germany to resume its reparation payments. Hitler stressed that France was the mortal enemy of the German nation. He looked forward to an alliance with Britain and Italy to isolate France, but he asserted in 1923 that Germany would have to rearm in order to make itself fit for an alliance.

This, then, was the kernel of his policy, to rearm Germany, and to strike out to achieve additional land in Europe and in the great world island of Europe and Asia. This meant attacking the Russian Slavs who had "contaminated" Austria. It also implied ultimately attacking France, England, and possibly the United States to get Germany its lebensraum.

Hitler's public position in the 1930s was moderate only in comparison with the rantings of Mein Kampf[2] Privately, on May

22, 1930 in a conversation with Otto Strasser, that was published in a pamphlet, he stated, "The Nordic race has a right to rule the world and we must take this racial right as a guiding star of our foreign policy." He added that cooperation with Russia is out of the question but that the interests of Germany demanded cooperation with England and later with the United States.[3] A few months later, he publicly repudiated in the strongest terms Germany's sole responsibility for World War I.[4] Another main theme used in his speeches to appeal to the German electorate was a necessity to stamp out Communism.

After he achieved power in 1933, his speeches became less extreme. In a May 17, 1933 speech in the Reischstag on peace he asserted Germany was willing to disarm completely if its neighbors did the same. His aim was to get a position of equality of Germany with the other nations. Other countries, he said, should not fear an invasion. Germany, he claimed, was willing to renounce offensive weapons if the rest of the world did the same.

Hitler instituted a rapid policy of rearmament, stating that Germans must be the first soldiers in the world. He rationalized it by saying that German armies would convince others to seek peace.[5] Hedgehogs, he asserted, do not attack unless threatened. Therefore, he said, Germany must arm in order to be left in peace.

One of his themes, which for a time blinded leaders like Prime Minister Chamberlain of Britain and other appeasers, was his appeal to the principle of self-determination. His takeover of Austria, and later Czechoslovakia, was excused on the basis of the Wilsonian principle of self-determination for the oppressed Germans, and in 1938, he was bragging that he had fought for and won the right of self-determination for 6 1/2 million Germans in Austria.

In answer to President Roosevelt's long peace appeal, Hitler on April 28th, told the Reischstag that since Versailles there had been 14 wars, none of them started by Germany. He accused the United States of six military interventions since Versailles and the Soviets of ten wars. Germany, he said, was no more to blame for World War I than any other nation. He said the states bordering on Germany assured him that they do not feel threatened. He said it was easy for President Roosevelt to make such a peace appeal since the United States had 15 times the living space of Germany.

At the same time he was telling this to the public, he was explaining his policy in confidence to close associates as follows. "War is life. Any struggle is war...What is war but cunning, deception, delusion, attack, and surprise?" He told them he was usually willing to use any weapon, including bacteria and gas to win in the war. He was willing to demoralize the enemy by murder, terror, sabotage, and then a gigantic attack. No agreements or international law would prevent him from using any advantage or instrument in order to achieve his ends.[6] He would not, he told his close confidantes, shrink from a war with Britain. He would also attack India and Canada. Although he might make an alliance with Russia, this would not stop him from attacking Russia after a victory in the west. Shattering the hordes of the Slav empire, he continued, would open the door to permanent mastery of the world. At the same time, after conquering Russia, he would have to develop a technique of de-population--removal of entire racial units in Russia. Nature is cruel, he said; therefore, we too must be cruel. This at first, he said, would not require extermination, but keeping their men and women separate for years to dam their natural fertility.

The public speeches of Hitler were cleverly designed to exploit the isolationism, wishful thinking, bad conscience, and pacifism of many people in Europe and the United States. This was reinforced by the historians' re-examination of the causes of World War I which indicated that other leaders and countries shared the blame. This fit in with historians' judgments that Versailles was a harsh peace that even violated its own proclaimed principle of self-determination, particularly in relation to Germany, which was reduced in size and power by the peace treaty. At the same time, Hitler's ideology, as watered down for public consumption, gave the Germans someone to blame for their economic and political difficulties. Moreover, Germany's big rearmament program created an economic dynamism that was the envy of economists in other countries who were struggling with answers to the world depression. Germany, in contrast, was putting people to work and becoming a major world power with the totalitarian guidance of the Nazis. Hitler bragged that he had come to power by constitutional means, which was true only if you did not look beyond the political facade which was backed by ruthless, political maneuvering including the use of terror. Moreover, he pictured the relatively democratic governments of Austria and Czechoslovakia, which he had overthrown, as dictatorships. Non-discriminating observers could find much to criticize in those two countries.

We will now trace the political steps by which Hitler took over the German government and the later steps as he conquered one country after another until British leaders finally drew the line at Poland. Hitler, flushed with success and his diplomacy of bluff, continued his drive for lebensraum by an attack on Poland, which brought about the European part of World War II. We will then look at how the United States was drawn into war with Japan, which made the war world-wide in scope.

Hitler's Rise to Power

The question of how Hitler achieved power is an unusually important question since Hitler dominated the action that led the world into World War II. My thesis is that World War II could be called Hitler's war. The conventional historical treatment points out how World War II started with Japan's invasion of Manchuria and Mussolini's invasion of Ethiopia. The fact that these aggressors got away with it certainly encouraged Hitler. I would argue, however, that Hitler was so fanatic and single-minded in his desire to achieve European and even world domination for the German race, that he would have proceeded close to the actual historical schedule even if the Manchurian and Ethiopian wars had not occurred. He certainly in all his speeches does not refer to these other wars as major factors in his thinking.

After the economic and political respite provided by the Dawes and Young plans to reschedule reparations payments and the Locarno detente between Germany and France, Chancellor Bruning, a strong but rather colorless statesman from the Center Party of Germany, was appointed chancellor. This was a period after the American stock market crashed, beginning a world depression that had a severe impact on the German economy. Table 6 reflects the snow-balling of the depression during the critical years in which Bruning was replaced and Hitler was able to achieve control. Many authors have attributed the growing strength of the Nazi Party to the promises of the Nazis to strengthen Germany's society, to bring order out of the economic chaos, and correct the injustices of the Versailles Treaty.

TABLE 6

THE GERMAN DEPRESSION AND THE RISE OF THE NAZI PARTY

	German Unemployment	Nazi Vote Percentage
1928	1,300,000	2.6
1930	3,000,000	18
1931	4,350,000	-
1932	5,200,000	33-37
1933	6,000,000	44

After serving his sentence for the 1923 putsch attempt, Hitler built up the Nazi Party by creating a shadow government structure throughout Germany down to small Nazi cells. He had learned from his putsch attempt the hazards of opposing the basic political system, including the German army and influential political groups, so he restrained some of the more radical of his followers, like Strasser, who were trying to create a proletarian, socialist mass movement. Hitler seized on the 1930 depression, blaming it on the Jews and the socialists, and used the rise in the Communist vote as a bogey to frighten the German middle class and also the

German army. As the depression deepened, he asserted that it was opening the eyes of the German people to the "swindles" of the Marxists and the Jews.[7]

Bruning's strategy to combat the depression was to obtain a drastic reduction in Germany's reparations payments joined with an agreement on the part of the Allies to permit German equality of armaments, thereby ending the Versailles' restrictions and strengthening Bruning's hand against the radicals including Hitler. Actually, he came very close to achieving this remarkable feat in the midst of the depression of the early 1930s. I remember in a speech that he gave at the University of Chicago after World War II his claiming if the United States and other nations had moved a little faster and cooperated with Germany on this matter, that he could have headed off Hitler's rise to power. Winston Churchill, in his book The Gathering Storm, makes the same point indicating that Bruning came within a few hours of achieving such an agreement with French, British, and American diplomats in Geneva. Churchill adds that if he had succeeded, he "might have led the German people into the enjoyment of a stable and civilized constitution and open, peaceful channels of intercourse with their neighbors."[8]

President Hoover did get Congress to call a moratorium of one year on international debts from December 1931 to December 1932, but Congress, in approving it, added that none of the debt should be cancelled. The U.S. role during this period was not something to be praised. The Hearst press and American senators were insisting that the U.S. not be a party to any international agreement to reduce German and European war debts to the United States.

In the midst of these negotiations, General von Schleicher, a key official in the Ministry of Defense, who had a great deal of influence with President Hindenburg, persuaded him to dismiss Bruning. One of Hindenburg's associates, von Papen, a former general staff officer and politician with no political backing, was appointed by Hindenburg to be Chancellor. Von Papen was able to rule by decree with the support of Hindenburg during the 1932 elections. Hitler threw himself into the campaign, and in July, 1932 elections more than doubled his strength compared to two years before. The Nazi's seats increased to 230 out of a total of 608 members and became the largest block of votes. The Communists increased their strength to 89 from 77, and the Catholic Center Party increased its strength from 68 to 73. The Social Democrats, as a second largest party, lost from 143 to 133.

At this point Hindenburg was still well in control of the situation, and he bluntly refused to accept Hitler's demand to become chancellor and take over key ministries and the head of the powerful and strategic Prussian government apparatus. Hindenburg pointed out that the Nazis were not trusted and that they should work with other parties to dispel that distrust.[9] Meanwhile, von

Papen had obtained a decree from Hindenburg to dissolve the Reichstag, which would permit rule by decree. Before he could present it, however, Hermann Goering, one of the Nazi leaders who was president of the parliament (Reichstag), permitted a motion of censure and the government fell, thus requiring new elections.

These elections were scheduled in November, 1932. In these elections, the Nazis lost seats, dropping from 230 to 196, while the Communist seats rose up to 100. The Socialists again lost some ground, and the Center Party remained about the same. Again, Hitler demanded the chancellorship and the right to rule by emergency decree, which could be granted by Hindenburg. Hindenburg still indicated he feared this would develop into a party dictatorship. Hindenburg then appointed Schleicher as Chancellor on December 2, but that government soon fell as a result of Hitler's Nazis and the Communist party voting against it.

On January 30, 1933 Hindenburg named Hitler as Chancellor with von Papen agreeing to be Vice-Chancellor. Von Papen hoped to control Hitler in the political deal in which Hindenburg agreed von Papen would accompany Hitler whenever he saw Hindenburg on official business. However, Hitler appointed Goering as Minister of Interior for Prussia, which controlled the police and the strategic area of Berlin. Von Papen was Premier of Prussia with no real power or political backing, and he was completely out-maneuvered by the Nazis. Hitler again got the government dissolved and called for new elections. By this time, the Nazis, with Goering's assistance, were terrorizing and arresting political opponents, fighting with the Communists, and taking advantage of their government backing to get political support for the Nazi party. In February, they exploited an incident, in which a Dutch half-wit set fire to the Reichstag, by blaming it on the Communists. Goering used this as an excuse to arrest leading Communists, who made up one of the major parties in the Reichstag.

In the March 5 elections, the Nazis, in the midst of all this confusion, repression, and economic distress, were able to obtain 288 seats or 44 percent of the votes. They combined with the right-wing Nationalist party to get a majority in the Reichstag. Hitler then, by further terror tactics and illegal pressure on Reichstag deputies, including the arrest of the Communist members, was able to railroad a two-thirds vote through the Reichstag giving Hitler's cabinet full legislative powers for four years. The vote was 444 for, and 84 against, all of whom were Social Democrats. Within a fortnight Hitler had appointed Nazis as governors of all the states and given them full powers. By July, the Nazi party was decreed as the only legal party in Germany, and in August, after Hindenburg died, Hitler became Reich Chancellor and head of the armed forces.

Hitler then bought off the military by immediately instituting a major program of rearmament for Germany and agreeing to disband his private Nazi para-military units.

Hitler was able to claim, even though the claim was not justified, that he had achieved power by constitutional means. His propaganda also claimed that the Nazis had been able to save Germany from a Communist revolution. By this time the worst of the world depression was over, and Germany, by insulating its economy from the rest of Europe, was able to start a massive rearmament program. This had the economic effect of putting the Germans back to work and causing Germany to lead Europe, not only in economic recovery, but in arms production. This helped consolidate his position for the explosive moves of Germany to conquer Europe and dominate the world.

Hitler with his propaganda stretched and distorted the facts so that many Germans as well as foreigners, thought his aims were to correct the injustices of the Versailles Treaty. Hitler's cynical manipulation of public opinion and his ability to lie for years and get away with it created a cynicism that still affects international politics. Many world leaders who remember Hitler still believe that international politics is a jungle where commitments are not to be trusted, that nations are justified in using any means to put down an opponent who could threaten their vital interests, and that any powerful aggressor is potentially a Hitler.

The saddest lessons derive from the fact that Hitler's rise to power was touch-and-go at certain critical periods. If the United States and other Western powers had been more forthcoming in adjusting the heavy burden of reparations payments, which were never paid anyway, the moderate Bruning might have survived Hitler's political offensive. As we will see, if the Western powers with Russia had opposed Hitler's moves into the Rhineland, Austria, Czechoslovakia, or Poland, this could have given the necessary margin of support to German generals who were plotting to overthrow him. Our task, however, is not to grieve over the "ifs" of history, but to move forward to analyze events and learn lessons that could prevent further world tragedies.

Hitler's War

A conventional treatment of World War II starts with the Japanese invasion of Manchuria and the failure of the League of Nations and the world community to stop it. Then, many historians proceed to the Italian war with Ethiopia and Mussolini's attempt to build an Italian empire and continue with Hitler's aggressive moves against Austria, Czechoslovakia, and Poland. Such an approach implies a chain of causation, but I would argue Hitler would have started the European conflicts even if Japan and Italy had never existed. Hitler, as evident in <u>Mein Kampf</u> and from the historical record, was determined from the beginning to dominate all of Europe, including Russia, and probably the world. At first, his aims were evident to only a relatively few people. Only a much smaller group of leaders realized the world was on the verge of nuclear weapons, and that a madman, such as Hitler, might have just succeeded in dominating the world.

Hitler's first target was Austria, a country where he was born. As early as July, 1934, a little over a year after he came to power, he was manipulating an Austrian Nazi movement to take over Austria. On July 25th, 154 members of the Austrian Nazi party dressed in Austrian army uniforms tried to initiate a coup by shooting Chancellor Dollfuss. The government had been forewarned to some extent by captured documents that such a scheme was under way, and Minister of Justice Schuschnigg rallied the police and military forces to arrest the rebels. More important, Mussolini mobilized four Italian divisions on the Brenner pass as a warning, since the Italians were reluctant to have a powerful and aggressive German neighbor on their border. Hitler quickly changed his prearranged propaganda announcements, and in the face of this show of force expressed regret and declared that this was entirely an Austrian affair.

By 1935 British and French leaders were increasingly concerned about Germany's growing power and Hitler's aggressive aims. They approached him in February, 1935 with a proposal for equality of armaments with the West and guarantees to eastern European countries, similar to the German guarantees to Western countries by Stresemann before Hitler came to power. Hitler played it cool and offered to discuss the proposals with the French and the British. Then, in a clever tactical move, he announced a month later that Germany was starting military conscription and would increase the German forces to 36 divisions, roughly one-half million men. This flouted the military restrictions of Versailles. The German generals were delighted, and Hitler made an impressive celebration of his decision, which provoked no serious challenge.

Predictably, the British, French, and the Italians objected, along with the League Council. Hitler, on May 21, 1935 replied with an impressive speech of peace. All he wanted was peace, he said, and he rejected the terrors of war. He asserted that the Nazi racial theory opposed including non-Germans into the Reich since that would weaken Germany and eventually bring about its defeat. War, he sanctimoniously said, destroys the flower of every nation. Germany, he asserted, does not want an <u>Anschluss</u> with Austria. He also pointed to the recent non-aggression pact with Poland. He added, that Germany renounced claims to Alsace-Lorraine, and it was ready toagree to any limitation on armaments with the British and French. He even pledged to abide by the demilitarization of the Rhineland, which was one of the provisions of the Versailles treaty.

In another clever diplomatic move to split the British and the French, Germany agreed in bilateral discussions with the British to limit the German fleet to 35 percent of the British fleet in tonnage. The British without even consulting the French agreed, even though observers like Winston Churchill pointed out that it was a meaningless concession by Germany. It would take ten years for German shipyards to build up to the level of 35 percent of the British fleet. This agreement abolished another Versailles provision.

Hitler continued to move on the diplomatic front by calling attention to the element of instability caused by the Franco-Russian pact. One year after it was concluded, Hitler used this as an excuse to withdraw his "peace speech" statement that Germany would not re-occupy the Rhineland. On March 7, 1936 German troops marched into the Rhineland in violation of its demilitarization under the Versailles Treaty. Again, Hitler accompanied this with a speech saying that this permitted Germany to regain its honor and that it would never break the peace. Foreign observers burdened with the guilt of the unjust terms of the Treaty of Versailles could not argue against a country moving its armed forces into its own territory, particularly when France had moved through this demilitarized zone to humiliate Germany in 1923. Blomberg, Hitler's Minister of Defense, was ready to retreat and even gave orders to do so if the French made a move, but no country demanded withdrawal.

On February 12, 1938 Hitler summoned Chancellor Schuschnigg of Austria to Berchtesgaden, Hitler's mountain retreat in Bavaria. He threatened Schuschnigg with an overnight invasion of Austria and a ruthless war if Schuschnigg did not yield to Hitler's demands, which included pardoning the Nazis who had been imprisoned in Austria, including Austrian Nazis in Schuschnigg's party alliance, and appointing a Nazi as Minister of Interior. Schuschnigg signed the protocol demanded by Hitler. Arriving back in Austria, however, Schuschnigg countered with a call for a plebiscite to take place within a few days. Hitler was furious and claimed it was a Communist plot. He threatened to invade immediately. Schuschnigg could find no international support, including Italy which was now aligning with Germany, so he resigned and permitted a pro-Nazi to take over as chancellor. The German army immediately marched into Austria and incorporated Austria as part of the Reich. As Churchill points out in his memoires, Germany was still in a weak position, so weak that its tanks broke down in clear weather on the road to Vienna. Nevertheless, Hitler, by one master stroke of deception and threat of force, had gained 6,750,000 Austrians for Greater Germany. On the map Czechoslovakia was now in a more vulnerable position with the new Germany facing it on three sides.

In 1937, Hitler began the planning to take over Czechoslovakia. The German general staff agreed, since such a move would

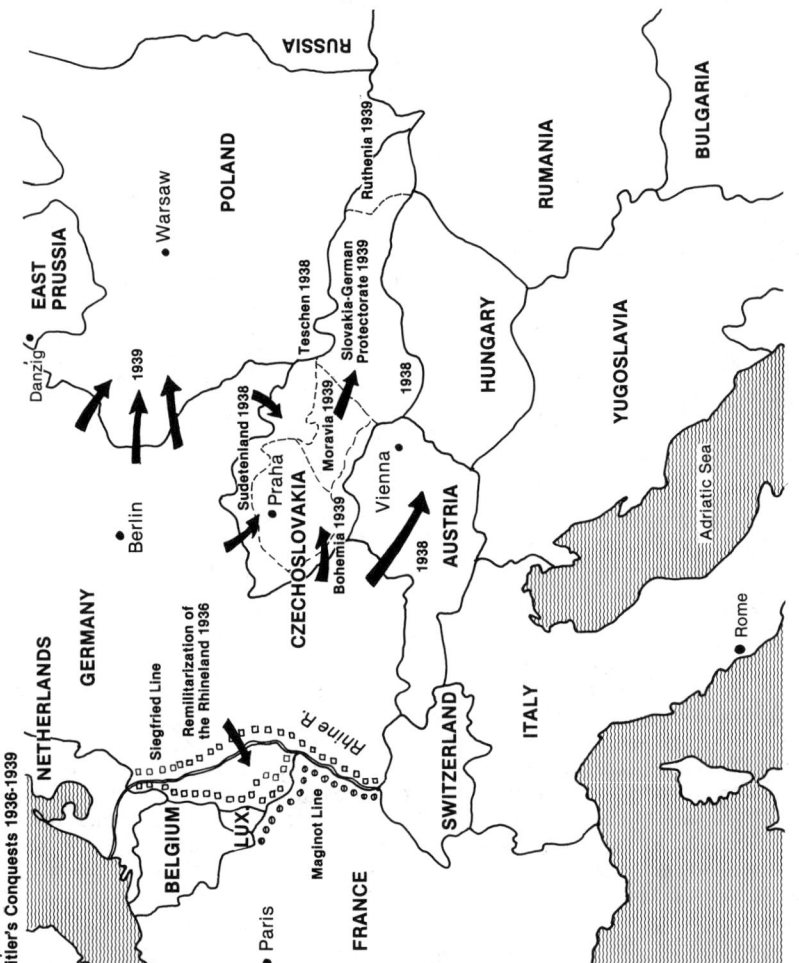

map 2
Hitler's Conquests 1936-1939

eliminate Czechoslovakia as a major military threat and as a base for possible action by Russia, Czechoslovakia's ally. Churchill's history and account of the critical 1936-1938 period praises the Russian policy of this era and severely criticizes that of Britain's Prime Minister Chamberlain. Particularly after the Austrian Anschluss the Russians sounded the alarm and proposed a conference of the major powers to implement the Franco-Soviet defense treaty within the framework of League of Nations action. During this period, the French were only lukewarm. Prime Minister Chamberlain of Britain delayed and would not agree to Churchill's proposal for a Franco-British-Russian alliance to stop the Nazis. During the consultations of this period, in September 1938, at the height of the Czechoslovakian crisis, the French asked Britain what help France could expect if the security of France were threatened. The reply from London was that it would provide only two divisions and 150 airplanes in the first six months of war. This was virtually the same as no help at all to France, which hesitated to challenge Germany when France could mobilize about 100 divisions.

Hitler's threat to invade Czechoslovakia resulted in an offer of Chamberlain to fly to Berchtesgaden to discuss the issues. Chamberlain's yielding to German threats by visiting Hitler to ask for a compromise had far reaching and disastrous effects. As Churchill points out in The Gathering Storm, the German generals had a plot ready to arrest Hitler. Their fear was that by his challenging Czechoslovakia with its 35 divisions, Hitler would have to withdraw troops from the Siegfried line next to France and open Germany up to a French invasion where French troops would outnumber the Germans almost 8 to 1. Moreover, such a move by Hitler might bring Soviet armies through Poland or Rumania to fight Germany, which at that point was not ready to fight in such a war.[10]

In Chamberlain's third meeting with Hitler at Munich, in which neither the Czechs nor the Russians were invited to attend, Chamberlain agreed to the evacuation by the Czech army of the Sudetenland border areas of Czechoslovakia populated by Germans, with an international commission to determine the final boundaries. Hitler added what later proved to be a meaningless commitment to consult to settle differences and not to go to war. At the same time, the post-war records indicate that Hitler and Mussolini, at that time, were secretly plotting to invade England.[11]

Because of dramatic success of his bluffs, not until late in the war did the German general staff conspirators again challenge Hitler's leadership. In a single year Hitler gained almost 10 million Germans without a fight.

President Benes of Czechoslovakia resigned after the Munich protocol with Hitler was signed. The British House of Commons, in a debate following Chamberlain's mission, approved it by a vote of 366 to 144. About 30 to 40 Conservatives, including Churchill, abstained.

Hitler's next objective was Poland, an attack which would precipitate the European war. By March, 1939 German troops marched into Prague and assumed control of Czechoslovakia, which was incorporated into the Reich. Slovakia had formally declared its independence after Munich, and Chamberlain used this as an excuse to say that the British were no longer bound by the guarantee of Czechoslovakia. On March 17, however, Chamberlain sharply attacked Hitler for his flagrant breach of faith. He asked rhetorically, "Is this in fact a step in the direction of an attempt to dominate the world by force?" Later on that month, Chamberlain stated that in the event of any action which clearly threatened Polish independence and which the Polish government accordingly considered it vital to resist for their national forces, His Majesty's government would feel themselves bound at once to lend the Polish government all support in their power. He added that the French government had made a similar commitment.

Churchill, in his memoires, recounts the sad tale of wrong judgements which British leaders had made up to this time in failing to oppose Hitler. These included Germany rearmed in violation of a solemn treaty, the Rhineland forcibly occupied, the Berlin--Rome Axis established, Austria devoured and digested by the Reich, Czechoslovakia deserted and ruined by the Munich pact with its fortresses and mighty Skoda arsenal in German hands, President Roosevelt's effort to intervene waved aside, Soviet Russia's willingness to join Western Powers to save Czechoslovakia ignored, and the services of 35 Czech divisions against the still unripened German army cast away. Still, Churchill continued, "if you will not fight when you can easily win without bloodshed and if you will not fight when victory will be sure and not costly, there may come a moment when you will have to fight with all the odds against you." "There may be even a worse case;" he adds, "you may have to fight when there is no hope of victory, because it is better to perish than live as slaves."^{12}

By May, 1939, Hitler made clear in meetings with his chiefs of staff, his aim was to expand Germany's lebensraum in the East to secure its food supply and to prepare for war by August against Poland. He doubted that he would be able to avoid a conflict with England, and he planned on sharp, annihilating blows to both England and France.

In August Hitler concluded a pact with Stalin, and shortly thereafter, on September 1, Hitler attacked Poland. On September 3, 1939 Britain and France declared war on Germany, implementing their commitment to Poland. Churchill did not blame Stalin for the German attack, although other observers pointed out that the

Nazi-Soviet pact of August, 1939 had permitted Hitler to attack Poland and then turn on France in the following year. Winston Churchill, both as a statesman and as an historian, blamed England and not Russia for the failure to build a coalition against Hitler. The British part of the March 31, 1939 Anglo-French guarantee of aid to Poland in the event of aggression by Germany would have had little meaning unless it had been included in the framework of a general agreement with the Soviet Union. On April 16, 1939 the Soviet government had repeated an offer for a united front of mutual assistance by Great Britain, France and the U.S.S.R. with guarantees to states in Central and Eastern Europe. However, Chamberlain and his foreign office had stalled. By May 4, Moscow had replaced the pro-west foreign minister Litvinov, with Molotov, a hard-liner who would negotiate an agreement with the devil if so instructed. Churchill muses that if Mr. Chamberlain on receipt of the Russian offer had replied "Yes. Let us three band together and break Hitler's neck," or words to that effect, the British Parliament would have approved the agreement, Stalin would have agreed, and the difficulties with the Poles and Rumanians, who feared Russian rescue, could have been worked out. Instead, there was a long British silence while the new foreign minister, Molotov, began exploring an arrangement with Germany.

The Russians feared they were a major target of German aggression. Hitler's Mein Kampf expressed his hatred for Bolsheviks, the Slavs, and what he called a Jewish domination of Russia. Moreover, his main object was to gain "lebensraum," or living space for the German nation, and Russia was the "heartland" for Hitler and his geopoliticians. Shortly after the Nazi-Soviet Non-Aggression Pact was negotiated on August 23, Hitler in only a temporary alliance with Russia attacked Poland and World War II, for most historians, began. It was not surprising the following May (1940) that Germany mounted its blitzkrieg to remove France from the military equation, although the quick success of the blow was amazing.[13]

Although Russia had tried to form an alliance against Hitler, in 1939 it was an accessory to Hitler's crime of aggression. It took over the eastern part of Poland as Hitler's troops took over the rest. Stalin then immediately forced the Baltic republics of Estonia, Latvia, and Lithuania to submit to Russian control. In October, 1939 he demanded that the Finns cede strategic parts of Finland to the Soviet Union to strengthen its defenses of the Leningrad area. When the Finnish Government refused, the Soviet Union invaded it without warning. The Finns resisted strongly, but by March they sued for peace, ceding strategic areas but retaining their independence. The Soviet Union still retains almost all the territory taken during that period.

Some Western leaders had hoped Hitler's next attack would have been against Russia and that these two totalitarian powers would destroy each other. It is not clear even at this date how widespread that view was and how much it affected British decisions before the attack on Poland. Probably those who write their memoires were not entirely frank on this point. Nevertheless, Churchill was clearly on the record for an alliance with the Russians against Hitler. It was natural after the attack on Poland that he was called to office as Chamberlain stepped down, and it was not surprising that a year later in June, 1941, when Hitler attacked Russia, that Britian offered to provide all assistance within its power.

In analyzing the causes of the war, it is not necessary to go into detail on the World War II military campaigns, which were a natural outcome of Hitler's war against the Eurasian heartland. Before we attempt further to analyze the patterns of causes of World War II, we will examine the side-shows of Manchuria and Ethiopia and then how the United States was drawn into the world conflict.

Italy's Attack on Ethiopia

Italy's attack on Ethiopia in 1936 and the Chinese invasion of Manchuria and China are often lumped together with World War II, but these wars would probably have occurred without Hitler. It makes sense, threfore, to treat them separately in analyzing the causes of war.

In 1906 France, Italy, and Britain entered into a tripartite treaty to maintain the independence of Ethiopia. At the same time the treaty allowed western powers to keep their business and investments in the area.

In 1917 Haile Selassie came to the throne and began a program of modernization of Ethiopia. However he did not create a modern army, and in 1935 all Ethiopia could muster for defense were primitive weapons including little better than matchlock rifles. Mussolini, in the hopes of reviving Italy's slumping economy and establishing an empire like other great nations of the world, trumped up charges about commercial discrimination and ordered an invasion of Ethiopia in 1935. This aggressive war broke not only the tripartite treaty of 1906 but the Covenant of the League of Nations and the Pact of Paris of 1928. The British and French, hoping to appease Italy and line it up against Hitler, offered it an economic mandate over Ethiopia, but Mussolini rejected it.

In response to the invasion the League Council announced that Italy had resorted to war under Article XII. It then prepared a list of sanctions as required in the Covenant, while Mussolini threatened reprisals on any countries applying them.

A coordinating committee under the League Council listed five different levels of sanctions including: 1) an arms embargo, 2) no credits to Italy, 3) no imports, 4) an embargo of certain raw materials, and 5) support to those states suffering economic loss.

Fifty of the nations appoved the first resolution, 49 approved number two, and 48 nations approved numbers both three and four which would involve an oil embargo. Proposal five, which would support states suffering economic loss, obtained only 39 votes. By November 18, 1935 sanctions against Italy were enforced by a large number of nations.

Meanwhile British Foreign Secretary Hoare and the French Foreign Secretary Laval drew up a secret plan to appease Italy by extensive cession of territory. Their motive was to get Mussolini on their side in order to oppose the threat of Hitler, which they saw as more important than Ethiopia. After Laval leaked the plan to the press, the sanctions fell apart, and Mussolini pressed forward with the attack against Ethiopia. By May, 1936 the war was over and Mussolini had annexed Ethiopia. By that time Hitler was threatening Europe with aggression, and in July, 1936 the League of Nations voted to end the sanctions against Italy. Italy then joined with Hitler in October in a pact called the Berlin-Rome Axis, which strengthened Hitler's position in his plans for aggression.

Italy, the first of the fascist countries, had in common with Germany and Japan an extreme nationalist ideology, and was ready to expand where international weakness appeared. Mussolini was jealous of Britain and France, which had achieved control of colonies in an earlier era. Mussolini convinced his people, who were seriously affected by the depression of the 1930's, that the path to power and prosperity was imperialism. Mussolini with totalitarian controls over society succeeded in his aggression against the poor and backward country of Ethiopia, estimating correctly the reluctance of the Western democratic powers effectively to oppose his moves. He then allied with Hitler in his aggression against Europe.

The Japanese Conquest of Manchuria

The Japanese drive to colonize Manchuria and other parts of China stimulated American opposition and finally the sanctions which triggered Pearl Harbor and American's entry into World War II. The Japanese attacks on China, which began at the beginning of the century, culminated in taking over Manchuria and other parts of China in the 1930's and early 1940's.

The Chinese province of Manchuria with its industrial resources was a rich prize for countries with colonial ambitions. Since the beginning of the century Russia and Japan had been exerting economic and military pressure on the province, but by 1930 Japan had achieved economic dominance there. Frustrated by the Chinese opposition and their boycott, the Japanese military brought the matter to a head in September, 1931 by secretly blowing up a small section of a railroad and then moving in troops to "establish order."

The attack was an initiative of Japan's armed forces. The Japanese prime minister, who opposed the action, was assassinated by a group of Japanese naval officers on May 15, 1932. The Japanese military then took over the responsibility for defense of a new state of "Manchukuo" and set up a puppet emperor. China appealed to the League of Nations, and the League Council asked both parties to withdraw armed forces from Manchuria.

Secretary of State Stimson, in cooperation with Senator Borah of Idaho, drafted a letter reminding Japan of its treaty obligations to respect the sovereignty of China and then brought the matter up before League Council. Although the United States was not formally a member of the League, it had participated in many League activities.

The League operated slowly sending a commission of inquiry under a Britisher, Lord Lytton. In March, 1931, a special session of the League voted non-recognition of Manchukuo, the Japanese satellite, in line with the proposal of Secretary of State Stimson.

By October 1932, the Lytton report was completed stating that the Japanese campaign was not justified and that the Manchukuo regime was a puppet. It proposed a compromise that China recognize substantial autonomy of Manchuria but that China retain sovereignty over Manchuria. Japan responded by giving notice of withdrawing from the League. In February, 1933 the League adopted the Lytton report.

Japan continued pressure against China, and in 1937 it invaded the South. In July 1937, its forces were attacking near Peiping, the capital. By the end of December, 1937 major cities and railroads of central China south of Manchuria were in Japanese hands. War was never formally declared, but the Japanese and Chinese armies continued fighting as Japan took over Shanghai, Canton and other South China cities ultimately forcing Chinese forces to retreat to what became their World War II headquarters at Chungking.

The Japanese drive into China was stimulated by a fascist type of ideology that mobilized the Japanese people to organize East Asia in a "co-prosperity sphere," a slogan for Japanese domination. It, too, grew out of the 1930 depression and the severe impact of falling trade on the Japanese economy. It was a case of Japanese imperialism dressed up in propaganda against Western imperialism under the banner of Asia for the Asians. Although the imperialistic drive was said to reflect a pressing need of Japan for new resources, Japan's unprecedented economic expansion after World War II with these foreign territories taken away demonstrated that the economic motive for the co-prosperity sphere had been a cover for a drive for prestige and power. The drive came to a climax with Japan's confrontation with the United States that triggered World War II.

How the U.S. was Drawn into World War II

It is easy for historians to slip into the post-hoc ergo propter-hoc approach in describing how the U.S. was drawn into World War II. They naturally take an orderly, chronological approach to events, and there was a natural progression from a neutral stand to an activist stand in supporting the British and Russian opposition to Hitler. By the time of Pearl Harbor U.S. Navy ships were escorting vessels on the way to Britain, and had suffered casualties in battles with German submarines. Moreover, 85 percent of the people in November 1941, expected the U.S. to be drawn into the European war. Many of President Roosevelt's advisors, as indicated in their memoires, wanted the United States to participate in the war against Hitler. Therefore, it is easy to conclude, as many do, that American leaders inevitably would have brought the United States into the European war.

As a minority view, however, I would maintain the obvious that the United States was drawn into the Asian and European wars by the Japanese attack on Pearl Harbor, and that we should start there in analyzing this question. Moreover, in this analysis I find no real evidence that Roosevelt was secretly plotting to draw the United States into war. His views seem to be that we would provide as much help as possible, short of active participation in the conflict, to Britain and the Soviet Union, and that he was stalling and trying to buy time in the negotiations with the Japanese. In any event, to analyze the issue we should look at the events that led into Pearl Harbor and then discuss the broader question of whether the U.S. was inevitably drawn into World War II. The critical decisions on our policy towards Japan centered on the discussions between the Secretary of State, Cordell Hull, and the Japanese ambassador to Washington, Kichisaburo Nomura, beginning in March, 1941, and the increasing pressures in the U.S. Government to cut back trade with Japan. The second critical areas of decision making took place in the Japanese cabinet, which was split between an aggressive faction led by the army and a faction led by Prime Minister Konoye that wanted to achieve an understanding with the United States.

Hull's talks with the Japanese at the time were only a sideshow compared to the series of escalating moves as the United States increased assistance to England in its critical struggle with Germany. In September, 1940, the U.S. had passed the U.S. Selective Service Act and by March, 1941, the U.S. Lend-Lease Act was in effect by which we could provide war material to England, and also Chiang Kai-shek's government, and settle later for the price. After their meeting with the President, Secretary of State Hull and the Japanese Ambassador Nomura began a series of about fifty meetings that took place after working hours in Secretary of State Hull's apartment. Hull, in his memoires, pointed out that he estimated that there was not one chance in 20, 50, or even 100 for agreement.[14] Japanese officials, particularly those who supported the army, were also pessimistic about the chances of reaching an agreement with the United States.[15] The United States was on record with Congress that Japan's new order in the Pacific meant economic domination by Japan and destruction of personal liberties of the conquered people and that this was of immense importance and concern to the United States. By the beginning of 1941, the United States had severely cutback on shipments to Japan of important metals and high octane gasoline. However, the United States still permitted shipments of petroleum. In June, 1941, in the middle of Hull's negotiations, Germany attacked the Soviet Union, which tended further to draw attention away from the negotiations with Japan.

By July, the discussions began to come to a climax. The United States was regularly intercepting and decoding the Japanese cables, including the instructions to the Japanese Ambassador. It was clear that the Japanese were preparing to move into Southeast Asia to take over French Indo-China, which was left dangling after Hitler had conquered France. Just beyond that was the rich Dutch East Indies, which had the oil production that Japan coveted. In fact, in July Japanese troops had occupied the southern part of China. Hull, who had retired to White Sulfur Springs to convalesce from an illness, saw this as a last move before a full-scale attack on the southwest Pacific. To show his displeasure, he even refused to see Ambassador Nomura when he came to White Sulfur Springs to proceed with the negotiations.

On July 26, a puzzling event occurred, which is understandable only when one looks at it in the context of the confusion that was occuring in Washington with Hitler's attack on the Soviet Union and Japan's massing to attack in the Far East. On July 21, Under-Secretary Welles, who had discussed the matter with the Cabinet and President Roosevelt, gave instructions to prepare an order to freeze Japanese assets. Dean Acheson gives the details in his <u>Present at the Creation</u>.[16] Acheson notes that the President did not want to cut off oil because he did not want to trigger Japanese aggression. However, apparently unknown to President Roosevelt, the order freezing Japanese assets had that effect. Three Japanese tankers came to the United States on the West Coast ports at the end of July, and after some dickering were able only to get bunkers because they could not obtain funds to pay for a cargo of oil. By August 5, Japan announced withdrawing its merchant marine from American trade because of these restrictions. Japanese demands in the talks with Hull at this time centered on the critical question of getting the United States to resume normal trade with Japan. The United States' major demand was that Japan withdraw from its aggression in China. The gradual U.S. trade restrictions and particularly the freezing of assets, which cut off the oil, brought the discussions to a climax. Actually, Japan had been anticipating a cut-back in oil supplies for several years and had extensive stockpiles and conservation measures in effect. It was estimated that the civilian economy could have lasted over a year and a half with normal peace-time consumption. However, the Japanese military had much greater requirements in mind because they needed huge supplies to take over Indo-China and to establish the East Asian Co-prosperity Sphere. Geopolitics was as popular in Japan as it was in Germany, and Japanese geopoliticians and policymakers envisaged a Co-prosperity Sphere for Japan incorporating former colonies extending from Japan to India. As noted above, Hull saw this as imperialism by Japan with a destruction of personal liberty. However, Japanese spokesmen and propaganda pictured it as a mutually beneficial arrangement to replace the colonial exploitation of the West. Actually, as history worked out, Japanese aggression in Asia and the Co-prosperity Sphere did bring about an end to the colonial system in Asia, but not in the way the Japanese envisaged.

By August, Ambassador Nomura and Prime Minister Konoye were frantic. They realized that the Japanese military had obtained a cabinet decision to use force if diplomacy did not succeed. As a final attempt to achieve agreement, Prime Minister Konoye and Ambassador Nomura began pressing Secretary Hull and the American Government to agree to a top-level meeting between President Roosevelt and Prime Minister Konoye. The peace faction in the Japanese government hoped by this maneuver to increase the prestige and power of their faction versus the militants in the army. The President, at first, took a favorable view, but after strong respresentations from Hull, took the position that he would not participate in such talks until the basic agreement was reached on a lower level.[17]

In complicated maneuverings in Tokyo Foreign Minister Matsuoka, a relatively militant and unfriendly foreign minister, was replaced by a more friendly Foreign Minister Toyoda. However, this did not soften the U.S. view toward summit negotiations. Ambassador Grew from Tokyo added his appeals to Washington for President Roosevelt to meet with the Japanese leader, but Cordell Hull was afraid it would result in another Munich, in which Roosevelt would reach some sort of a bland agreement with the Japanese about China without representatives of China present.

In October, the Toyoda cabinet fell and was replaced by the military cabinet headed by General Tojo, which carried Japan into Pearl Harbor. Planning and preparations for Pearl Harbor had been taking place since the beginning of the year.[18] On November 5th, soon after taking over, Tojo sent a message to Ambassador Nomura that was intercepted by the United States that it was absolutely necessary if an agreement was to be reached, that it be completed by November 25th. It was clear to the United States by that time Japan would make aggressive moves if there were no agreement in the discussions. Japan's final proposal included the following key phrases:

> Japan to withdraw her troops from Indo-China when peace was restored between Japan and China or an equitable peace was established in the Pacific areas; Japan and the United States to restore their commercial relations to those prevailing prior to the freezing of assets, and the United States to supply to Japan a required quantity of oil; and the United States to refrain from such measures and actions as would prejudice endeavors for the restoration of peace between Japan and China.

Japan did not agree to withdraw troops with this final proposal, but only "to make no armed advance into any region in Southeast Asia and the Southwest Pacific area." Secretary Hull saw this as a commitment to restore U.S. trade in strategic commodities to Japan, while Japanese troops remained in Manchuria and much of southern China. At the same time, the United States would be bound not to supply aid to China while negotiations on the restoration of peace between Japan and China continued. Secretary Hull responded with ten proposals, including a non-aggression pact among the governments principally concerned in the Pacific, a trade agreement between the United States and Japan on liberal terms, and a unilateral commitment by Japan to withdraw her armed forces from China and Indo-China.

U.S. forces in the Far East had been put on alert status prior to this, and on November 27th, a "war warning" was sent to commanders of U.S. forces in the Far East including those in Pearl Harbor. The Japanese messages intercepted by the United States indicated naval movements towards southeast Asia, but none of the American leaders, including military commanders, anticipated the attack at Pearl Harbor. They thought the ships, that in fact were sailing to attack Pearl Harbor, were still in Japan. On December 7, 1941, Japanese planes attacked Pearl Harbor, devastating the largest part of the Pacific fleet, but fortunately key U.S. aircraft carriers were out on maneuvers and were not harmed.

Hitler, in accordance with the Tri-Partite Pact with Japan and Italy of September 27, 1940, over the objections of his foreign minister, joined Japan by declaring war on the United States. The Pearl Harbor attack and the declaration of war by Germany made it easy for the President and the U.S. Congress to recognize that a state of war existed with the Axis Powers. World War II had engulfed the major powers of the world.

Why the World Went to War Again

Hitler on November 28, well before Pearl Harbor, was urging Japan through his foreign minister to go to war against the United States. He promised if Japan did this, Germany would join Japan in accordance with the Tripartite Pact. On December 7, Hitler's first reaction at the news of Pearl Harbor was delight, exclaiming now we cannot lose the war. "Now we have a partner who has not been defeated in three thousand years."[19] His speech requesting the Reichstag to declare war against the United States was drowned in cheers. Only later on second thought did Hitler regret the action which removed the Japanese threat from Siberia, because of Japan's war with the United States, and allowed Russia to transfer more troops to defend itself against the Nazi attack.

Japanese politics are often subtle and hard to define, but there is little doubt that the Japanese military led Japan into World War II. The Japanese navy struck at Pearl Harbor hoping to destroy the major part of the U.S. Pacific fleet and its ability to oppose the establishment of the Co-prosperity Sphere. The question to be addressed is how the Japanese military achieved a position of power where they could make such a fatal mistake.

As Japan rushed into the modern world in the latter part of the 19th century, the Japanese military achieved high prestige by their success in taking over Taiwan in 1895 and Korea in 1905. Although Japan was about the last to enter into the colonial race, these were major colonial gains. The Japanese military and business interests continued to penetrate Manchuria, and in 1931 Japanese troops took over Manchuria, China's richest industrial area. Japan not only succeeded in establishing a puppet state under the economic control of Japan, but it successfully ignored the protests of the League of Nations.

The Japanese military had a powerful political position. They controlled their own budget, and their Minister of War, a military man, had the right to see the Emperor on policy matters without going through the Prime Minister. In effect, the Prime Minister could not fire the Minister of War.

During the economic disruption of the early 1930's, extreme nationalist organizations of army officers assassinated one prime minister in 1932, and attempted a coup in 1936. They did not succeed in the coup, but they did intimidate civilian officials. The army moved in to Manchuria over the opposition of Japan's civilian ministers, including the Prime Minister, and during the 1930's and the early 1940's the Army successfully resisted civilian control of their military operations and preparations for war. The Emperor gave some indirect and weak support to the civilian peace faction, but would not take a stand against the military, which avoided presenting key decisions to him. In the final months before the war the Emperor was informed of developments. On December 1st, in a meeting with the Emperor, Prime Minister Tojo said that it was necessary for Japan to go to war. The Emperor gave no reply and did not, therefore, prevent him from proceeding. The military, therefore, took advantage of the highly disciplined Japanese society, which revered the Emperor and did not question the actions of his government.

Other obvious questions are: Did the American authorities make reasonable efforts to forestall the war and what can be learned from the "ifs." Cordell Hull can be faulted for persuading the President not to meet with Konoye. Conceivably, if Franklin Roosevelt had reached some sort of an agreement with Konoye, he could have gained enough prestige to fight off the political influence of the military and avoid war with the United States. It is difficult to see how the United States would have fought for French and Dutch colonies in the Far East when it had not joined in the war against Hitler, which was directed against its closest ally, England. Moreover, the United States might have developed a nuclear bomb and ended the war in Europe with that terrible instrument, and then could have contained Japanese expansion without a war. Few if any could foresee this possibility in 1941. In fact, our top leaders feared that Hitler would get the nuclear weapon first.

Hull was probably realistic, however, in realizing that no agreement was possible with Japan's powerful military faction. It is hard to imagine their withdrawing from China, with no force there effectively to oppose them. The Japanese military seemed to be more firmly entrenched than Hitler, and it is difficult to see how American diplomacy could have drastically shifted the political balance in Japan. The attack on Pearl Harbor, however, was a reckless and foolish act, and conceivably Japan, if it had been diverted from that attack, might have moved into the Far East without bringing the United States directly into an Asian and European War. There is little doubt, therefore, that just as the three emperors were responsible for World War I, totalitarian leadership of Japan, as well as of Germany, was responsible for plunging the world into World War II.

Causes

Although there is no argument that Hitler was to blame for World War II in Europe, the controversies arise about who helped him ride to power and who created the conditions that permitted the Nazis to take over Germany. Certainly, old President von Hindenburg, 84, who at the very end was senile, is responsible for appointing Hitler as Chancellor. President von Hindenburg had resisted Hitler and even had lectured Hitler when he demanded Hindenburg appoint him as Prime Minister after the elections of November 19, 1932, in which the Nazi party again proved to be the strongest party in Germany. However, two months later Hindenburg yielded to the pleadings of two people he apparently trusted - von Papen and Hindenburg's own son. In January, 1933 Hindenburg offered Hitler the Chancellorship and von Papen the Vice-Chancellorship. Apparently von Papen thought he could control Hitler since one of the conditions was that von Papen would accompany Hitler any time he saw Hindenburg. Also, von Papen, as part of the deal, became Prime Minister of the very powerful state of Prussia. Unfortunately, von Papen underestimated Hitler in thinking that he could control Hitler. Von Papen had virtually no political or paramilitary backing in comparison to Hitler, who had the powerful Nazi party with its storm troopers at his command. Von Papen did not even have the confidence of the Center Party from which he originally came. Thus, von Papen, and to a lesser extent, another political conspirator, General Schleicher, also have some degree of responsibility for the political maneuvering that brought Hitler to power.

When we go beyond this, the matter becomes quite controversial. The Social Democrats, the Communists, and many other observers would attribute much of the blame for the rise of Hitler to backing by big business interests. Certainly some businessmen did provide financing to Hitler and towards the end gave him backing along with the military and millions of Germans. Actually, however, the business financing dried up in the critical period just before Hitler became Chancellor, and it was only when Hitler made a deal with von Papen that von Papen was able to persuade them to renew their backing for Hitler.

The culprits for the Japanese attacks on Pearl Harbor are about as easy to determine as those to blame for the European war. Prime Minister Tojo, the former war minister, was the one that gave the final order for Pearl Harbor. The Emperor was informed and did not object so he, too, must assume blame for that attack. During the 1930's, the army operated almost as an independent branch of the government, responsible only very vaguely to the Emperor, and the military was the major political force that drove Japan into Manchuria and into the further attack on China. Thus, as in the case of World War I, old and ineffective leaders permitted the hawks to make decisions that caused disaster.

The Ideas and Ideologies of the Two World Wars

In both World War I, and World War II, it was the authoritarian or totalitarian governments that decided on aggressive war and took the aggressive acts. In World War II the German and Japanese government carried their peoples into war on a wave of a fascist ideology of extreme nationalism that pictured them as master races destined to rule other peoples. It is true the Japanese had no mass movement like the Nazi Party, but other institutions of Japanese society instilled similar racist ideas and discipline. Both German and Japananese totalitarian movements had a hatred of

Western nations and their values, which supported democracy, religion, and international law.

There are striking differences in the pattern of the ideas and ideologies of the two World Wars, as can be seen from Table 1. World War I was based on false conceptions and poor judgements of leaders who did not intend to trigger a European or a world war. World War II, on the other hand, was caused by the aggressive leadership of Germany and Japan. Table 1 reflects a pattern in World War I of bad judgements of the three emperors and the leaders of their countries. Germany and Austria-Hungary thought they could teach Serbia a lesson without triggering a big war. The Czar hoped to deter Austria-Hungary by mobilization, and Germany overreacted to the threats of mobilization. Underlying their moves was a determination to protect their alliances and other interests and their feuds with the opposing alliance. In the realm of ideology the dominant ideology was the extreme nationalism of the Serb terrorists who assassinated the Archduke, and a form of nationalism by which the Austro-Hungarian emperor and his officials were determined to maintain the empire intact. All of them were swept along in the last few days by enthusiastic nationalisms reflected in their news media and popular demonstrations in support of the nations and their stands against an opposing alliance. All but a few of the leaders underestimated the suffering and destruction that would be caused by the war.

World War II was dominated by the aggressiveness of the Nazi and Japanese leaders who wanted to create a form of imperial rule for their own country. These rulers were overly-optimistic about their own strength, and, particularly in the case of Japan, they underestimated the reactions of their opponents. Both of them promoted, through their propaganda, feuds with other nations whom they opposed. In this propaganda the German and Japanese leaders combined ideologies of fascism and extreme nationalism in promoting their aggressive policies. There was no parallel to this before World War I. Hitler, in particular, played on the themes of anti-Communism and racist ideologies to a degree almost unimaginable in today's world. Japan's nationalism was based on a state religion glorifying Japan and the Emperor, and in a sense it was racist since the Greater East Asia Co-prosperity Sphere was designed to substitute Japanese imperialism for that of the White imperialist nations. Part of the Japanese drive was due to a resentment of the racial discrimination which they, as a nation, had faced in their dealings with the United States and other nations.

The United States' entry into World War I and World War II deserves separate treatment in analyzing the underlying causes. On balance, Germany was committing aggressive acts in World War I by sinking U.S. shipping since, in large part, the United States' right to continue such commerce during war was recognized under international law. However, Germany's position was understandable since Britain was blockading Germany in a manner that could not be defended under conventional international law, and Germany, in a sense, was retaliating by setting up a blockade by submarine. Table 1 shows a U.S. determination to maintain a right of freedom of the seas in World War I as a major cause for U.S. entry into that war. Also, a minor cause was Wilson's desire to "make the world safe for democracy," which played a minor part in his decision to recommend entry into World War I.

Similarly, the United States' policy of acting as an "arsenal of democracy" and supporting the territorial integrity of China triggered the extreme Japanese reaction of attacking Pearl Harbor. The United States, in maintaining this right and in opposing the aggressive designs of dictators, cut back on trade of strategic goods necessary to military operations to the point where the Japanese struck out in frustration at Pearl Harbor. In terms of causes of war, however, U.S. acts should not be placed in the same category as the aggression of Japan and Germany since the right of countries collectively to defend themselves is recognized under international law.

Table 1 highlights the fact that World War II was the beginning of the wars of ideologies. This was supported by new media technologies which permitted leaders to saturate their people with ideological poison. Hitler's fascism was based on a extreme anti-Semitism, claiming the Jews were at the root of all evil. His attacks against Communists played a part in his success in preventing many European leaders, at first, from opposing his rearmament and expansion of greater Germany to include Austria and Czechoslovakia. All this was in the framework of the geopolitician's claim that the German master race had the right to dominate the world island of Europe and Asia in order to obtain lebensraum. Hitler concealed his aggressive design with speeches and propaganda about his desire for peace and his intention to redress the unfairness of the Treaty of Versailles. He also appealed to the ideals of self-determination of Germans, claiming that the Germans of Austria and of Czechoslovakia wanted to be united in the greater German Reich.

To a lesser extent, Japan promoted its ideology of a Greater East Asia Co-prosperity Sphere. This ideal was based on a mixture of nationalism, and state religion glorifying the Japanese race intensified by anti-Western practices of racial discrimination. This served to unite the Japanese leaders and people behind the Japanese aggression. But the propaganda at first did not spill over the borders to nearly the extent that the German propaganda did.

In terms of actions and instruments of aggression, the mobilization schedules and alliances were major factors helping start World War I. In World War II, Hitler and Prime Minister Tojo of

Japan, used the aggressive instruments of alliances, mobilization, media, and military instruments. Hitler, particularly, used terrorism, clashes, surprise attacks, as instruments of force for his aggression. His honoring the alliance with Japan helped bring about his downfall.

Towards the end of the table, we see one common pattern to both World War I and World War II. These wars were caused by authoritarian leaders - emperors in World War I and dictators in World War II. Since World War II, there has been perhaps too much of a tendency to criticize democracy because of its ability to rally people to causes and to military action in defense of a country or in support of certain principles. However, it is clear from the record that democratic rulers played no important part in starting World War I and World War II, the two most terribly destructive wars of this century.

Much of history since World War II reflects the lessons learned from the two wars. By the 1940's, leaders and historians were well aware of the connections between the economic disruption of the early 30's and the growth of radical movements like the Nazis that achieved power in Germany. President Roosevelt's determination not to create a network of war debts helped bring about the concept of "Lend-Lease," which permitted the United States to ship war material to Britain without burdening it with impossible debts. The problem of how much Britain should repay or return was left to after the war. Also during World War II the constitutions of the International Monetary Fund and the International Bank for Reconstruction and Development were negotiated to help manage the economic problems after the war. To date the International Monetary Fund has played a key part in managing international monetary transactions to prevent the currency flights and instability that lead to the economic disasters of the 1930's. The Marshall Plan of economic aid to reconstruct Western Europe was also inspired by the lessons of World War I, and it helped provide a solid base for European economic recovery. Finally, the Schuman Plan, which resulted in the establishment of a common market in coal and steel and later for all products, grew out of the determination of Jean Monnet, who believed that such an economic union would prevent a future war between Germany and France. The above major economic initiatives created a structure for a strong and economically healthy Europe after World War II.

The United Nations, which was established after 1945, grew out of a determination not to permit the mistakes of the 1930's to reoccur. It was based on the principle of universal membership so that all major powers would unite together to prevent war. It provided a forum where the powers could meet within a few hours to meet a threat to security. It was based on a commitment of all members to prevent the smaller countries from being swallowed up one by one by another Hitler. We will evaluate the U.N.'s success at the end of this book.

The strong alliance system centered on NATO was also a lesson learned from World War I and II. The unified command of NATO is designed to prevent Soviet aggression. Moreover, 240,000 U.S. troops plus British and other units are stationed in Europe under a NATO command to deter war. The contrast between this and the relatively weak and ambigious alliance system of the 1930's is striking.

Finally, there were measures taken in setting up German and Japanese democracies to prevent them from again becoming aggressor nations. As part of the bargain for regaining its sovereignty, Germany accepted the ABC agreement, which prohibits it from developing atomic, bacteriological, or chemical warfare weapons. Japan is also committed to a similar type agreement and, moreover, its constitution prohibits it from developing an aggressive military force. Japan has strictly abided by the provisions of its constitution, even though it could amend it if it wished, and the Japanese self-defense forces have no aggressive capability. Japan only spends one percent of its gross national product on the military, which is far below that of other industrial nations. Moreover, both Germany and Japan are tied by the series of treaties and agreements to permit joint defense forces to be stationed on their soil. Most of the American forces in Europe are in Germany, while Britain maintains two divisions on the Rhine. Similarly, Japan is committed under a mutual defense treaty to have U.S. forces stationed on its soil. This has been a matter of political controversy, but, in recent years with the United States recognizing the right of Japan to terminate the treaty at any time with one year's notice, the political controversy has subsided. There has been no major political move to get American troops out of Germany or Japan. With the above political, economic, and military measures, the United States and other allied powers have indirectly acknowledged their negligence that led to World War II. Their blame, generally, is one of omission and not commission, and, in any event, cannot be compared with the blame of Hitler and Tojo.

We will now look at the major wars since World War II, many of which were directly related to the changes and problems that arose from that conflict.

NOTES

[1] C.P. Kindleberger, The World in Depression 1929-1939 (New York: Penguin, 1973).

[2] Norman H. Baynes, The Speeches of Adolf Hitler, April 22 to August 1939 (London: Oxford University Press, 1942).

[3] Ibid., Vol. II, pp. 988-989.

[4] Ibid., p. 996.

[5] Ibid., p. 1545.

[6] Herman Rauschning, The Voice of Destruction (New York: G.P. Putnam's Sons, 1940), pp. 1-10.

[7] William Shirer, The Rise and Fall of the Third Reich (New York: Simon and Schuster, 1961), Chapters 5 and 6.

[8] Winston S. Churchill, The Gathering Storm (Boston: Houghton Mifflin Company, 1948), pp. 64-65.

[9] William L. Shirer, The Rise and Fall of the Third Reich (New York: Simon & Schuster, 1961), p. 237.

[10] Winston S. Churchill, The Gathering Storm, (Cambridge: Houghton Mifflin Company, 1948) pp. 311-318.

[11] Ibid., p. 318.

[12] Ibid., p. 348.

[13] A. J. P. Taylor in The Origins of the Second World War (New York: Athenium, 1983) argues that since Hitler's immediate demands against Poland were for Danzig and the corridor, where pro-German sentiment was strong, the British and other powers might have worked out a compromise and avoided the war, particularly if they had lined up with Russia. It is true that Hitler was a master improviser, but he seemed determined to subjugate Poland, as he did Czechoslovakia, and move against Russia; so I accept the historians' majority view that Hitler's ambitions were too great to be contained by any reasonable compromises.

[14] Cordell Hull, The Memoires of Cordell Hull (New York: MacMillan Company, 1948) p. 987-989.

[15] Prince Fumimaro Konoye, Memoires of Prince Konoye, March 1942, from Paul S. Burtness and Warren U. Ober, The Puzzle of Pearl Harbor (Evanston: Row, Peterson, and Company, 1962) pp. 94-123.

[16] Dean Acheson, *Present at The Creation* (New York: W. W. Norton, 1969) pp. 22-27.

[17] *Memoires of Cordell Hull*, pp. 1024-1028.

[18] Gordon Prange, *At Dawn We Slept*, (New York: Penguin, 1961).

[19] John Toland, *Adolf Hitler* (New York: Balantine Books, 1976), pp. 950-53.

CHAPTER 5

The Korean War

The Korean War and other wars after World War II took place in a world much different from the one that spawned the two world wars. The nuclear bombs that destroyed Hiroshima and Nagasaki gave a frightening picture of how civilian populations could suffer in the next war. Germany's V-2 rockets, jet planes, and cruise missiles developed near the end of the World War II indicated that the United States was losing its geographic buffer and in a few years would be less than 30 minutes away from devastation in a nuclear war. As Russia expanded its nuclear arsenal after 1949, the Cold War confrontation of the two superpowers dominated war and peace issues.

Most nations of the world, including those formed from the old colonial empires, temporarily supported policies of collective security after World War II. They incorporated this ideal in the Charter of the United Nations, hoping that the UN would provide a framework to maintain peace. In the first decade after the wars most nations presented the difficult problems to the UN. Great Britain turned over the conflict in its Palestine mandate to the UN, and the U.S. presented the UN with the problem of how to achieve a unified Korea. Both these issues led to wars.

How It Started

Korea had been a colony of Japan's since the beginning of the century, but with the flowering of anti-colonial sentiment in the World War II era, it was natural the U.S. should work toward granting it independence. During World War II, in connection with the United States' request for Russia to enter the war against Japan, the United States and Russia agreed on a Korea that would be free and independent of colonial control from Japan. The war, however, ended much quicker than expected with the dropping of the atomic bombs in August, 1945. The Russians, as agreed, moved to occupy Manchuria and the northern part of Korea to the 38th parallel, where agreement had been reached to divide occupation zones before the war ended. The Soviets immediately installed Korean leaders trained in Russia, Soviet advisors, and Soviet-equipped forces. The U.N. General Assembly proposed a reasonable solution --that Korea be unified by free elections monitored by the U.N. The Soviet Union did not accept the U.N. proposals and refused to let U.N. observers observe conditions in North Korea or monitor elections there. The U.N. could not try to enforce its mandate on the Soviets without shattering the world organization and endangering world peace, so its observers monitored elections only in the South. In the elections, Syngman Rhee was elected president, and the U.N. General Assemnbly in December, 1948 recognized the South Korea government as the legitimate government. South Korea, however, could not join the U.N. as a regular member because the Soviets blocked Korean membership by a veto in the Security Council.

In line with U.N. Security Council and General Assembly recommendations, the Soviet armed forces withdrew from the North in 1949, and the United States followed suit in the South. As the U.S. withdrew in 1949, it left only 500 officers of a military advisory assistance group, plus equipment for about 50,000 troops, or four divisions. At that point, the U.S. military and the U.S. National Security Council were confident that South Korea could hold its own against the North. The South had a population of twice the North and military forces, at that time, approximately the same size as those of the North.

The war began on June 24, 1950 with a major invasion by the Soviet-equipped North Korean army. U.N. observers in South Korea were there to provide unbiased reports to the U.N., and it was soon evident that the invasion was out-and-out aggression in flagrant violation of international law and the United Nations Charter. We will examine the origins of the war, the way it was expanded from a collective-security operation against North Korea to a major war involving Communist China, and then the lessons to be drawn from the experience, including the value of U.N. system in the crisis.

Nikita Khrushchev, in his memoires, gives probably what will be the closest to an inside account of the origin of the Korean War as we will ever get.[1] Khrushchev states that about the time he was transferred from the Ukraine to Moscow at the end of 1949, Kim Il-sung arrived to consult with Stalin. Kim's proposal was that "the North Koreans wanted to prod South Korea with the point of a bayonet." He anticipated that the first poke would touch off an internal explosion in South Korea and that the power of the people would prevail. Khrushchev continued that naturally Stalin could not oppose the idea because it appealed to his conviction

map 3
The Course of the Korean War

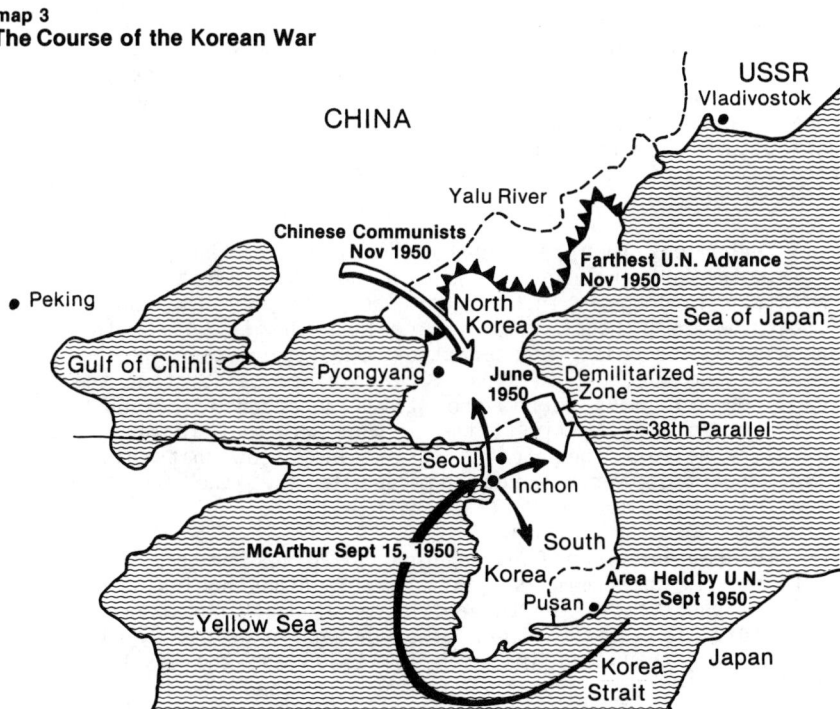

that this would be an internal matter which the Koreans would settle among themselves. The idea also appealed to Khrushchev, who explained that the North Koreans wanted to give a helping hand to their brethren who were under the heel of Syngman Rhee. Stalin told Kim to go home and come up with a more concrete plan. Kim later returned to Moscow and assured Stalin of the plan's success. Stalin believed if the war were fought swiftly, intervention could be avoided. Khrushchev stated in his memoires that no real Communist would have tried to dissuade Kim Il-sung from his compelling desire to liberate South Korea from reactionary American influence. To have done so, Khrushchev said, would have "contradicted the Communist view of the world."

Mao Tse-tung was also in Moscow during Kim's initial trip and supported Kim's plan. Mao, according to Khrushchev, also was of the opinion that the United States would not intervene since the war was an internal matter. At a dinner of these leaders, Khrushchev reported that Kim said that Korea with this move would get agricultural products in the South such as fish, rice, and other food to combine with the raw materials for the Korean industry from the North.

Khrushchev then related how the plans did not go as hoped. First, the internal uprisings did not materialize. Then the MacArthur landing in Inchon near Seoul cut off the North Korean forces, which by that time had reached the tip of South Korea. MacArthur's surprise counterattack completely changed the character of the war. At this point, Khrushchev says, after the Americans began to move north, Chou Enlai appeared in Moscow to discuss what to do. At first, the opinion was that it was fruitless to intervene, but then it was agreed in Moscow that China should give support to North Korea in order to save the situation from disaster. (See Map 3).

Information from Congressional hearings on the Korean War confirm that the Communists were making plans beginning early in 1950 for the attack. By the end of 1949, North Korea had four infantry divisions and a number of border guard brigades. The fifth division was activated in March 15, 1950, and the sixth on April 17, 1950. The sixth was the one that launched the initial attack in June. However, training was underway for additional divisions, because by July 20th, about six weks after the attack began, they had the seventh through the fifteenth divisions in action. Meanwhile, South Korean forces were completely outclassed. U.S. reports indicated that they had no heavy weapons, no tanks, and only sixteen training aircraft. North Korea, on the other hand, had modern equipment, including heavy Russian tanks.

How the Korean War Became a United Nations War

The President's first decision on the Korean War was to approve Secretary of State Acheson's proposal to ask for an emergency session of the U.N. Security Council. This was a natural reaction of the President, who had been an ardent supporter of President Wilson's proposal for a League of Nations after World War I, and who had given strong support to the United Nations as soon as he became president. Truman, in his early presidency, had been determined that the United Nations would not suffer the fate of the League and fail for lack of Congressional support. He personally briefed the U.S. delegation, and then kept in close touch with the delegates at San Francisco as they completed negotiation of the U.N. charter. After the U.N. was formed, President Truman used it as an instrument to maintain peace. For example, the United States made a major fuss in the U.N. Security Council at the beginning of 1946 when the Soviets did not withdraw from Iran, as they had promised to do when World War II was ended. Similarly, Truman supported the U.N. decision for establishing the State of Israel, for investigating the invasion of Greece by guerrilla groups from the neighboring Communist countries, and for designing a plan to control nuclear weapons.

Truman's strategy in 1950 of mobilizing the defense of South Korea through the United Nations was aided by the Soviet boycott of the U.N.; the Soviets had withdrawn six months earlier in objection to Chiang Kai-shek's government claiming to represent China in the U.N. Security Council. Without a Soviet delegate on the Council to veto a resolution, the United States was able to mobilize support of the world body, first to call for a ceasefire, and, two days later, to call on other U.N. members to furnish such assistance to South Korea as necessary to repel the attack. The Soviets appeared to be caught off balance by the Security Council's action. Their reading of the Charter from a strict legalistic point of view was that action of the Security Council required an affirmative vote of the Soviet Union, which was one of the "permanent members," and their absence then would prevent action by the Security Council. The United States and other members with a constructive interpretation of the Charter decided that a negative vote was needed by a permanent member to block action. That elastic interpretation of the Charter has come to be generally accepted. The President then made an announcement that in line with the U.N. resolution, the United States was ordering its air and sea forces to support the Korean government troops. A few days later he ordered U.S. ground troops to help defend Korea.

Truman's memoires state that in the first policy meeting with top officials of the State Department and Defense Department, "There was no suggestion from anyone that either the United Nations or the United States could back away from it. This was a test of all the talk of the last five years of collective security." Truman added that he was very aware of the parallel between the Korean attack and the way in which aggressors had taken over Manchuria, Ethiopia, Austria and Czechoslovakia at the beginning of World War II. He states:

> "Communism was acting in Korea just as Hitler, Mussolini, and the Japanese had acted ten, fifteen, and twenty years earlier. If the Communists were permitted to force their way into the Republic of Korea without opposition from the free world, no small nation would have the courage to resist threats and aggression by stronger Communist neighbors. If this was allowed to go unchallenged it would mean a third world war, just as similar incidents had brought on the Second World War. It was also clear to me that the foundation and the principles of the United Nations were at stake unless this unprovoked attack on Korea could be stopped."[2]

Secretary Dean Acheson, in ruminating about the war, thought of it in power politics terms rather than in internationalist terms. In his memoires, Acheson stated the invasion by North Korean troops did not amount to a casus belli--a reason to declare war against the Soviet Union. However, he added,

> "Equally plainly it was an open, undisguised challenge to our internationally accepted position as a protector of South Korea, an area of great importance to the security of American occupied Japan. To back away from this challenge in view of our capacity for meeting it, would be highly destructive of the power and prestige of the United States. By prestige, I mean the shadow cast by power, which is of great deterrent importance."[3]

John Foster Dulles, who became the next Secretary of State and who, at that time, was one of Acheson's advisors, strongly backed Truman and Acheson in this decision. A few weeks later the Security Council appointed General MacArthur as Supreme U.N. Commander. The U.S. and South Korean forces aided by relatively minor contingents from 15 other countries waged war under the U.N. flag.

Later, we will examine the role of the United Nations as an instrument of repelling aggression and of peacemaking. The major point of this section is to note that Truman entered the war under the provisions of the U.N. Charter. He saw it as a police action, an action to repel aggression, and as support of the principle of collective security on behalf of the world community.

China Enters the War

United States leaders looking at the war from the U.S. point of view were surprised at the massive Chinese intervention in November, 1950 in the Korean War. On the other hand, the Chinese leaders must have been puzzled that the United States did not take their warnings seriously. We will look at this issue from both viewpoints. The attacks by Chinese "volunteers" expanded the

Korean conflict from a U.N. police action to a major war, and set the stage for a U.S.-Chinese confrontation in Asia that lasted two decades. It also confirmed suspicions of U.S. leaders that the Communists were out to take over Asia and thus helped trigger future actions that brought the U.S. into the Vietnam War.

Secretary of State Dean Acheson traces convincingly in his memoirs the steps he and others took to reassure the Chinese that the U.S. had no intention of threatening Communist China after the Chinese Communists took over the mainland in 1949. His account, incidentally, also indicates how other U.S. leaders, and particularly General MacArthur, were giving completely different signals to the Chinese.

On February 7, 1949 Acheson met with 51 Congressmen to explain U.S. policy toward China. Asked to predict events, he replied that when a great tree falls in the forest one cannot see the extent of the damage until the dust settles. Congress and the press seized on this statement, and Acheson was saddled with "wait until the dust settles" as an explanation of U.S. policy toward China. During 1949, the Chinese Communists completed their rout of Chiang's forces, and it was clear from public statements that the United States indeed was waiting until the dust settled.

On January 5, 1950 Truman confirmed this by stating:

> The United States has no predatory designs on Formosa or on any other Chinese territory. The United States has no desire to obtain special rights or privileges or to establish military bases on Formosa at this time. Nor does it have any intention of utilizing its armed forces to interfere in the present situation. The United States will not pursue a course which will lead to involvement in the civil conflict in China.
>
> Similarly the United States Government will not provide military aid or advice to Chinese forces on Formosa. In the view of the United States Government, the resources on Formosa are adequate to enable them to obtain the items which they might consider necessary for the defense of the island. The United States Government proposes to continue under existing legislative authority the present ECA program of economic assistance.

Acheson followed up on January 12, 1950 with a speech on China policy that has been cited by many historians an an invitation to the North Koreans to invade the South. The major thrust of the speech, however, was to distance the United States further from Chiang's regime. Acheson's speech went along the following lines. No one in his right mind could believe the Chinese Nationalist regime had been overthrown by superior military force. Chiang was opposed by only one faction, the ragged, ill-equipped, small Communist force in the hills. Chiang had controlled the greatest military power of any ruler in Chinese history, supported by economic backing by the United States. Four years later it had melted away and he was a refugee on a small island off the coast. The almost inexhaustible patience of the Chinese people, Acheson continued, had ended. They had not overthrown the government--there was nothing to overthrow, and they had simply ignored it.

Acheson then elaborated on the historic differences and friction between Russia and the Chinese. Finally he turned toward the question of military security and described the U.S. line of defense which extended "along the Aleutians to Japan and then goes to the Ryukyus....to the Philippines." This was precisely the defense perimeter that General MacArthur had traced earlier in a public interview in Tokyo. Acheson added, if an attack occurred in other areas of the Pacific, "the initial reliance must be on the people attacked to resist it and then upon the commitments of the entire civilized world under the Charter of the United Nations, which so far has not proved a weak reed to lean on by any people who are determined to protect their independence against outside aggression."

The speech and particularly the description of the U.S. defense line, which left out South Korea, received little attention at the time. Khrushchev in his memoires about the Moscow meetings planning for the Korean War does not mention it. Nevertheless, in retrospect it was ambiguous and not a wise statement to make. On the other hand, it made clear U.S. policy clearly was not to intervene further in the Chinese civil war.

As indicated above, the North Korean attack was initiated by President Kim Il-sung of North Korea and Stalin, with China initially on the side lines. China did not even have diplomatic relations with North Korea, which was clearly in Russia's orbit. Acheson's initial recommendations for action, approved by the President, was that the U.S. Air Force and Navy should confine their defense to south of the 38th parallel. By June 29, 1950 however, the President authorized them to include targets in North Korea. General MacArthur was authorized to use U.S. ground forces to secure ports, airfields, and communications at Pusan in the extreme south.

General Chiang immediately offered up to 33,000 troops to help defend South Korea. Truman initially expressed an interest, but Acheson's opposition to widening the war and weakening Chiang's position on Formosa carried the day, and the United States declined the offer. From the U.S. leaders' point of view, our policy then was to insulate the Korean conflict from the Chinese Communists' war with Chiang Kai-shek. However, from the

Chinese Communists' point of view, U.S. policy was not so clear and it soon took an ominous turn.

On July 31, soon after General MacArthur as supreme commander mobilized defenses in South Korea, he visited Chiang Kai-shek on Taiwan. In talking to the press MacArthur indicated one subject discussed was "effective military coordination between Chinese and American forces." Chiang then triumphantly assured the press that victory was assured "now that we can work closely together with our old comrade in arms," a reference to MacArthur who had been supreme commander in the Asian theater during World War II. Time magazine after the visit quoted a reliable source at MacArthur's headquarters as saying that MacArthur believed the Korean War would be useless if the United States did not fight Communism wherever it arose including backing Chiang, the British in Hong Kong, and the anti-Communists of Indo-China, Thailand and Burma.

MacArthur on August 25, then, in a message to the Veterans of Foreign Wars accused those of not wanting to defend Formosa as advocating appeasement and defeatism. He asserted it would not alienate Oriental psychology on continental Asia to follow resolute leadership. This statement was in direct conflict with President Truman's assurances to the U.N. that our action in Korea was limited and not designed to expand the conflict to China. President Truman in a sharp message ordered the General to withdraw his, message to the Veterans of Foreign Wars, which he did. At this point even those knowledgeable about how the U.S. government works would have been uneasy about the possibility of the U.S. again getting involved in a conflict between Chiang's and Mao Tse-tung's Communist forces.

MacArthur's prestige as a leader rocketed in the next few weeks when he completely reversed the course of the war. The North Korean forces had swept down the penninsula and cornered U.S. and South Korean forces on a small beachhead at Pusan. On September 15 MacArthur launched an amphibious operation on the northwest coast of South Korea, 200 miles north of Pusan that cut off the North Korean forces and caused them to retreat in disorder to the north. (See Map 3.)

Buoyed by this success the Pentagon agreed that he should pursue the North Korean forces into North Korea and finish the war. Truman approved instructions along this line on Septeber 27, but with the important condition that there be no entry of major Soviet or Chinese Communist forces into the conflict; if they did, MacArthur was to assume a defensive posture.

On October 2 the Indian Ambassador Panikkar from Peking warned the United States that China would probably enter the war if U.N. forces (forces other than those of South Korea) crossed the 38th parallel. On September 30 and October 10 Foreign Minister Chou En-lai announced that "the Chinese people would not stand idly by" in such an invasion.[4] The United States received similar messages from Moscow and Stockholm.[5] Truman interpreted the messages as an attempt to head off a U.N. resolution calling for a unified Korea. Despite the warning, the U.N. on October 7 approved a resolution calling for a "unified, independent and democratic government" of Korea. It was clear from the discussion of the resolution that its sponsors interpreted it as authorization for MacArthur to cross the 38th parallel, and the same day that the resolution was passed, U.S. forces reportedly entered North Korea.[6]

On October 15, President Truman, uneasy about the Chinese threat and hopeful of clearing the air with MacArthur, met him at Wake Island. In the meeting MacArthur assured the president that Chinese troops would not enter the war, and if they did, they would be destroyed.[7] At about the same time the Pentagon issued basic orders preventing American troops from entering the North Korean provinces adjacent to China. On October 24, however, MacArthur, sensing complete victory, ordered American troops to drive toward the Chinese border with the aim of ending the war by Christmas. In response, Chinese volunteer forces in a surprise attack against elements of the U.S. Eighth Army caused heavy casualties and then withdrew. MacArthur undaunted ordered his units forward. A few weeks later, as U.S. troops approached the border, masses of Chinese troops attacked causing initially heavy losses of American and South Korean forces.

General Ridgway assumed command under MacArthur, and it was a month before he succeeded in regrouping and stabilizing the fighting close to the 38th parallel at approximately the present border between North and South Korea. The final act of the Truman-MacArthur drama came in April, 1951 when Truman fired MacArthur for writing a letter to the minority leader of the House of Representatives, again supporting the use of Chinese Nationalist troops in the conflict and more forceful action in Korea. MacArthur came home to a hero's welcome in the United States, but President Truman had asserted his authority on the Chinese issue.

The point is, from the point of view of Truman and Acheson the U.S. made it clear to the Chinese it had no intention of intervening in the Chinese Civil War, and that U.S. objectives were to bring an end to the war with a unified Korea. MacArthur, supported by important Republican leaders, gave opposite signals on China which could have alarmed the Chinese. President Truman, nevertheless, bears the ultimate responsibility for the decision to send non-Korean troops into North Korea, which was the factor triggering the Chinese attacks on U.N. forces. The U.N. also shares in this responsibility by virtue of the General Assembly resolution authorizing MacArthur's action.

The Threat of Nuclear War

The Korean War was the first major war started in the nuclear era. The Soviets exploded their first nuclear bomb in August, 1949, and in January, 1950 Truman ordered the development of the first U.S. fusion bomb. The necessity of keeping the Korean War contained and from escalating into a nuclear conflict, therefore, was a major concern of Truman and other top leaders. A minor nuclear crisis occurred at the beginning of December, 1950, after the initial Chinese attack by "volunteers." This surprise attack caused a disorderly retreat of MacArthur's forces. At that time MacArthur, after landing at Inchon, near Seoul, had driven on into North Korea and was approaching the Chinese border. At the end of November, the Chinese volunteers attacked in force and MacArthur sent back an alarming secret message, that without a cease-fire or a new policy of air attacks and blockade of China, reinforcements from the United States and Formosa, and the possibility of using atomic weapons in North Korea, he would have to evacuate his forces."[8]

The nuclear issue broke into the media at the President's press conference of November 30, 1950. At that conference President Truman made the remark that he would take whatever steps were necessary to meet the military situation. One of the reporters asked "Will that include the atomic bomb?" Truman replied, "That includes every weapon that we have." "Mr. President," the reporter shot back, "You said 'every weapon that we have.' Does that mean there is active consideration of the use of the atomic bomb?" "There has always been active consideration of its use," Truman told him. "I don't want to see it used. It is a terrible weapon and it should not be used on innocent men, women, and children who have nothing whatever to do with this military aggression. That happens when it is used."[9]

To make sure that no one would misunderstand, Truman issued a separate statement after the press conference. The statement said that

> "consideration of the use of any weapon is always implicit in the very possession of that weapon. However, it should be emphasized that, by law, only the president can authorize the use of the atom bomb, and no such authorization has been given. If and when such authorization should be given, the military commander in the field would have charge of the tactical delivery of the weapon. In brief, the replies to the questions at today's press conference do not represent any change in the situation."

These statements, which were featured in the British press, alarmed Britain's Prime Minister Atlee, who made a hurried visit to Washington, D.C. a few days later for formal talks. During the meetings Prime Minister Atlee queried the President about his intention on the use of the nuclear bomb. At the end of the meetings Truman, in a communique, made the following statement:

> "The President stated that it was his hope that world conditions would never call for the use of the atomic bomb. The President told the Prime Minister that it was also his desire to keep the Prime Minister at all times informed of developments which might bring about a change in the situation.[10]

During the meetings Undersecretary Lovett phoned from the Pentagon reporting that radar screens of some air defense installations in the far north reported large formations of unidentified planes approaching. U.S. fighter planes were sent up to check on the report and alerts were flashed to air centers in New England. At that time it would have taken Russian bombers about two or three hours to reach Washington, D.C. The U.S. precautions were limited to defensive measures and the President proceeded with his meeting with Atlee as scheduled. About one hour later Secretary Lovett notified the President that the report had been error. Some unusual disturbance in the Arctic atmosphere, or geese, had been picked up as enemy planes.

Perhaps the world came close to a nuclear conflict at this point. It would have been easy for the President to have overreacted and put offensive nuclear bombers into the air. Conceivably, Russian leaders could have also reacted and the world could have been led into war by a mobilization and use of nuclear weapons like it was led into World War I by the mobilization and use of conventional military forces. However, as Truman notes in his memoires,[11] every decision he made in connection with the Korean conflict had one aim in mind, "to prevent a third world war and the terrible destruction it would bring to the civilized world. This meant that we should not do anything that would provide the excuse to the Soviets and plunge the free nations into full-scale all-out war." Not only did he exercise cool judgement with regard to the reported flight of Soviet bombers, but this aim kept him from expanding the conflict by using Chinese forces from Taiwan that Chiang Kai-shek offered to throw into the Korean battle.

Today, in a crisis of a threatened attack the time for decisions is minutes and not hours. In a twelve-month period, 1979-1980, there were three false alarms by radar of a Russian attack, and fortunately American leaders did not overreact by alerting their forces in such a way that it would threaten the Soviet Union. We will discuss this nuclear issue in more detail in Chapter 8, where we analyze the usefulness of the U.N. and its instruments for deterring war.

Assigning the Blame

The obvious instigator of the Korean War was Kim Il-sung, backed by Stalin and Mao. All of these leaders saw the war in terms of supporting a "Korean national liberation movement" in a struggle against capitalist oppressors of the South. As Khrushchev said, no good Communist could have refused to support Kim's proposal to prod South Korea with the point of a bayonet. Although as in many other wars the nationalist virus started the infection, the communist ideology lowered any resistance to the proposals for an attack.

From a non-Communist point of view, the attack was blatant Communist aggression against a state recognized by most of the world's nations. Kim and Stalin hoped by quick action they could overrun South Korea and portray the attack as an internal Korean affair. They made classic misjudgements of their opponents, and they were surprised by the strong U.S. reaction, which was supported by most of the world's nations.

Truman's aim in opposing aggression was to maintain the principle of collective security on behalf of the world community represented in the United Nations. His Secretary of State, Dean Acheson, saw the situation in power terms--reacting with military force after going through the motions in the UN and thereby deterring the Communists from further aggression. The Chinese intervention also was a classic power move. The Chinese did not want to see a powerful and hostile nation, the United States, controlling North Korea next to the Chinese industrial heartland of Manchuria. They avoided a direct challenge to the most powerful nation in the world by calling their troops "volunteers."

The lessons of the conflict for U.S. and Western leaders were far-reaching. To them, the attack was a close parallel to Hitler's aggression and evidence that the Communists would take advantage of weaknesses to commit aggression. The whole framework of alliances in the Far East with Japan, 1951; ANZUS, 1951; Philippines, 1951; Korea, 1953; Republic of China, 1954; and SEATO, 1954 in large part was a reaction to the Communist aggression. The Korean attack even had indirect effects in Europe of helping Secretary Acheson persuade NATO countries to strengthen that alliance by the rearmament of Germany.[12] Kim Il-Sung's attempt to spread Communism by force also convinced Truman that we should rearm and support Chiang Kai-shek's stronghold on Taiwan, which claimed to represent all of China. Another of Truman's counter moves was to escalate support to France in its battle against the Communist forces in North Vietnam. This proved to be a first step toward U.S. participation in the Vietnam War.

Perhaps the most important result of the war was psychological. The attack convinced many doubters that Communism was a world movement led by the Soviet Union that would take advantage of weakness, and that arms and alliances were the only effective way to contain Communist expansion. The Korean War gave strong political support to NATO and the Far East alliance systems, and consolidated the Cold War. Thirty years later we will see that the Russian invasion of Afghanistan gave a similar stimulus to rearmament against a perceived Communist threat.

NOTES

[1] Khrushchev's memoires were smuggled out of Russia in the form of tapes he had dictated after he was forced out of office by Brezhnev. They were widely published in summary form in Life and later in two volumes by Little, Brown, and Co. At first they were greeted by some suspicion, but as explained in the introduction to the second volume, they were subjected to extensive voice print tests by an independent agency. These tests confirmed that they were genuine, and Russian scholars generally accept them as Khrushchev's authentic dictation of his memoires. Although he denied that he had negotiated with Life and Little, Brown, and Co., the wording of the denial indirectly confirmed that a set of memoires did exist on tape. Perhaps more so than some memoires, they attempt to justify his position in history, but at the same time they provide a wealth of information that scholars rarely get on Communist policies.

[2] Harry S. Truman, Years of Trial and Hope (Garden City, N.Y.: Doubleday and Company, 1956), p. 333.

[3] Dean Acheson, Present at the Creation (New York: W. W. Norton & Company, 1969), p. 405.

[4] New York Times, October 1, 1950, p. 1.

[5] Truman, op. cit. pp. 361-362.

[6] New York Times, September 29, 1950, p. 1; October 5, 1950, p. 1 and October 8, p. 1.

[7] Acheson, too, had told the press there was reason to believe Chinese troops would not enter the war. New York Times, October 5, 1950, p 4.

[8] Dean Acheson, Present at the Creation (New York: W. W. Norton, 19 p. 477.

[9] Truman, op. cit., p. 395.

[10] Ibid. p. 396, 413.

[11] Ibid., pp. 395, 405.

[12] Acheson, op. cit., pp. 435-437.

CHAPTER 6

The Arab-Israeli Wars

The Origins

The origin of the five wars between Israel and its neighbors is described in Genesis, the first book of the Hebrew Torah and the first book of the Christian Bible. According to these scriptures, about four thousand years ago, after Abraham led a tribe of nomads from the land of Ur to the area now controlled by Israel, God promised the area where Abraham settled to him and his descendents forever and promised to create there a great nation for the Hebrews. The Old Testament is full of battles between the Hebrews (or Jews) and the original inhabitants of that land, and the conflicts have continued until today. Some of their battles involved the Philistine tribe, who lived there and who probably gave the name Palestine to the area.

This promise in the Jewish Torah is the basis of the burning nationalism that brought the Jews back to their Holy Land. The Zionist movement was founded in 1897 by Theodore Herzl to encourage Jews to escape from the anti-Semitism of France and other countries and to return to their Biblical homeland. Jewish immigration into Palestine increased after World War I and became a flood after World War II, when Jews fled from the memories of Hitler's Holocaust.

The first major break-through of the Zionist movement in establishing a home in Palestine for the Jews was the Balfour Declaration of 1918. The British Foreign Secretary Arthur Balfour, in gratitude for Jewish support in World War I, wrote a letter to Lord Rothschild, the leader of the Jewish community in Britain, with the following pledge:

> His Majesty's Government views with favor the establishment in Palestine of a national home

for the Jewish people and will use their best endeavors to facilitate the achievement of the object, it being clearly understood that nothing shall be done which may prejudice the civil and religious rights of existing non-Jewish communities in Palestine or the rights and political status enjoyed by the Jews in any other country.

During World War I the British had also made a commitment in the McMahon correspondence to the Arab religious and political leader, Sharif Hussain, an ally in the war against Germany. This pledge supported the formation of Arab nations from the Ottoman Empire, which at that time was waging war against Britain along with the Central Powers. There were reservations in this correspondence about certain districts in the general area of Palestine, but few of the Arabs read the fine print, and they believed that the British had committed that land to them.

Under the British post-war mandate of Palestine, which required Britain to report to the League of Nations on its management of the area, the Jews and Arabs squared off for battle. In 1920, Haj Amin Husseini, a young Arab nationalist, incited an Arab street mob to turn on the Jews in Jerusalem, and on Easter Sunday six Arabs and six Jews were killed in the riot. Haj Amin escaped arrest and fled to Trans-Jordan, the present state of Jordan. However, the British High Commissioner overlooked this crime and appointed Haj Amin as the Grand Mufti or religious leader of Palestine. The Islam religion extends into all social and political activities of its adherents. With his new position and British backing, Haj Amin was able to be elected to the Supreme Moslem Council of Palestine, controlling all religious funds. During the early years of the mandate he built up a powerful political machine where he could approve all official appointments in the mandate area. At the same time, he reportedly was responsible for major riots protesting Jewish immigration. The Jews also organized during this period and retaliated against the Arab terrorism in line with the Torah's admonition of an eye for an eye and a tooth for a tooth.

During World War II, Haj Amin went to Germany and collaborated with Hitler. After the war he returned to Egypt, where he had once attended college, to take over the leadership of the Arab opposition to Jewish immigration into Palestine.

After World War II Jewish immigration into Palestine flooded over quotas set by the British. The Jews were fleeing from the memories of Hitler's terror, where six million Jews were killed in the concentration camps and gas ovens of the Nazis. In protest against the British immigration restrictions, Menachim Begin and other Jews joined in the Irgun to mount a campaign of protest and

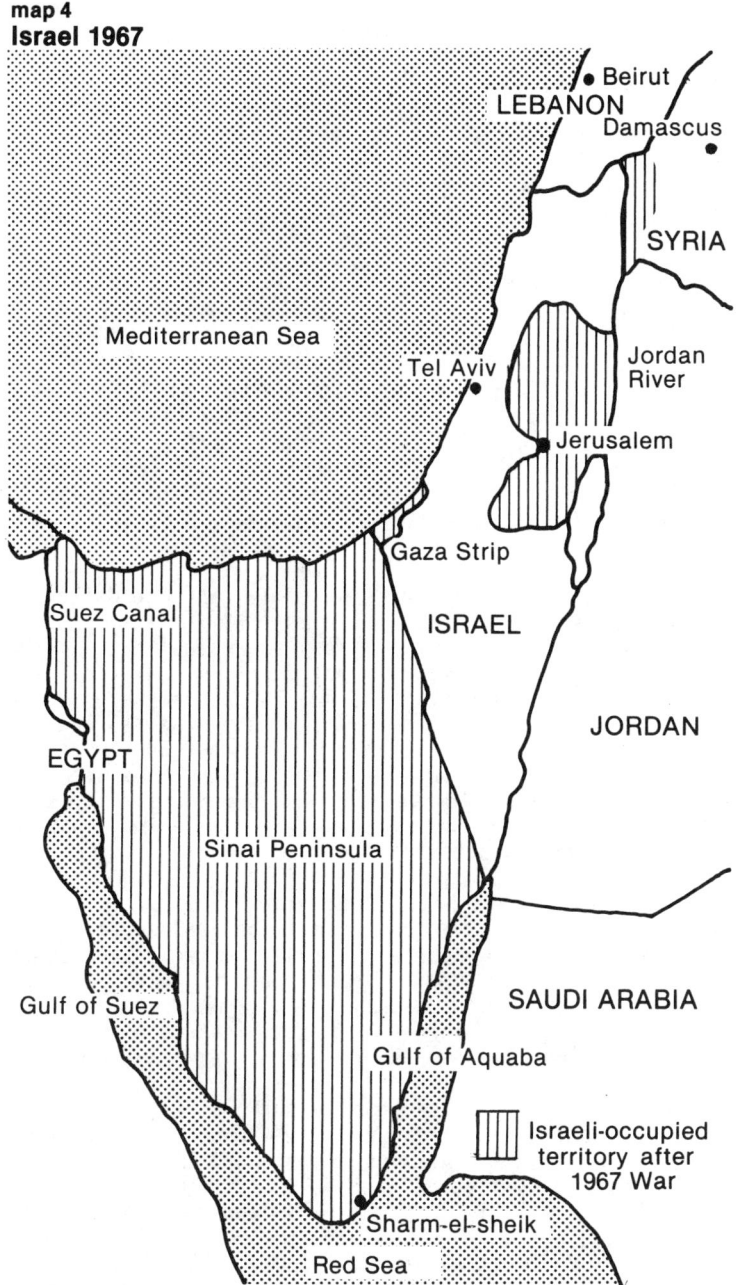

assassinations against the British and against the Arabs who had mounted a terrorist campaign under the leadership of Haj Amin. As the violence increased, the British finally gave up on their efforts to establish peace in the area. On April 2, 1947 the United Kingdom in a note to the United Nations, which had inherited mandate problems of the League of Nations, said the Palestine question should be placed on the agenda of the next General Assembly since Britain would withdraw its forces in May, 1948. The note also suggested that a special committee be convened to study the question.

The U.N. called a special session between April 28 and May 15, 1947 and chose a special committee to recommend a solution. It was composed of the smaller powers - not the big five of the Security Council. The committee after extensive consideration, including hearings in Palestine, submitted its report on August 31, 1947. The major proposal was by Canada, Czechoslovakia, Guatemala, the Netherlands, Peru, Sweden, and Uruguay. Both this proposal and the minority proposal by India, Iran, and Yugoslavia, recommended the partition of Palestine into Arab and Jewish states with Jerusalem under international control. Australia abstained from making a recommendation.

In September, 1947 the General Assembly, as a committee of all member states, heard the views of the United Kingdom, the Arab Higher Committee, and the Jewish Agency for Palestine. The United Kingdom said it could not impose a policy on Palestine by force of arms. The Arabs indicated that they would oppose the partition of what they considered their territory, while the Jewish Agency said it would accept the partition plan. On November 29, 1947 the General Assembly adopted the plan by a vote of 33 to 13 with ten abstentions, a few votes over the required two-thirds. Count Folke Bernadotte, President of the Swedish Red Cross, was appointed by the U.N. as mediator to put the plan into effect.

It was clear to Jewish and Arab leaders that there would be war as a result of the U.N. resolution. The Jews accelerated preparations by purchasing weapons and smuggling them into Palestine. Haj Amin's answer on December 1, 1947 was to provoke a riot in Jerusalem spread by rumors that two Arab women had been raped by the Jews. The British forces did not intervene to stop the looting and burning of Jewish shops.

In December, leaders of seven Arab nations (Egypt, Iraq, Saudi Arabia, Syria, Yemen, Lebanon, and Trans-Jordan) met in the Egyptian Ministry of Foreign Affairs to prepare a plan of action. They represented forty-five million Arabs, thirty times the population of the Jews in Palestine. They commanded five regular armies; any one of the three major armies of Iraq, Egypt, or Trans-Jordan fully committed to the fight in Palestine could have probably defeated the Jews. However, the Arab leaders were overconfident and split by rivalries. Egypt was most concerned about its position in the Suez Canal and with its relations with the British, who patrolled the Canal. Iraq's leader, Nuri-Said, had as a major aim to annex Syria; Syria, realizing this, did not want Iraq's forces to march through it on the way to Palestine. King Abdullah, of Trans-Jordan did not have his heart in a war against the Jews; he hated Haj Amin, and he was disdainful of King Farouk, the weak leader of Egypt. Most of all, he wanted to annex part of Palestine on the West Bank, and to control at least part of Jerusalem in line with the U.N. partition plan. With these divisions, the Secretary General Abdulrahman Azzam Pasha, the Secretary General of the Arab League, was able only to get a lowest common denominator of a resolution which called on Haj Amin to wage guerrilla warfare against the Jews with Arab support until the British mandate ended. This suited Haj Amin, whose aim was to put himself into a position to control Palestine after the Jews were driven out.

The Arab leaders were high on rhetoric but low on material support for the guerrillas of Haj Amin. The Jewish strategy was to hold every collective farm (kibbutz) with the help of their secret army, the Haganah. Most of all, their strategy was to dig in and control Jerusalem, their holy city. Haj Amin was fully determined to strangle the Jewish community in Jerusalem, and with this in mind, organized a series of attacks led by his cousin on convoys of supplies to Jerusalem. The British convoys were not molested, but the Jewish convoys with food, supplies, and weapons for Jerusalem were attacked during the next few months along the vulnerable forty-mile Jerusalem road.

The December, 1947 meeting of Arab leaders in Cairo appointed Ismail Pasha, a Syrian, as the leader of the Liberation Army. During the next few months thousands of volunteers converged on Damascus from all over the Arab world to help form the force to liberate Jerusalem. However, funds and ammunition were short, and discipline poor. Meanwhile, during that 1947-48 winter, the Jews managed to keep convoys moving to Jerusalem despite heavy losses from Haj Amin's guerrilla forces.[1] On May 14, 1948 the mandate of the United Kingdom expired, and the Jewish leader Ben Gurion proclaimed the new Jewish state under the name of Israel. On the following day the Arab states attacked Palestine. The causes and motives of the war were clear--conflicting nationalisms reinforced by religion.

The Arabs could not get their act together, while the Jews fought tenaciously to hold on to Jerusalem and their exposed settlements. After about two months of fighting, with both sides nearing exhaustion, they agreed to a cease-fire in line with a Security Council resolution. During the next thirty days of the cease-fire, the Israeli forces were able to smuggle in large quantities of conventional weapons and to refurbish their exhausted food and military supplies in Jerusalem. When the fighting resumed, the Jewish forces, strengthened in numbers and equipment, were able greatly to increase the territory under their control. The Arab nations, threatened by a disastrous defeat, agreed to another cease-fire and truce under the supervision of the U.N. mediator, Count Folke Bernadotte. When he was assassinated by Jewish terrorists, an American, Ralph Bunche, was appointed in his place. In February, March, and April, he arranged separate truces between Israel and Egypt, Lebanon, and Jordan, and finally Syria on July 20, ending the first Arab-Israeli war. The truce recognized Jewish control of an area more than double the area of the original proposed U.N. partition plan. This laid the basis for a strong Israel, but fueled the burning resentment among the Arabs that was the basis for future Arab-Israeli wars.

The 1956 Suez War

The Suez War of 1956 was the last major fling of British and French leaders at regaining an imperial position in the Mideast. Israel was a willing partner, determined to break the tightening Arab blockade. During 1952 to 1956 Nasser took over supreme power of the revolutionary movement in Egypt, which had toppled King Farouk. Nasser was the head of a group of nationalist army officers who were determined to end the dominant role of the British in Egypt. As Nasser consolidated his power, he established himself as leader of the Arabs in their continuing struggle against Israel. His Radio Cairo blanketed the Mideast with propaganda against Israel and reinforced Egypt's position as a natural leader of the Arab world.

By the end of 1953 Egypt had cut off all cargoes to and from Israel going through the Suez Canal. It then tightened the screws by blockading the Straits of Tiran, which cut off Israel's last direct access by ship to Asia. Tensions in the Mideast remained high as Arab guerrillas attacked Israel from neighboring states, and as Israel retaliated.

Britain recognized the power of the nationalist movement under Nasser by agreeing in 1954 to withdraw its forces from the Suez Canal. The U.S. encouraged this move on legal and political grounds. The last British soldier left the Suez Canal area in June, 1956. The Canal, however, was still run by the private British-French Suez Canal Company, and Britain was still responsible for the protection of the Canal under an Anglo-Egyptian treaty of 1955.

President Nasser was determined to build up Egypt's military strength in his crusade against Israel. Nasser, at first, tried to get arms from the United States, but failing this, he made a major arms deal with the Russians on September 27, 1955. This alarmed Britain, France, and the United States, and it made a particularly strong impact on Israel. Israel was outnumbered about 20 to 1 by the Egyptian population, and Israel's leaders believed that Egypt's acquisition of modern Russian arms represented a "stunning acceleration" of rearmament in the Middle East that soon would tip the balance "drastically" against Israel.[2] Chief-of-Staff General Dayan pressed for a major military move to take over Sharm-el-Sheikh, which controlled the Straits of Tiran, and the Gaza Strip, where many of the Arab terrorist raids originated.

Ben Gurion had returned as head of Israel's Defense Ministry early in 1955, and he and its director general, Shimon Peres, laid the groundwork for the supply of French arms to the Israeli army. In January, 1956 Guy Mollet formed a new French cabinet with the Radical Socialists as a major coalition partner. This party was deeply concerned with France's Algerian problem, and Radical Socialist leaders hated Nasser, who was the major supplier and supporter of the Algerian rebels. Guy Mollet and his socialist party were also favorably disposed toward Israel as a socialist state.

In May and June, 1956 top Israeli officials met with the French Defense Minister to propose massive deliveries of arms to Israel and discuss joint action against Egypt. Just after these visits the Suez Canal issue boiled over. Secretary of State Dulles, after a long period of negotiating with Egypt, suddenly withdrew a U.S. offer of aid to help build the Aswan Dam; this was a major project on the Nile that would provide water and irrigation for Egypt's economic expansion. Dulles' action reflected exasperation over Nasser's arms deal with the Communist Bloc, Nasser's strong opposition to British and American efforts through the Bagdad Pact to build an alliance of Arab nations against Russia, and Nasser's recognition of Red China, all of which were at cross-purposes with U.S. diplomacy.

Nasser retaliated on July 26 by nationalizing the Suez Canal. This infuriated Anthony Eden, the British Prime Minister, and French leaders who felt they had been "had" by Nasser's easing British forces out of the canal zone, and then immediately taking over control of the historic lifeline to Asia. The fact that Nasser offered to reimburse the owners of the assets of the Suez Canal Company did not lessen the blow. The day after the nationalization was announced, the French foreign minister and military experts flew to London to plan joint action against Egypt.[3] They found support from Anthony Eden, the Prime Minister, although his Cabinet was reluctant to force the issue. Eden saw Nasser as another Mussolini. Nasser had not only opposed the CENTO alliance but he had encouraged Jordan, another key British ally in the Middle East, to dismiss Glubb Pasha, the British Commander of Jordanian forces.[4]

In one sense Nasser had made a brilliant move because international law was on his side. In fact, President Eisenhower and Secretary of State Dulles for this reason did not contest Nasser's right to take over the Suez Canal. Their tactic was to start a series of negotiations to set up an organization that would guarantee the Canal would remain open and ensure its efficient operation. At the same time, Eisenhower and Dulles attempted to calm Anthony Eden and dissuade him from using force against Egypt.

British and French leaders were determined to try to unseat Nasser and to try to regain control over the Canal, but the British, particularly, were deterred by Eisenhower and Dulles' strong objections to the use of force and by their negotiations to establish an international regime for the Canal. French, British, and Israeli leaders met secretly, and French leaders proposed a way out of the dilemma. Israel was to act first with a military action to threaten the Canal, and then British and French forces were to take over the Canal, ostensibly in accord with the 1955 Treaty by which Britain retained the right to protect the Canal when threatened by war. During the secret negotiations it was apparent the British and French gave priority to unseating Nasser over keeping the Canal open, which could have been accomplished by the Dulles negotiations.[5]

In the midst of the negotiations to establish an international regime for the Canal, on November 2, Eisenhower and Dulles were informed that the Israelis had opened an attack in the Sinai. At the same time U-2 intelligence planes and other information indicated that the British and French were mobilizing forces in the Eastern Mediterranean to support the Israeli attack. Without hesitation, the United States called an emergency meeting of the U.N. Security Council, and Dulles drafted a resolution demanding a cease-fire and withdrawal of forces from Suez. The resolution was strongly backed by other U.N. members including the Soviet Union, but it was blocked in the Security Coucil by the French and British vetoes. British and French forces attempted to take over the Canal as planned. The issue was then transferred to the General Assembly, which strongly supported the majority opinion of the Security Council that all forces should withdraw from the Suez Canal area. Canada drafted a resolution asking for an international force under the command of the United Nations to separate the combatants. The vote on this resolution was 57 to 0. The first units were organized and placed in Egypt by November 15.

The Suez crisis took place during the confusion of the Soviet invasion of Hungary. On October 28, as Israel was beginning its invasion, the Security Council took up the problem caused by the new, revolutionary Prime Minister of Hungary, Nagy, informing the U.N. Secretary-General that Nagy was demanding the withdrawal of Russian troops, which had invaded Hungary. The Security Council was blocked by the Russian veto, so that the General Assembly took up this issue and by a vote of 50 to 8 demanded the withdrawal of foreign forces from Hungary. Eisenhower, meanwhile, was campaigning for re-election as President and he summed up the issues posed by these crises as follows: "We cannot - in the world, any more than in our own nation, subscribe to one law for the weak, and another for the strong." Thus, he and Dulles were supporting the U.N. Charter by opposing aggression whether by a traditional enemy or by close historical allies.

Anthony Eden's action against Nasser stirred up a hornets nest of opposition in Britain, particularly among the Labor opposition. At times proceedings had to be suspended because of the booing and disorder caused by their opposition to the aggressive British moves against Egypt.[6] Pressure mounted on him to resign, which he finally did on January 9, 1957, at his doctor's suggestion.

Eisenhower accompanied his stand with strong diplomacy in the United Nations against the U.S. allies. The U.S. Secretary of the Treasury indicated Israel's action would affect our aid programs to Israel including private donations of aid to Israel, which benefited from tax deductions in the United States. Egypt, at the outbreak of the hostilities, closed the Canal and its vital oil traffic by sinking thirty-two ships in the Canal so that Britain and France were faced with a cold and harsh winter with greatly reduced petroleum supplies. Britain and France, therefore, faced the need for economic and petroleum assistance to make up for the shortage of oil caused by blocking the Suez Canal. This, plus world disapproval, reflected by an overwhelming vote in the United Nations against their action, caused them to back down.

Israel was the first to yield after it had achieved control of Sharm-el-Sheik. Britain and France then agreed to halt their military actions soon after the Israeli action. Some historians have alleged that Russian threats to intervene played an important part in causing Britain, France, and Israel to end their aggression. A close reading of the record, however, indicates that the Russian threat did not come until a week after hostilities started and after Israel had agreed to a cease-fire. Although Russian intervention was in the back of the minds of those acting during the crisis, there is little evidence that this was the major consideration in the key decisions of Eisenhower and Dulles to support the U.N. Charter by opposing aggression and pressuring the aggressors to withdraw.

By March 16, 1957 Israel had completely withdrawn from the Sinai, which it had taken during the hostilities. It did this with assurances that freedom of navigation would be maintained through the Straits of Tiran. This condition later played a key part in the 1967 war ten years later.

Under the good offices of the International Bank the Suez stockholders reached agreement with Egypt, whereby it would pay $81 million for the Suez Canal Company's assets in the Canal area, while the stockholders could keep all external assets. Simultaneously, Britain unfroze 400 million pounds that it had blocked when Nasser nationalized the Suez Canal. By April 24, 1957 the U.N. managed to raise ships sunk in the Canal, and the Canal was open for traffic.

The Suez War was an unfortunate last fling of colonialism or neo-colonialism on Britain's part that was not in the main stream of other Arab-Israeli conflicts. Britain and France thought they could get around international law with a few subterfuges, and they were greatly surprised by the strength of the U.S. action in support of the U.N. and its principles of non-aggression.

Israel viewed the war as retaliation, since Egypt had blockaded the Straits of Tiran. However, Israel too, was surprised at the strength of the U.S. and world reaction against its moves against Egypt, and at one point Israel was even threatened with a resolution that would have expelled it from the United Nations. Eisenhower maintained a steady course - support of the United Nations and of international law as a guide to the solution of the problem. This involved confronting the United States' closest allies and lining up with its historic enemy, the Soviet Union. Despite the complications of the invasion of Hungary and presidential elections, the crisis was solved relatively quickly. However, the war added to the underlying tensions that erupted in the 1967 war.

The 1967 War

Israel fired the first shots in the 1967 war, yet many observers blame Nasser for the conflict. To understand Israel's position in relation to the neighboring states, which were its enemies, it is helpful to look at Table 7 which compares their military manpower and population. It is obvious from this table that Israel was outnumbered about 40 to 1 in terms of its population and greatly outnumbered in military manpower. Nasser's initial action, therefore, to move a major part of the Egyptian army up to the border of Israel and the Sinai, coupled with similar moves from his Arab allies on Israel's borders, threatened Israel's existence. His bellicose statements forced Israel to mobilize its limited manpower, thereby robbing farms and factories of necessary labor. Nasser's next move to blockade Israel's only outlet to the Far East, the Straits of Tiran at the mouth of the Gulf of Aqaba, was an act of war under international law. This gave Israel the excuse to retaliate. As we will see, Nasser and other Egyptian leaders realized this and our first major question, therefore, centers on why Nasser took these steps.

TABLE 7

MIDDLE EAST POPULATION AND MANPOWER - 1967

	Military Manpower	Population
Israel	75,000*	3,000,000
Egypt	310,000	35,000,000
Syria	110,000	7,000,000
Jordan	60,000	2,600,000
Iraq	95,000	10,000,000
Lebanon	15,000	3,100,000
Saudi Arabia	40,000	8,500,000

*Mobilization to 400,000 is possible in 72 hours.
Source: International Institute for Strategic Studies, The Military Balance, (London).

Anwar Sadat, who succeeded Nasser as President of Egypt, describes vividly the political events that influenced Nasser to take this decision. In the year preceeding the war General Amer, the commander of Egyptian forces, was gaining more and more political power and directly challenging Nasser's ability to govern. Anwar Sadat describes Nasser's despair a few months before the decision to go to war as follows:

"I am worried," Nasser told Sadat. "My dear Anwar, the country is being ruled by a gang of thieves,...and I cannot carry on like this. I cannot continue to be President, to hold such a serious responsibility, while it is Amer who actually rules the country and does precisely what he wants. I think it is better for me to go, and perhaps concentrate on my duties as chairman of the Arab Socialist Union (the only political organization). I'm willing to hand the Presidency over to him and to answer for everything that has taken place up to the minute of my departure." A few days later, one of the political leaders made a formal request that Nasser step down and let Amer be Premier. Nasser replied that he would agree to this if Amer gave up his command as head of the armed forces. Amer made no reply to this proposal, which would have undermined the base of his political power.

A few months later, Sadat continues, many Arab brothers criticized Egypt for leaving the Tiran Strait open to Israeli navigation. At one point Amer sent a telegram during a visit to Pakistan demanding that this strait be closed to Israeli navigation. Nasser later convened Egypt's Supreme Executive Committee at the end of May 1967, which was attended by Amer, to discuss the issue. During the discussion, Nasser said that if we close the Straits, war would be 100 percent certain. He turned at that point to General Amer and asked if the armed forces were ready. According to Sadat, Amer replied, "Everything's in tip-top shape." All including Sadat, except one of the Executive Committee, voted for closing the Straits.

Sadat explains that Nasser "was eager to close the Straits so as to put an end to the Arab maneuverings and maintain his great prestige within the Arab world." A few pages later, in assessing the conflict, he stated that the Amer-Nasser conflict played a major role in bringing about the terrible disaster."[7]

After the disaster of the 1967 wars, Sadat, six years later was to fall prey to the same type of nationalist fever.

Table 7 shows Israel's basic vulnerability and helps explain the reason it decided to strike first. Only by complete mobilization of its population for war could it put together a force of 400,000 adequate to counter the Arab threat. Such a mobilization would severely hinder economic and other activities in Israel.

On May 14, 1967 Israeli intelligence warned its leaders of massive Egyptian forces moving into the Sinai. On May 17, President Nasser requested the U.N. forces which separated Egypt and Israel to leave. A few days later 80,000 Egyptian troops and 800 tanks were moving in the Sinai towards Israel's border. On May 22, Nasser announced that the Straits of Tiran were blockaded, and on May 26 in a public press conference, Nasser pledged to destroy Israel. (See Map 4.)

The Soviet Union played an important role in goading Nasser to take this action. Anwar Sadat reported that on a visit to Moscow on May 20, Russia's deputy Foreign Minister had told him that ten Israeli brigades were concentrating on the border of Syria, which was Egypt's closest ally. When Sadat got back to Cairo, he found that Soviets had also informed Nasser of this. According to Sadat, this played a part in Nasser's decision, but Sadat's later accounts of the cabinet decision do not mention these false reports. These reports were also repeated in Russian propaganda. Israel, to counter the reports, invited the Russian ambassador to tour its northern border to see for himself the reports were not true. The Soviet ambassador refused. Also, the United States and other powers assured Egypt that the Soviet reports were false.[8]

On May 26, Nasser declared Egyptian and Syrian forces unified under one command. On May 30, Jordan joined its forces in this command when King Hussein flew to Cairo and signed a defense pact with Nasser. Iraq joined with the Arab armies on June 4, and moved an armored battalion and a mechanized brigade into Jordan. Meanwhile, Moshe Dayan, the commander of the 1956 war, was pressing Israel to strike first with the aim of destroying the Egyptian armies in the Sinai. On June 1, he was appointed Minister of Defense. After debating the issue, the Cabinet gave him the authority to strike first at a time of his own choosing.

There is another major question to address in determining the reasons for the war and why it was not headed off. Many observers and even historians blame Secretary-General U-Thant for agreeing to Nasser's demand to withdraw U.N. forces, which separated the future combatants. U-Thant, however, was at the mercy of the countries contributing to the U.N. contingents, and three of them insisted on withdrawing their forces in line with the Egyptian request. Secretary-General U-Thant did bring the matter up before the U.N. Security Council and the General Assembly, which was meeting in a special session at that time. The records show that he stressed the dangers of war, but that the U.N. did not take action to meet Israel's major demand to keep the Straits of Tiran open to Israeli shipping.

It is puzzling that the United States did not receive more criticism for its failure to act in this crisis. After the 1956 war it had made a commitment to keep the Straits of Tiran open, and it had reaffirmed that commitment only a few months before the war broke out. President Johnson's own memoires describe the delays of U.S. diplomacy as it attempted to get the U.N. to act, its major allies to help form an international naval force, and Congress to support U.S. action to break the Egyptian blockade of the Straits of Tiran. With its overwhelming naval power the U.S. could have kept the Straits open, but Johnson's memoires reveal a lack of understanding of Israel's vulnerability and the urgency of the crisis. Johnson made assurances to Israel, but they were not strong, and they did not satisfy the Israeli leaders that he was serious about keeping the Gulf open to their shipping. Moshe Dayan's memoires indicate, moreover, that perhaps he secretly was glad that Israel had a clear excuse to smash the Egyptian threat without the long, drawn-out negotiations that would have resulted if the United States had acted more forcefully. Johnson, at this period, was in the midst of the political turmoil caused by the wide-spread opposition to the Vietnam War. Perhaps a year or two earlier he would have had the confidence to take the initiative in this crisis, but his political position in his eyes was so weak that he dallied in the hope of developing congressional and international backing for using U.S. naval forces in the Middle East.

Israel achieved complete tactical surprise in its attack, and in the first day of fighting wiped out three-fourths of the Egyptian Air Force, about one-half of the Syrian Air Force, and all of the small Jordanian Air Force, with minimal losses to Israeli planes. This gave it the air cover for its ground offensive and air attacks against Egyptian tanks. In an incredibly short period of six days the Israeli armed forces had swept up to the banks of the Suez Canal, taken over the strategic Sharm-el-Sheikh, and captured the strategic Golan Heights from Syria that had been used to shell settlements in Galilee. Israel's forces also easily captured East Jerusalem and swept to the West Bank of the Jordan. This gave Israel control over the Arab population of the West Bank that has become the major issue preventing a peace settlement in the Middle East.

Thus, Arab nationalism, based on a claim to the lands of Israel, goaded Nasser to take the offensive. Perhaps the most important pressures were the internal political pressures mounted by General Amer, who challenged Nasser's leadership. External Arab pressure also played a role in goading Nasser to lead an Arab crusade against Israel. Nasser did not want to lose his status as the leader of the Arab nations in their struggle against Israel.

Nasser's threat to attack Israel and his belligerent act of closing the Straits of Tiran in the eyes of most observers justified Israel's surprise assault. As a result the Arab armies suffered a humiliating defeat and Israel almost trebled in size as a result of its conquests. In the south it took over the huge military buffer of the Sinai desert. In the northeast it controlled the Golan Heights, which had been used by Syria to harrass agricultural settlements in Galilee. In the east Israel took over part of Jerusalem and the West Bank of the Jordan, again making defense much simpler from a military standpoint.

General Amer was the goat of the war, responsible for a lack of military preparedness for the Israeli assault. He was arrested by Nasser, and Amer later committed suicide in humiliation.

The most important political result was the conquest of the West Bank of the Jordan, which has remained the focus of Israel's dispute with Arab neighbors since the 1967 war.

The 1973 War

Israel's stunning victory in 1967 and its determination this time to hold on to its gains made the fourth Arab-Israeli war virtually inevitable. Sadat, who after Nasser's death assumed the presidency, was completely devastated by Israel's victory and resolved to show the world Egypt could fight. Sadat's personal humiliation and "search for identity" is summarized in his memoirs entitled In Search of Identity:

> I myself was completely overwhelmed by our defeat. It sank into the very fabric of my consciousness so that I relived it day and night. As its real dimensions were daily revealed to me, my agony intensified--and my sense of helplessness. I shut myself up for three whole weeks at my home near the Pyramids, concentrating on the recent events and trying, with all the fortitude I possessed, to weather the fierce campaign of denigration launched by both friend and foe against our armed forces.
>
> Doubts were cast on our fighting ability. It was alleged that the Egyptians were not fit for fighting, that no further wars could ever be fought for the recovery of our land and the restoration of our honor. If it were true, I thought, it could mean death and destruction for our people for thousands of years to come---we might even end up in the same predicament as the Red Indians of America. What a disgrace and humiliation...I was brought up to love and believe in Egypt, and to have infinite faith in the Egyptian man. Would all this now go overboard? If it did, I would too. For in that case I could never recognize the man I call myself, never know who I really was, but must live without identity--a stranger

among strangers. Would such a life be worth
living?

I had to break out of the moral dilemma in
which I found myself so suddenly. That Egypt
should survive became my dominant passion. I
wanted to ascertain whether we were able to
fight or not and indeed could think of nothing
else.[9]

Sadat then sought out one of the Egyptian generals wounded in the battle, who recounted how his unit had mounted a successful counterattack during the 1967 war. From his account and others Sadat became convinced that confusion in the high command was responsible, not the Egyptian soldiers' willingness to fight. He became determined it was his duty to help Egypt's struggle to survive.

On taking power after Nasser's death in 1970, Sadat's Minister of Finance informed him Egypt was "almost bankrupt," and Egypt's desperate economic plight strengthened Sadat's resolve to redress the 1967 defeat. He was faced with a dilemma since Egypt was largely dependent on Soviet arms and military advisors, yet he was concerned about the attempts of some of these advisors in conspiracy with a group of Egyptian officials to take over the government. Sadat then ordered the 20,000 Russian advisors to leave Egypt in the summer of 1972. By cutting these ties with the Soviets Sadat hoped to enlist the support of the United States in getting Israel to return the Sinai peacefully. However Dr. Kissinger, the key U.S. official, was too engrossed in the Vietnam War, reestablishing ties with China, and other issues to devote much attention to Egypt's problems.[10] Moreover, cutting those ties with the Soviet Union lulled both the United States and Israel from taking Egypt seriously as a military threat to Israel. Sadat explains his views in his memoirs as follows:

I worked hard on the problem, of course, making
use of every possible resource. Throughout 1971
and 1972 the real dimensions of our economic predi-
cament were not very clear to me. Only five days
before the October War I asked the National Security Council to face the reality and learned that
our economy had fallen below zero. This would have
frightened anyone in my position, I am sure, but I
tried to think about it calmly and took my decision.

I do not believe that most people in my position
would have plucked up enough courage to take a decision of any sort, but I was confident that the key
to everything--politically, economically, and mili-
tarily--was to redress the situation following from
the 1967 defeat, so as to regain our self-confi-

dence and the world's confidence in us. The economic situation was merely one of the dimensions of the problem.

The basic task was to wipe out the disgrace and humiliation that followed from the 1967 defeat. I reckoned it would be 1,000 times more honorable for us--40,000 of my sons in the armed forces and myself--to be buried crossing the Canal than to accept such disgrace and humiliation. Posterity would say we had died honorably on the battlefield...and posterity would carry on the struggle.[11]

President Sadat then issued explicit orders to prepare plans for a counterattack against Israel. Even his military commanders at first did not take him seriously, but Sadat determined to carry through with the attack. Moshe Dayan and other Israeli leaders were convinced Sadat would attempt to regain the Sinai, but the Egyptian attack on Israel's sacred holiday of Yom Kippur in October, 1973 caught the Israeli army off balance. Supported by Syria, Jordan, and other Arab nations, Sadat's forces breached the Israeli defense line on the Canal and established his Egyptian third army on the east bank of the Canal, recapturing Egyptian territory that had been conquered by the Israelis.

Israel, after a brutal battle in which most of its tanks and a large number of aircraft were destroyed, managed to cut off the Egyptian Sinai salient in the last hours of the war. Secretary of State Kissinger with a major diplomatic effort assisted the United Nations in establishing a truce.

The terrible potential for escalation of the Arab-Israel conflicts was demonstrated on October 24 when the United States received a Russian threat they would police the cease fire unilaterally if the U.S. did not participate in such an effort. The Soviet threat was reinforced by U.S. intelligence reports that the Soviets were alerting seven airborne divisions and possibly sending ships into the Mediterranean Sea with nuclear weapons. Kissinger late at night after consulting briefly on the telephone with Nixon, who was preoccupied with the Watergate crisis, instructed the Secretary of Defense to raise the alert status of U.S. nuclear forces with the intention of using the resulting movement of forces to send the Soviets a message. The Soviets did not dispatch troops to the area, and Kissinger was able to get the cease-fire reinforced with U.N. forces and calm the crisis without a dangerous further escalation of threats.

Israel's heavy losses in the war forced it to treat Egyptian demands with a new respect, and over the next few years a series of withdrawals and finally a peace settlement was negotiated under President Carter at Camp David providing for Israel to give up all of the Egyptian territory it had conquered. Israel did not, however, give up the Gaza Strip, the Golan Heights, and the West Bank of the Jordan, which contained almost a million Palestinian Arabs, who were demanding a right to form their own nation in this territory.

Israel's refusal to give back this land to Arab control set the stage for Israels' prolonged struggle with the Palestinian Liberation Organization, which continued to carry the Arab banner for regaining the lost territories for the "Palestinians."

The War In Lebanon

In the 1970s the focus of the conflict between Israel and the Arabs shifted to Lebanon. In September, 1970 the PLO assisted by Syrian PLO tank units tried to unseat King Hussein of Jordan, but he rallied the Jordanian army and forced the PLO rebels and their families out of Jordan into Lebanon. (This was the origin of the "Black September" name for certain PLO terrorist units.) The PLO refugees from Jordan settled mostly in Beirut and southern Lebanon near the border with Israel, close to Palestinian refugee camps already there.

The oil-rich Arab states financed PLO purchases of weapons from Russia, which not only enabled the PLO to shell Israel from Lebanon, but also successfully to take over military and political control of much of southern Lebanon. Lebanese authorities were not able to challenge PLO rule, but Lebanese Christian forces supplied by Israel attacked the PLO units and set up centers of political and military control. Southern Lebanon became almost a no-man's-land of continual strife.

Former Secretary of State Kissinger explains the subsequent move of Syrian forces into Lebanon as follows: "Despite strenuous avowals of its devotion to the Palestinian cause, Syria in 1976 sent its army into Lebanon to prevent a PLO victory over the Lebanese Christians and indigenous Moslems."[12] He gave as the reason for Syria's move its fear of having a radical Palestinian state on its borders in addition to its long-time enemy Iraq. The Syrian forces in Lebanon, which were under the flag of the Arab League, barely managed to contain Lebanon's civil war, and clashes continued between various factions. The PLO continued raids and shelling of Israeli settlements from Lebanon.

On March 15, 1978 following a Palestinian commando raid in Israel, Israeli forces invaded southern Lebanon. A few days later the Security Council managed to establish a truce with the help of the United Nations Interim Force in Lebanon (UNIFIL) with the aim of getting Israeli forces to withdraw and of assisting the Government of Lebanon to reestablish its authority over the area. UNIFIL forces patrolled only a narrow sector in Lebanon along the

Israeli border, and they were not able to prevent further clashes there between the Christian and Moslem forces or terrorist attacks against Israel, and retaliatory attacks by Israeli forces.

In July, 1981 Philip Habib, the U.S. Middle East negotiator, arranged a cease-fire between Israel and Lebanon, and for almost a year there was a lull in the PLO attacks and Israeli retaliation. This cease-fire was broken in June, 1982 with the attempted assassination by a Palestinian group of the Israeli ambassador to London. Israel reacted by shelling PLO camps in Lebanon, and the PLO responded by again shelling settlements in northern Israel. On June 6 Israeli forces mounted a major attack in southern Lebanon, slicing through the UN zone patrolled by UNIFIL, and destroying and attacking PLO camps up to the outskirts of Beirut. After a few sharp exchanges with Syrian forces, during which Israel shot down over 60 MIG aircraft and destroyed Syria's surface-to-air missiles in Lebanon, Israeli and Syrian forces declared a cease-fire. This permitted Israel with the aid of Lebanese Christian troops to concentrate on mopping up PLO centers of resistance and on beseiging and surrounding the major PLO headquarters in Western Beirut.

Israel offered to withdraw its forces as soon as the Lebanese Government reasserted authority, which included disarming the PLO, and as soon as Syrian forces withdrew from Lebanon. Israel also invited the United States and others to patrol Southern Lebanon. They refused, but Israel withdrew its forces anyway. It continued periodic patrols in a narrow security zone inside Lebanon.

At the end of 1987 there was still no peace. Israel's attack had forced PLO forces to evacuate from southern Lebanon to friendly Arab nations, but some PLO elements were still in Lebanon. United States forces had withdrawn after 241 U.S. marines were killed in a suicidal attack on their Beirut headquarters. Syrian forces with the agreement of the Lebanese government had moved into western Lebanon and Beirut. Israeli forces continued periodic raids across the border, and Lebanese religious and political factions continued their skirmishes.

The Roots of the Wars

Jewish nationalism opposed by Arab nationalism, both reinforced by religious claims and cultural differences, are the roots of the long history of wars in the former area of Palestine. The cynicism developing out of these wars has submerged ideals of peace and cooperation, and power politics dominate policies in the area. However, the people's weariness of war plus common ideals of the Moslem, Jewish and Christian religions helped President Sadat, Prime Minister Begin, and President Carter negotiate the Camp David peace treaty, which finally brought peace to Israel and Egypt in 1979. This peace has been violently opposed by Arab nationalists in other areas of the Middle East, because it neutralized Egypt as the most powerful Arab opponent of Israel in the area.

The history of the Arab-Israel wars is replete with misjudgements of their opponents by leaders. The Arab leaders in the 1948 war grossly misjudged the ability of the Jewish settlements to defend themselves, and after the war Israel staked out a claim to nationhood twice as large as the UN partition plan, which Arab leaders had tried to defeat.

Israeli, French, and British leaders also grossly misjudged the reactions of world leaders, and particularly the United States, in the 1956 war, when the United States rallied the U.N. in opposition to their aggression against Egypt. Probably the most serious underestimation of the enemy was made by Nasser and his leaders in 1967. The successful Israeli rebuff to Nasser's aggressive acts brought Israel to control the Sinai, the West Bank, and the Golan Heights. After the war Arab nationalists insisted their claims to regain the Sinai, Gaza, the West Bank, and the Golan Heights were non-negotiable.

Oil and strategic lines of communication are behind the intense power politics in the region. The major powers of the world have indicated that a continued supply of petroleum is a vital interest, and almost every major confrontation there threatens to involve forces of the superpowers. Thus, although economic interests are not the cause of the conflicts, they continually threaten to escalate the clashes out of control.

Hopefully the 1956 war over the Suez Canal was the last major outbreak there of the classic colonial-type war. That conflict fanned the flames of Arab nationalism and helped ignite the 1967 war. That war, in turn, not only brought about the 1973 war, but Israel's maintenance of its territorial gains ignited the resistance of the Palestine Liberation Organization and its terrorist activities. Israel managed to make peace with Egypt, which strengthened Israel's position, but the PLO seized the Arab banner of the struggle against Israel. The Middle East with its history of cynical and ruthless power politics is one of the likely spots for the next major war, which could flame out of control into World War III.

What are the lessons to be learned from these conflicts and what are the prospects for the future? Certainly there has been no dampening of the fires of nationalism or the desire of the Arabs to get their land back. Most nations, however, are willing to recognize Israel's pre-1967 boundaries as established by the United Nations, and they refuse to recognize Israel's occupation of the West Bank of the Jordan and of the Gaza strip. Egypt is continuing to negotiate sporadically for Israel to return this territory, but Egypt has been isolated by most other Arab nations who resented its making a peace settlement with Israel over the

Sinai. Israel's leaders, battered and bloodied by four wars by neighbors who far outnumbered them in population and military potential, refuse to give up all the land Israel conquered, some of which provides a buffer against its neighbors. It insists on iron-clad guarantees of peace and protection before giving up further territory to Arab self-government, and it is consolidating control over the West Bank.

After 1979, the Arab nations were split in conflicts among themselves, and Israel's position, therefore, improved considerably. The major split isolated Egypt from most other Arab states because of its peace treaty with Israel, which removed the major Arab threat to Israel's existence. This seriously weakened the bargaining power of Syria and other nations wishing to regain the West Bank for the Palestinians. As we will see, the second major split occurred over the Iraq-Iranian War, in which the conservative nations - Jordan, Saudi Arabia, and the Gulf States--lined up against Libya, Syria, and Yemen, which supported Iran.

The future was murky in 1987, but it appeared that Israel would not give up buffer areas and the Arab states would not make peace until changes were made in the Mideast power equation. Such changes were in process. The PLO was split between Syrian and Arafat factions. The important elements of Mideast leadership had changed. Prime Minister Begin of Israel had resigned, and there were strong voices in the new coalition calling for an international conference to settle the Arab-Israel dispute. Hosni Mubarak, who replaced Sadat after his assassination in 1981, had resumed Egypt's relations with Jordan. Secretary of State Schultz was "on a roll" with agreement on an intermediate nuclear arms treaty with the Soviets, and with cooperation with the Soviets in the United Nations to settle the Iraq-Iran War. He planned to visit the Middle East to revive the Arab-Israel peace process. Nevertheless, the Middle East remained a danger spot with classic signals of war planning, arms races, terrorism, clashes and hostile propaganda poisoning the atmosphere.

NOTES

[1] Larry Collins, Dominique Lapierre, O Jerusalem (New York: Pocket Books, 1973); Glubb Pasha, A Soldier with the Arabs (London: Hodder and Stoughton, 1957); and Moshe Dayan, The Story of My Life (New York: Werner Books, 1966).

[2] Moshe Dayan, op. cit., p.224.

[3] Ibid., pp. 224-260; Michael Bar-Zohar, Ben Gurion (New York: Delacorte Press, 1977), p. 228-230.

[4] Townsend Hoopes, The Devil and John Foster Dulles (Canada: Little, Brown & Co., 1973), p.335.

[5] Dayan, and Bar-Zohar, op. cit.

[6] Hoopes, op. cit., p. 376.

[7] Anwar el-Sadat, In Search of Identity (New York: Row & Harper 1977), pp. 168-169, 172 and 194.

[8] Sadat, op. cit., pp. 171-172; Dayan, op. cit., p. 366.

[9] Sadat, op. cit, p. 184

[10] Edward R. F. Sheehan, "Step By Step in the Middle East," Foreign Policy, Spring 1976, pp. 3-70.

[11] Sadat, op. cit., p. 215.

[12] Henry Kissinger, "From Lebanon to the West Bank to the Gulf," Washington Post, June 16, 1982, Editorial Page.

CHAPTER 7

The Vietnam Wars

The Vietnam wars demand analysis since they involved the United States in the longest and most controversial war in its history. To analyze them as part of a study of war among nations, we focus on the ways they escalated into an international war involving the United States. We could say there were three wars in Indochina after World War II, with the second civil war escalating into the third, an international war involving the armed forces of the United States and other nations.

The First Two Vietnam Wars

The first Vietnam war was a colonial conflict of the forces led by Ho Chi Minh, supported by Chinese equipment, against the French colonial army in Indochina. Ho's insurgent forces operating from a Chinese sanctuary won a dramatic victory over French forces at Dien Bien Phu in 1954 at a critical time when an international conference was meeting at Geneva to establish a truce in Indochina. Under the 1954 Geneva Agreement Ho won a major political victory--the establishment of the Democratic Republic of Vietnam in the northern half of Vietnam above the 17th parallel. As a result of that agreement the French withdrew from the North and began phasing down their support of South Vietnam, which became recognized as a separate country by over 90 nations.

At the height of the Dien Bien Phu crisis, Eisenhower made the famous April 7, 1954 speech referring to Indochina as a domino, which if toppled would cause other countries of Southeast Asia to fall. This domino theory was a simplification of policy statements contained in a National Security Council paper approved before the outbreak of the Korean War in 1950 and repeated in policy papers thereafter; these papers had provided a basis for increasing aid to the French in the fight against Ho. After the 1954 agreement,

123

the French withdrew their forces as a result of financial pressure, requirements for troops to defend their colonies in North Africa, and the pressure of President Diem, who disliked the French presence. The United States, at the insistence of Secretary of State Dulles and President Eisenhower, provided the military equipment and advisory personnel to fill the gap after the French withdrawal.[1]

The second war, from 1954-1958, was a civil war waged mainly by President Diem's government with U.S. military equipment and advice against about 15,000 Communist cadres and other rebels who remained in South Vietnam after the Geneva agreement. These Communists and their supporters, who looked to political leadership of the North, hoped to help win the all-Vietnam elections promised under the 1954 Geneva agreement. However, President Diem refused to hold the elections, announcing in July, 1955 that free elections would be impossible in the North. From 1955-1958 a relatively low-scale insurgency broke out in opposition to Diem and his government's repression of Communists and those suspected of being Communists. Communist cadres were leaders of the revolt, but at first there was only propaganda support from North Vietnam.

The third war began about 1959 when North Vietnam pledged support to the southern revolutionary movement aimed at overthrowing the Diem government. Communist groups assassinated thousands of local officials in the South and increasingly took over control of rural areas. In 1965, President Johnson began escalating U.S. participation in the war until U.S. combat units in the area totalled about one million men. This chapter will focus on the way in which this third war escalated and the causes for it.

As with other wars, we will look first at those who initiated the attack or aggression against another nation and then analyze how the United States and other nations got involved. Technically, the third Vietnam War as an international war was initiated by North Vietnam supporting the insurgent movement in South Vietnam, a nation recognized by most of the governments of the world. Many have criticized the United States for intervening in this war by assisting South Vietnam, and later by giving a green light to the coup against Diem, and we will, of course, evaluate this issue.

How The Third Vietnam War Began

Ho Chi Minh, the leader of Vietnam's Communist Party, dominated the history of Indochina and Vietnam after World War II. His background and ideology provide the key to his success in leading a nationalist revolution against the French and unifying Vietnam over the opposition of the most powerful country in the world.

Ho Chi Minh was born in 1890, the son of an official of the imperial administration at the time Indochina was coming under French control. His father was one of a small, nationalistic group of officials in Indochina who refused to learn the French language. Ho became active in anti-French activities. Ho attended Indochina's only Vietnamese high school in Hue, but he was forced to leave because of his anti-French activities. He sailed for France in 1911, worked temporarily in London, and even visited Harlem in New York. He became a socialist in France after World War I, and in 1920 he helped found the French Communist Party.

Ho deeply resented French colonial control, and the Communist Party's ideology on colonialism appealed to him. He became the French Communist Party's colonial expert, writing articles for the Communist media. Ho travelled to Russia in the early 1920's and joined the Comintern, continuing his anti-colonial writing. The Soviets sent him to China in the mid 1920's as an interpreter for the Russian agent, Borodin, who helped set up Chiang Kai-shek's military academy. At that time, Ho trained a number of Vietnamese political agitators and sent about 200 to Indochina.

During World War II he helped in China to organize resistance against the Japanese in Indochina. At that time he made contact with American military intelligence, which provided arms and ammunition for the anti-Japanese fight. He, of course, concealed his Communist connections and was able to assume the leadership of Vietnamese troops that took over Hanoi from the Japanese. However, war soon broke out between Ho's forces and the French, who resumed control of South Vietnam. The French forces drove Ho's forces back into the jungle. His forces continued to control the countryside and, in desperation, the French forces tried to lure the Communist forces into an open fight. In 1954 they dug in at Dien Bien Phu, which was well fortified, and invited attack since they thought they could be supported by air. They miscalculated, however, and Ho's forces with military equipment provided by the Chinese, including heavy artillery brought in over the mountains, gave the French colonial forces a stunning defeat.

This came at a critical time when the major powers concerned with Vietnam (China, Britain, France, Russia, the United States, and India) were meeting in Geneva to arrange a settlement of the war. In the Geneva Agreement these powers agreed to divide Vietnam at the 17th parallel, permitting Ho Chi Minh to set up a government in the north with a separate state in the south. Ngo Dinh Diem, premier of the government in the south under Emperor Bao Dai, to the surprise of most observers, consolidated his control and forced Bao Dai to abdicate. The Geneva Agreements also provided for general elections to be held in July, 1956, under the supervision of an international commission. Under the Agreements France was to withdraw its troops at the request of the government concerned. The United States assumed the task of advising the new

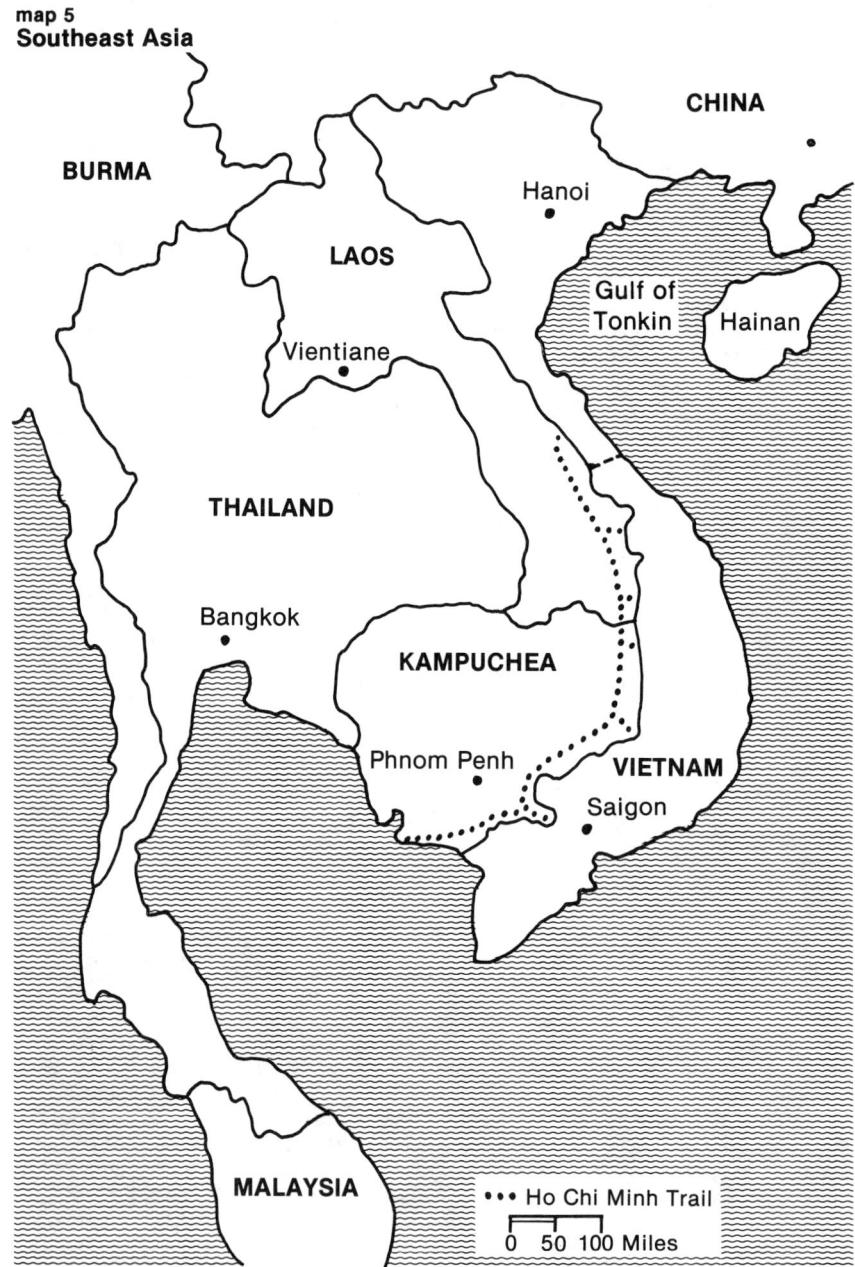

Diem government and providing it with military supplies, while the French were eased out of Vietnam.

Ho's speeches indicate that he was confident he could use these agreements to his advantage. Ho's government trained and indoctrinated the 50,000 Cadres transferred to the North, and took over the leadership of those left in the South to oppose the Diem regime.

Both his background and speeches indicate that he was a confirmed Communist, determined to install a Communist system throughout all of Vietnam and to promote Communism throughout the Far East. For example, in writing for the Russian party newspaper, on April 18, 1955 in praise of Lenin, Ho stated that Lenin gave working people suffering from imperialist oppression "the miraculous weapon to fight for their emancipation--the theories and tactics of Bolshevism." He asserted that Lenin's popularity and doctrine were closely linked to all the successes of the "camp of peace and democracy" which stretched from the Elbe river to the Pacific ocean, and from the Arctic poles to the tropics. He then noted that the main task of North Vietnam was to consolidate peace, complete the land reform, to improve its economic life, and to stabilize the livelihood in every respect in the territory north of the 17th parallel, while continuing the political struggle in the south. His speeches during the 1955-1956 period indicate his concern for consolidating the land reform and political organization of North Vietnam in preparation for the struggle with the "American imperialists and their agents" in the south. He was confident that the Communists would be victorious although the political struggle would be long and hard.

Ho's speeches strengthened the image prevalent in the West that the war in Vietnam was part of a Communist movement to take over all of Asia. For example, on November 3, 1957 he said that the Russian October revolution "shattered the fetters of imperialism, destroyed its foundation, and inflicted on it a deadly blow. Like a thunderbolt, it has stirred up the Asian peoples from their century-old slumbers. It has opened up for them the revolutionary anti-imperialist era, the era of national liberation." He said, "the October revolution gave an impetus to the movement of national liberation, which has become a surging wave in all eastern countries: China, India, Indonesia, Vietnam, etc." He added, "the colonial system of imperialism is collapsing beyond remedy; the question of total liquidation of the colonial system is the foremost one. The peoples of the east are rising up against their aggressors and are determined not to let anyone oppress them."[2]

General Vo Nguyen Giap, Commander in Chief of the Vietnam People's army, was as ardently Communist in his speeches as Ho. General Giap, in People's War, People's Army, described the long range strategy of the North Vietnamese as follows: a war against imperialists starts with a stage of contention, goes through a period of equilibrium, before arriving at a general counter-offensive. He stressed that only a long-term war would enable them to utilize their political strength to the maximum. His strategy was to attack only when success was certain, refusing to give battle when it was likely to incur major losses.[3] It was clear from the speeches of these and other North Vietnamese leaders that they never wavered in their intention to take over South Vietnam and force the United States to end its support to that government. The fact that the Republic of Vietnam in the south was recognized by most countries of the world as a separate nation did not impress the Communist leaders of North Vietnam. To them, Vietnam should be unified, and diplomatic recognition was only an imperialist trick to enable the United States and other powers to exploit South Vietnam.

The North Vietnamese continued to call for the elections proposed by the Geneva Agreements. President Diem, in the fall of 1956, announced, however, that he would not agree to such elections because there was no way that they could be free in the North. Ho Chi Minh would not permit United Nations' supervision of elections in the North, and since under the Communist system, elections there would be virtually 100 percent for Ho Chi Minh, Diem saw that his regime would stand no chance in all-Vietnam elections.

Ho continued to call for a "peaceful" solution to the issues on the basis of the Geneva Agreement, but in his definition a peaceful solution was support of Communist insurgents short of open invasion by the North Vietnamese forces. Thus following 1957, and particularly in the period 1959 and after, cadres were infiltrated from the North with military equipment to carry on the revolution against the Diem regime. Officials of the Diem regime were the targets of assassination. Communist cadres were responsible for killing thousands of village leaders and school teachers who were associated with the Diem regime during the late 50's.

The Diem regime after 1957 managed to keep control over much of the area through repressive measures against Communists and suspected Communists. There is a major controversy over whether Diem's repression triggered the rebellion or whether the Communist terrorism triggered Diem's repression. These two conflicts were probably self-reinforcing. It seems clear, moreover, that Ho and other Communist leaders never wavered in their determination to take over the South by escalating measures of force.

A major question remains, however, of why Ho was so successful. Communist doctrine and ideology call for wars of liberation all over the world; why was there such strong support in South Vietnam? A related question is whether it was essentially a civil war or an international war depending on support by the Communist regime of North Vietnam.

Insights into the reasons for the Vietnamese support of the war are provided by a series of interviews carried out by the RAND Corporation, which was under contract to the U.S. Defense Department. Between August, 1964 and December, 1968, RAND conducted about 2,400 interviews with Vietnamese, mostly Viet Cong and defectors from the Viet Cong. The RAND interviewers were mostly professors aided by interpreters. They tried to disassociate themselves from the South Vietnamese government and to assure privacy to those being interviewed. RAND estimates that privacy was assured in about half of the interviews, but that it was poor in many of the other interviews. RAND also notes that those interviewed were suspicious that the South Vietnam government was involved. Although the interviews were not perfect, there are about 62,000 pages of useful data about the views of those who were leading the rebellion against the Diem government.

The RAND analysts report that about 90,000 of the insurgents who fought against the French travelled north after the 1954 Geneva Agreements. In the North, they were "regrouped" under Hanoi's leadership and trained in techniques of insurgency. These "regroupies" later became the "steel frame" of the insurgent organization in the South. A smaller number remained in the South. These had varying degrees of allegiance to the northern Communist movement, but it was clear from the interviews that they recognized the leadership of the North. Their task, at first, was to organize for the elections, and they indicated that they were looking forward to the chance to re-unify Vietnam. However, in July, 1955 President Diem said free elections were impossible. About the same time, Diem initiated a program of repression against the group that remained in the South. He classified people in three categories - (A) The most dangerous Communist Party members, (B) Party members of lesser importance, and (C) The loyal citizens. The Saigon authorities with the aid of local officials initiated an active program of repression of the A and B categories. Many of the local officials, according to the interviews, abused their power, arresting and even killing some of the group that remained in the South. Those who were interviewed complained particularly about harassments such as stealing their ducks and chickens or forcing them to work on certain projects without pay.

After 1959 Communist leaders in the South increased the pressure on former party members to join in opposition to Diem. Some who were harassed by both Communist leaders and Diem's officials gave up and fled to the jungles where, at least, they could not be reached by the Diem government. They established base areas in the Plain of Reeds in the South and in other areas between 1955 and 1959. By 1959, the Vietminh were successfully using coercion to get new recruits on a larger scale.

The major theme used by the Communists combined nationalism, Communism, and hatred of the Diem regime. The Diem regime was called a puppet of the American imperialists who had taken over "colonial" control from the French. It was alleged that the French and the Americans had the same goal "to invade Vietnam, enslave people, and exploit human labor and resources to enrich the totalitarian capitalists in their own countries." Another Communist theme was that the U.S. capitalists were interested in subjugating Vietnam to obtain its raw materials. Communist China and Russia, on the other hand, were pictured as friendly members of the Socialist Camp. All of the propaganda pictured Vietnam as one nation.[4]

To sum up, Ho's indirect aggression against South Vietnam was based on a Communist theory which foresaw the ultimate victory over "colonial" forces. It was a struggle between nationalists because Diem also was an ardent Vietnamese nationalist and was by no means a puppet of the French, Bao Dai, or the Americans. Ho, however, had the advantage of a powerful Communist doctrine on colonialism and a powerful Communist apparatus, which generated support from the people. Thus, the burden of blame for the Vietnamese War and the prize for the victory of North Vietnam goes to Ho Chi Minh.

Many critics would claim the war was essentially a civil war to unify North and South Vietnam and that the United States, therefore, should not have intervened. They would add that the presence of U.S. military units in South Vietnam gave a powerful boost to Communist propaganda claims that the United States was trying to take over colonial control from the French.

Within the framework of international law, however, and particularly Western perceptions, the war was an international war against the Republic of South Vietnam. South Vietnam during the 1960's was recognized diplomatically by about 90 nations, some of which also recognized North Vietnam. South Vietnam was also a member of many international organizations including the International Monetary Fund and International Bank. Thus the Republic of Vietnam was being attacked by another nation, which was Communist--the Democratic Republic of Vietnam. The reason for the United States' involvement in helping defend South Vietnam will now be analyzed.

U.S. Participation in the Vietnam Wars

When President Truman decided to provide aid to the French forces in Indochina, the Chinese Communists had just taken over mainland China, and he believed an aid program was necessary in order to stop the spread of Communism in Asia. Eisenhower continued the limited U.S. support to the Republic of South Vietnam of about 600 military advisors, as permitted under the Geneva Agreement, plus a large program of military aid. Although the involvement under Eisenhower was miniscule compared to the later escalation under President Johnson, Eisenhower strongly reinforced the views that Vietnam was a keystone of Southeast Asian stability. Eisenhower made his famous statement for supporting South Vietnam on April 7, 1954: "the loss of Indochina will cause the fall of Southeast Asia like a set of dominoes." This domino theory was an over-simplified view of American leaders that the push into South Vietnam was a part of an overall Communist strategy of setting up Communist governments, and that the fall of Indochina would threaten other neighboring countries. As noted above, Ho Chi Minh frankly admitted this goal, and American leaders would have been naive not to have taken his statements seriously.

Eisenhower, nevertheless, refused to commit the United States to a unilateral defense of South Vietnam. As the French faced the prospect of a serious loss at Dien Bien Phu in early 1954, Eisenhower insisted on the following three basic requirements before the United States could provide major military assistance--the first was "a legal right under international law; second, was a favorable climate of free world opinion; and, third, favorable action by the Congress."[5] Congressional leaders supported these conditions. The first requirement about a legal right under international law would require an urgent request by the French, which Eisenhower said would have to reflect the desire of the people of Indochina. Eisenhower believed this should have included a French commitment to grant independence to the associated states in Indochina (Vietnam, Laos and Cambodia.) John Foster Dulles went on an urgent mission to London and Paris to test the second condition - "a favorable climate of free world opinion." Secretary Dulles found that the British were not willing to commit troops and the French were not willing to commit themselves to granting independence to the Indochinese states. Eisenhower with his fundamental concept of constitutional government, therefore, decided that there was no justification for the U.S. to intervene with U.S. troops. Dulles, as an alternative proceeded later to negotiate the SEATO treaty, which after it was approved did provide a basis for U.S. policymakers in the future to help defend Indochina from a Communist attack. South Vietnam was protected under a protocol to the Treaty, although it was not a member.

After the Geneva Conference, when South Vietnam was split off from the North, President Diem was able to establish a stable government without U.S. intervention, and it was not until six years later that his regime was seriously threatened by the Communist insurgents supported from the North. Thus, Eisenhower, with a characteristically conservative policy, postponed the decision on how to support Diem, leaving Presidents Kennedy and Johnson to face the problem of how to react to an accelerated program of subversion directed from North Vietnam that had been stimulated by Diem's repression in the South.

President Kennedy's escalation of the U.S. commitment to Vietnam was minor compared to the massive escalation that took place under President Johnson. Kennedy's position was summarized in a National Security Memorandum of April 1961, which restated the goals established by Truman and Eisenhower and gave further momentum to the U.S. government effort. That NSM described the U.S. aim in Vietnam as follows:

> To prevent Communist domination of South Vietnam; to create in that country a viable and increasingly democratic society, and to initiate, on an accelerated basis a series of mutually supporting actions of a military, political, economic, psychological and covert character destined to achieve that objective.[6]

The NSM was an activist memorandum calling for an acceleration of actions on a broad military, political, economic, psychological and covert front. W. W. Rostow, who was Kennedy's special advisor on Southeast Asia and a key figure in the drama, describes Kennedy's rationale in the Diffusion of Power as follows. Kennedy told Rostow that if we walked away from Southeast Asia, the Communist takeover would produce a debate greater than the loss of China. He added that we would be also violating a treaty commitment to the area (the SEATO treaty). This, he said, would result in a rise of left-and-right-wing isolationism and a loss of confidence in the United States. Kennedy feared that Khrushchev and Mao would then act to exploit a shift in the world balance of power. Kennedy was afraid that Burma might fall and that China, allied with Vietnam, would be able to threaten the boundary of India. He concluded that the United States, when it finally reacted, would be in a world crisis - possibly a nuclear crisis.[7]

The above, in essence, was an elaboration of the Eisenhower domino theory, only in a more intellectual form. A critic could point out that Communist China would hardly want to threaten India through a third party -- Vietnam -- and then do it the very difficult geographical way through the mountains and jungles of Thailand and Burma. Although Kennedy's geopolitics were poor, he recognized the threat of Ho Chi Minh's call for a revolution of former colonial areas in Asia, and regarded it as a challenge of expanding world Communist movements threatening South Asia.

President Kennedy, when groping around for a policy for Vietnam, sent W. W. Rostow, his Special Assistant for National Security Affairs, Maxwell Taylor, a military advisor, and others on a mission to survey the situation. The major question that Kennedy assigned Rostow, was whether the people of South Vietnam wanted an independent, non-Communist future or whether they would prefer Ho Chi Minh. Rostow concluded after consulting and interviewing people at different levels of society, including the opponents of Diem, that the villagers wanted most of all security -- to be left alone. They complained that both the central government and the

Communists took their sons and money for war. The Communists, at that time, were using terror techniques to recruit and to demonstrate that Communism was the wave of the future. Few Communist cadres had read Marx, Lenin, Mao, or even Ho Chi Minh but they grasped the simple idea of Communism as a system of equality for the people. Rostow reported, therefore, that there was no massive popular desire for Communism. Even the anti-Diem figures were not calling for a unified North Vietnam under the Communist regime of Ho Chi Minh. Rostow, however, missed the key element in the equation -- how the Communists were exploiting the intervention by the United States, which was pictured as an imperialist power.

The Taylor-Rostow report concluded that the war had to be won by the Vietnamese. They recommended an advisory structure on a large scale and a build-up of air support for Vietnamese military operations, including helicopter and combat aircraft. They also recommended a military task force with engineering capabilities, which could also carry out military operations. President Kennedy accepted much of the report, except that he balked at adding an engineering unit to which the Pentagon would give combat assignments. Biographers report that Kennedy's strategy, at that time, was to stall and to limit U.S. intervention to the approximately 15,000 "advisors," who were assigned for these accelerated programs in line with the National Security Memorandum. The above recommendations were not far reaching enough to satisfy Rostow and other top White House and Pentagon advisors who wanted the United States to take a more active role in supporting South Vietnam.[8]

The Rostow report, as far as it went, was substantially correct. The summary version in his book, however, left out or failed to stress that there was a deep seated anti-colonialism feeling among the Vietnamese people. The Communists, as noted in the previous section, were playing on the theme that the Americans were in Vietnam to replace the French colonialists. Both at that time and in retrospect it is clear that one of the major political factors that weakened the South Vietnamese regime was the dominant role played by the Americans. With the level of 15,000 U.S. advisors, the Communists were able to persuade the villagers that Diem was a puppet of the Americans. Before Kennedy was assassinated, American officers were accompanying patrols on military missions with instructions to fire back if attacked. American pilots were flying helicopters and other planes to support the Vietnamese troops. Americans were the target of both military and propaganda attacks.

A turning point came in 1963 when Kennedy, his top advisors, and the American TV audiences were horrified by Buddhist monks burning themselves to death in front of TV cameras. Diem, however, ignored American approaches urging him to institute democratic reforms and remove his brother from head of the police, who were persecuting the Buddhists. Washington then instructed the Saigon Embassy secretly to give the green light to plans of Vietnamese generals to overthrow Diem. A few months later their coup was carried out, and to the horror of Kennedy and his advisers Diem was brutally killed. Although the U.S. had actually not instigated the coup or planned it, the U.S. had given its approval secretly. This laid the basis not only for a succession of military dictatorships but increased the U.S. commitment and responsibility for subsequent events in Vietnam.[9] Some critics picture the U.S. as an aggressor after the Diem assassination and dominating the subsequent conflict over the unification of Vietnam.

A few weeks later Kennedy was assassinated, and President Kennedy's advisors began to prepare plans for the new president to escalate drastically U.S. participation in the war. The major question remaining is how did President Johnson bring about a massive escalation of the American military role in South Vietnam. This made the conflict a wider, international war rather than just one between two Vietnamese nations.

President Johnson was a leader seasoned by World War II, who saw how failure to stop Hitler early in his career resulted in disaster. It is not surprising that Johnson, therefore, was ready to take a hard line towards the Vietnamese aggression. In 1961, as Vice President under President Kennedy, he reported back to the President after a trip to Southeast Asia with the following conclusions:

> The battle against Communism must be joined in Southeast Asia with strength and determination to achieve success there -- or the United States, inevitably, must surrender the Pacific and take up our defenses on our own shores. Asian Communism is compromised and contained by the maintenance of free nations on the sub-continent. Without this inhibitory influence, the island outposts Philippines, Japan, Taiwan have no security and the vast Pacific becomes a Red Sea.[10]

Unfortunately, Vice President Johnson did not carry over into his later presidency the following good advice he offered in his 1961 memorandum to President Kennedy:

> "Asian leaders--at this time--do not want American troops involved in Southeast Asia other than on training missions. American combat troop involvement is not only not required, it is not desirable. Possibly Americans fail to appreciate fully the subtlety that recently-colonial peoples would not look with favor upon governments which invited or accepted the return this soon of Western troops."[11]

Johnson concluded that the key to policy is confidence in the United States and there "is no alternative to United States leadership in Southeast Asia."

As history shows, his views changed in one important respect three years later when he became President and sent massive U.S. troop support to South Vietnam. By that time the internal political situation in South Vietnam had deteriorated with one coup following another, and with intensified insurgent action. Intervention with U.S. troops was encouraged by his many advisors, who were inherited from the Kennedy Administration. They were confident men, who thought they knew how to face down the Communist threat after their successes in Berlin, Laos, and the Cuban missile crisis. Johnson was impressed with their background: McNamara, former President of the Ford Motor Company; McGeorge Bundy, Dean of Harvard and flashingly brilliant; Walt W. Rostow, a prominent Harvard intellectual; Dean Rusk, with his long experience in foreign affairs including former head of the Rockefeller Foundation; Maxwell Taylor, a smooth, educated, military diplomat who was former chairman of the Joint Chiefs of Staff; plus the impressive military establishment of the Pentagon. President Johnson was a powerful leader, but, deep down, he probably was not confident about international affairs and his background as a self-educated ordinary politician from Texas. George Ball, Undersecretary of the State Department and the only dove in the top echelons, said that "Johnson did not suffer from a poor education; he suffered from a belief he had a poor education." Johnson had not yet had his Bay of Pigs where he had learned how to question the advice of top military, intelligence, and foreign policy experts. Thus, after President Johnson received a strong mandate in the November, 1964 elections, he was swept along by the advice of top advisers and by his machismo into a massive escalation of the Vietnam war.[12]

The most widely read version of the Pentagon Papers, the documentary history of U.S. participation in the Vietnam War, is the New York Times edition. Although it contains many documents, the Times edition still summarizes much of the massive official Pentagon study of the war. The Times version has been criticized by observers because it indicates that planning for escalation of the war was well under way before the 1964 elections, and that top officials took advantage of events to put the plan into effect after Johnson was safely elected. The much more complete version of Congressman Gravel, in my view, shows that second-level planning officials were supporting a relatively minor escalation of the war in 1964, and that the center of gravity for decisions shifted to the White House after November, 1964 elections in which Johnson was swept back into office.[13] White House advisors such as McGeorge Bundy and Walt W. Rostow, and the Secretary of Defense early in 1965 encouraged the President to "bite the bullet and take command." Buoyed by favorable public reaction to his

135

hardline reaction to the 1964 Gulf-of-Tonkin incident, Johnson instituted a major escalation of U.S. troop commitments to the Vietnam War in 1965.[14]

The Tonkin-Gulf crisis, and the public and Congressional support he received for the Tonkin-Gulf resolution reinforced Johnson's tendencies to be a hawk. The Tonkin-Gulf incident grew out of two series of military operations that took place near the port of Vinh, about half-way up the coast of North Vietnam. The first were commando operations with the code name 34-A, which were under the control of the U.S. Military Assistance Command in South Vietnam. The second was a series of patrols designed to gather electronic intelligence from North Vietnam, that took place in approximately the same area under the control of the U.S. Navy. Although the two operations were not coordinated, the North Vietnamese obviously assumed they were.

The U.S. considered its destroyer patrol as being clearly in international waters. To the North Vietnamese the Gulf of Tonkin was "their lake" and the destroyer patrols during a war were a threat. (Map 5) The North Vietnamese were not concerned with legal niceties and attacked the destroyers with torpedo boats. The attacks were repelled by the destroyer Maddox on August 2, 1964, which then withdrew to the middle of the Gulf. On the night of August 4, while sailing in the Gulf, the Maddox again came under attack, or thought it was under attack. There was some confusion because it was stormy, and, moreover, the operators of the sonar equipment were confused by signals, some of which they realized later were echoes of their own engines.

The reports of the attack arrived at the White House in the morning. The President convened two National Security Council meetings that same day, one which had been previously scheduled. The President obtained NSC approval for a strike, and the U.S. attack on oil storage facilities and military installations took place later that day. That evening the President met with Congressional leaders, and in a message to Congress the next day President Johnson asked for approval of a resolution that became known later as the Tonkin-Gulf resolution. The resolution had been drafted earlier in anticipation of such a crisis.

The resolution was passed overwhelmingly in the Senate by 88 to 2, and by the House by a vote of 416 to 0 on August 10. The resolution gave the President what virtually amounted to a blank check for action in Vietnam. The preamble referred to the deliberate and repeated attacks on United States naval vessels present in international waters and noted that these attacks were part of a campaign of aggression by North Vietnam against its neighbors. Section II of the resolution had the following paragraph:

> The United States regards as vital to its national interest and to world peace the maintenance of international peace and security in Southeast Asia. Consonant with the Constitution of the United States and the Charter of the United Nations and in accordance with its obligations under the Southeast Asia Collective Defense Treaty the United States is therefore prepared as the President determines to take all necessary steps including the use of armed force to assist any member or protocol state of the Southeast Asia Collective Defense Treaty requesting assistance in defense of its freedom.

This paragraph gave the President the authority to use armed force to assist any of the SEATO nations covered by the Treaty. Senator Fulbright of the Foreign Relations Committee, who shepherded the resolution through the Senate, answered Senator Cooper's question on the Senate floor as follows:

> Senator Cooper: "Then looking ahead if the President decided that it was necessary to use such force as could lead into war, we will have that authority by this resolution?"
>
> Senator Fulbright: "That is the way I would interpret it. If a situation later develops in which we thought the approval should be withdrawn, it would be withdrawn by a concurrent resolution. That is the reason for the third section."

The resolution not only passed through Congress with virtually no opposition, but it received the overwhelming endorsement of the American people. This was reflected in a Harris public opinion poll which in July, before the Tonkin-Gulf resolution, showed that 58 percent of American people disapproved the way President Johnson was handling the war. On October 10, 1964, soon after the resolution, 85 percent approved. This one act reversed the unfavorable opinion towards his handling of the war. This came at a high point of the presidential campaign, and the popularity generated by his stand helped provide the momentum that carried him to an easy victory over his opponent, Senator Goldwater.

During the campaign President Johnson pictured himself as a peace candidate and Barry Goldwater as the hard-line, pro-war candidate. On August 29, in a political speech in Texas, President Johnson explained that the U.S. policy was limited to furnishing advice, giving counsel, and providing South Vietnam with equipment to help themselves, while not enlarging the war. As far as public support was concerned, Johnson appeared to have two options--holding steady as proposed in his election campaign, or escalating if challenged, as in the Tonkin-Gulf crisis.

Soon after the 1964 elections President Johnson took the escalation option. In February, 1965 the Vietcong raided the U.S. airfield at Pleiku and two smaller installations killing nine Americans and wounding over one hundred. McGeorge Bundy was in Vietnam at the time, and he came back to Washington convinced that the U.S. had to demonstrate to the Communists a will to defend South Vietnam. A memo to Johnson set forth the classic view of the hawk:

> There is one grave weakness in our posture in Vietnam which is within our power to fix--and that is a widespread belief that we do not have the will and force and patience and determination to take the necessary action and stay the course.[15]

Johnson supported this theme of demonstrating the U.S. will to fight in a July 28 press conference: "We intend to convince the Communists that we cannot be defeated by force of arms or superior power." The conflict had escalated to the test of wills and of national prestige in a battle to stop Communism, which meant the U.S. was directly and not indirectly involved.

In March the President ordered 3,500 marines to help defend the U.S. air base at Pleiku. From then on the build-up continued even faster than Ambassador Maxwell Taylor, former Chairman of the Joint Chiefs of Staff who had been assigned to Saigon, wanted. By the end of 1965 there were 179,000 American soldiers in Vietnam, and a year later the number had risen to 389,000. In 1968 the number peaked at about 540,000. (See Figure 2.) Altogether, including naval supply forces and forces in adjoining countries, the U.S. military in Southeast Asia approximated one million at the height of the war.

It is not necessary to describe the subsequent tragic history of the war since we are focusing on factors causing it and the U.S. intervention. It is useful, however, to summarize the events which set the stage for the climax when North Vietnamese forces shattered a truce by defeating South Vietnamese forces and forcing the remaining American advisors and diplomatic personnel to flee.

As draft calls mounted in 1967 to meet the expanding U.S. commitment to Vietnam, opposition to the war developed and major demonstrations were organized. One of the largest of the early efforts was in October, 1967 when 55,000 anti-war militants marched on the Pentagon. In the following months Senator Eugene McCarthy, who opposed the war, entered the race for Democratic nomination for President. In February of the following year he

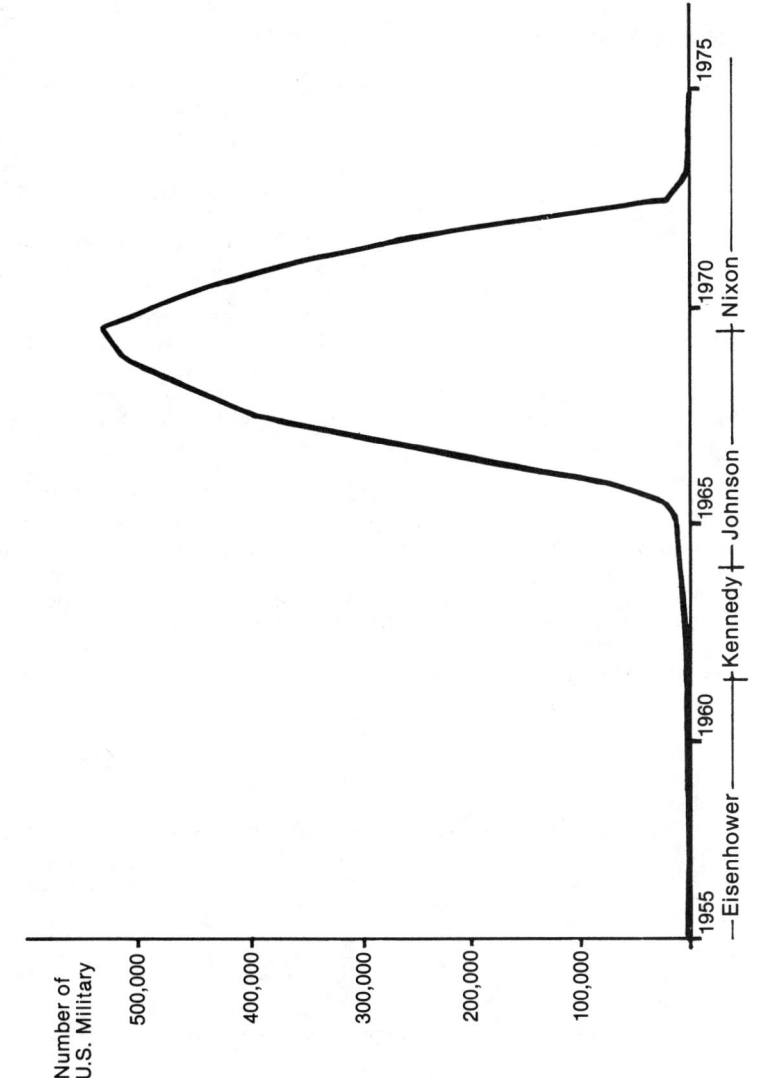

figure 2
Total U.S. Military Personnel in Vietnam 1955-1975

administered a stunning political defeat to President Johnson in the New Hampshire primaries. President Johnson withdrew from the presidential race in the following month.

President Nixon won the election in November, 1968 promising to end the war "with honor". In the summer of 1969 he announced a plan to withdraw the troops gradually from Vietnam with the aim of turning over the conduct of the war to the Vietnamese.

The withdrawal continued at a fairly steady rate, except for a break in 1970. At that time, President Nixon authorized a major attack against major sanctuaries used by North Vietnam in the Fish Hook area of Cambodia about 70 miles from Saigon. (Map 5) Nixon announced that this renewal of fighting by the United States' ground forces joined by those of South Vietnam would be temporary and that all U.S. ground forces would be withdrawn from Cambodia by June 30. The renewed offensive by U.S. forces caused an uproar in the United States. The Senate, in protest against the danger of escalation, passed the Cooper-Church amendment prohibiting funds for operations in Cambodia beyond the June 30 deadline. This was the first time that the Senate had made such a restrictive vote while the U.S. was at war. In 1972 the U.S. Congress repealed the Tonkin-Gulf Resolution, which reflected the growing public and media opposition to the Vietnam War.

In 1969 Kissinger, as the President's National Security Advisor, had begun secret truce talks with the Vietnamese in Paris, but they made little progress. In March, 1972 the North Vietnamese forces began a major invasion of South Vietnam from the North. This was turned back by the South Vietnamese forces, assisted by a U.S. blockade of Hanoi and bombing of North Vietnam. The North Vietnamese offensive failed militarily, but it reinforced political opposition to the war in the United States.

By the end of 1972, considerable progress had been made in the peace talks, and Kissinger made an optimistic statement right before the elections about "peace at hand." However there was another set-back to the negotiations, and President Nixon with Kissinger's concurrence resumed bombing of North Vietnam. Apparently the pressure worked, because in January, 1973 the final agreements were concluded between Kissinger and Ambassador Le Duc Tho on behalf of the Democratic Republic of Vietnam.

The major elements of the complicated series of agreements included the following:

1. There would be a cease-fire on January 27, 1973.

2. There would be no reinforcement of troops in the South by any of the participants.

3. All U.S. prisoners of war would be returned in 60 days.

4. There would be complete withdrawal of U.S. military personnel in 60 days. This did not include U.S. advisors attached to the South Vietnamese military forces.

5. The agreement set forth the aim of re-unification by peaceful means through negotiations between North Vietnam and South Vietnam. A "National Council" would organize the elections.

6. There would be an International Commission of Control and Supervision with 1,160 supervisory personnel to control and supervise the truce agreement. It would be aided by joint military commissions to check on specific provisions.

At this time, President Nixon wrote President Thieu of South Vietnam that "you have my absolute assurance that if Hanoi fails to abide by the terms of this agreement, it is my intention to take swift and retaliatory action." President Nixon's public statement was not quite so strong saying that "we shall continue to aid South Vietnam within the terms of the agreement, and we shall support efforts by the people of South Vietnam to settle their problems peacefully among themselves." Kissinger, in explaining the agreement to the press, also made a similar pledge of continuing aid to South Vietnam. Later when he was criticized that this went beyond the authority of the President, who would require Congressional authorization for aid, Kissinger explained that the idea of not being able to carry out such a commitment did not occur to President Nixon and Kissinger. In his memoires Kissinger pointed out that after fighting and losing 45,000 men, for the United States to then stand aside while the peace treaty was being violated, would be such a drastic action it would "be the end of diplomacy."[16]

North Vietnam did violate the agreement and continued to build up its forces, which were well known in the Nixon and Ford administrations and duly reported in the press. At the same time Congress was moving to further restrict the power of the Executive Branch to renew the war. On June 30, 1973 it voted to cut off funds for all U.S. military activity in and over Indochina, effective the 15th of August, 1973. On November 7, 1973 the far-reaching War Powers Resolution requiring Congressional approval or a declaration of war for the President's use of troops overseas was passed over the President's veto. The Resolution stated the only case in which the President without legislative authorization could order U.S. troops into battle was when the United States or its forces were attacked.

Meanwhile, Hanoi continued its build-up, and by the middle of 1974 it was estimated there were 185,000 of its soldiers in South Vietnam compared with 140,000 in January, 1973. Hanoi continued to improve the Ho Chi Minh Trail and, as later reports indicated, began to prepare for the final offensive. Meanwhile, Congress was severely cutting back the financial aid to South Vietnam. In 1973, it appropriated $2.2 billion to support South Vietnam; in 1974, $1.0 billion. At the end of 1974, the Ford Administration requested another $1.5 billion for the Vietnam War. However, the Democratic Congress, supported by some of the Republicans, cut this request to $.7 billion during the fall of 1974 and the spring of 1975. Meanwhile, the world-wide inflation raised the cost of petroleum products 400 percent, as well as ammunition by almost a third. Administration reports indicated that the reduced U.S. support for military supplies cut the South Vietnamese firepower by 60 percent and their air force missions by 40 percent. Their use of ammunition was reduced to less than one-third of 1972.

On January 8, 1975 the North Vietnamese forces in violation of the truce, overran Phuoc Long Province about 70 miles from Saigon. This fact was noted by an official U.S. government spokesman and in the U.S. press, but there was no U.S. military reaction. There were no threats of renewed bombing or blockading of Hanoi. Instead, during this period the U.S. Congress continued withdrawing financial support for South Vietnam.

The above signals were read clearly by both North and South Vietnamese. Ambassador Graham Martin, in charge of our embassy in Vietnam during this period, was bitter about the failure of the U.S. Congress and the U.S. media to support an adequate military aid program to South Vietnam in line with our previous commitments. He and friends of mine who were on his diplomatic staff during this period, confirmed to me that this severely affected the morale of South Vietnamese officials, commanders, and soldiers.

The above signals were also read clearly by the Communist leaders of the North Vietnamese forces. Reporters of the Far Eastern Economic Review carried out interviews with senior officers of the Vietnam People's Liberation Army after the fall of Saigon in April, 1975. These were not formal interviews for the record, but the officers spoke freely to the reporters. These officers said that preparations for the final offensive had started more than a year before the final fall of Saigon in 1975, since in their view it was clear Saigon would not implement the Paris Agreements of 1973. These officers continued that at the end of 1974 they had tested the water by the successful attack on Phuoc Long and its capital. They continued:

> This proved the incapacity of the puppet army to defend even a provincial capital against our offensive and popular uprising and confirmed our assessment that due to internal and international developments, the Americans had lost the will, if not the capability to intervene militarily.[17]

They were surprised by the muted response of the American government. They reported that Communist leaders in the South, the high command, then concluded that the time was ripe for victory. They said:

> Of course, we did not totally exclude the possibility of U.S. military intervention, but we were convinced the balance of forces was decidedly in our favor and that we would be able to defeat a renewed American intervention.[18]

The People's Liberation Army of North Vietnam brought from the North about 17 of their 19 regular army divisions for the final offensive. The South Vietnamese were outgunned, and their resistance folded rapidly in a calamitous retreat to the South. In about six weeks they were completely defeated, and Ambassador Graham Martin ordered an evacuation of the relatively few U.S. officials and personnel left in South Vietnam plus almost 200,000 South Vietnamese officials and their families who had been closely associated with the United States. The evacuation by the U.S. military was carried out with amazing success despite the fact that South Vietnamese resistance to attacks was collapsing.

Causes

Ho Chi Minh was the dominant leader of the Communist forces that used the ideologies of Communism and nationalism to win the three Vietnam wars. Ho had hated colonialism since his youth and had been attracted by the Communist doctrine, which to him provided the "miraculous tool" to fight the imperialists. His forces won the first war against the French colonial authorities, and in 1954 the Geneva Agreement, endorsed by major world powers, provided for establishing the Democratic Republic of Vietnam in the North under his leadership. Ho had mounted his offensives from sanctuaries in China and with equipment provided by the Chinese and Russians, in addition to that captured from the French.

President Diem of South Vietnam shares the blame for starting the second war from 1954 to 1958 which merged into the third, international war. Villagers' resentment against Diem's policies of trying to weed out the Communists left in the South after the 1954 Geneva Agreement stimulated resistance, and Ho and North Vietnam's leaders were able to manage the rebellion. Interviews with prisoners of war indicated their resentment of pressures, threats, and violence of the Diem officials. As the Communists resisted and were reinforced by cadres and equipment from the North, there was a vicious circle of violence as Communists assassinated thousands of local officials and Diem's forces intensified police and military action to put down the rebellion. During this second war, even before North Vietnam gave major support to their comrades in the South, Ho saw the insurgency as part of a world Communist movement to take over the colonies and former colonies of Asia.

President Kennedy, President Johnson, and other top policymakers also pictured the conflict in South Vietnam as part of a Communist thrust to dominate Asia, although other officials recognized important nationalistic and anti-foreign political elements underlying Ho's successes. By 1960 Ho's open support had made the war international in character as thousands of cadres infiltrated from the North, and as the North built major supply lines to the South. The violence and terrorism of the war intimidated the Southern villagers and prevented programs of social and economic reform that American advisors thought were essential to winning the support of the people.

The United States involvement was mostly economic and military-equipment aid until President Johnson took over major responsibility for waging the war. President Truman with the lessons of World War II fresh in his mind had provided military equipment and financial support to the French with the aim of helping them stop the spread of Communism beyond China. President Eisenhower and Secretary Dulles had continued and reinforced this containment policy with SEATO after Ho's forces took over North Vietnam. During Kennedy's short term as president the North Vietnamese intensified their support of the insurgency in the South and took over its leadership, but Kennedy refrained from sending U.S. combat units to Vietnam.

President Johnson, alarmed by what he saw as the deteriorating position of South Vietnam and egged on by his top advisors, decided to bring the direct military might of the United States against what appeared to be a much weaker enemy. The enemy refused to be enticed into conventional battles and responded by stepping up the guerrilla war. As U.S. draft calls and casualties mounted, American public opinion and Congressional support for the war melted away. President Johnson withdrew from the presidential race in 1968 rather than face almost certain defeat.

Some blame the disaster of increased American participation in the war as a result of commitments beginning with Truman to help South Vietnam defend itself against Communist aggression. Others blame Johnson for committing U.S. troops to a political and military morass where they were branded as imperialists--such a battle, these critics say, could only have been won by the South Vietnamese themselves. The combination of nationalism and Communism which bolstered the Communist forces was a much more powerful political doctrine than the anti-Communism and collective security slogans of the defenders.

President Nixon in an attempt to achieve "peace with honor" withdrew American troops while reinforcing the ability of the South Vietnamese forces to defend themselves. The strain on American patience proved too great and in the final months, as Congress cut back on appropriations for military supplies to South

Vietnam, the North Vietnamese forces finished the war in a full-scale conventional offensive.

In these three wars Ho Chi Minh and his successors had no illusions about the strength of their enemies, and they prevailed as a result of a correct assessment of American political vulnerability. They gave no evidence of wavering or yielding on their ultimate goals during their drawn-out negotiations with Secretary of State Kissinger.

After signing a cease-fire and a framework for peace in 1973, North Vietnam cynically tested the water by capturing the entire province of Phuoc Long near Saigon later in 1954. There was only a muted American response and a continuation of the withdrawal of U.S. financial support from the Southern forces. The final offensive of North Vietnam caused the collapse of South Vietnam's military resistance and morale in less than six weeks. It helped to end President Nixon's and President Ford's administrations with a humiliating defeat.

There is widespread agreement among political observers that the United States attempted too much. It saw its role as a world policeman with the duty of stopping the spread of world Communism. This perception of a threat was reinforced by statements of Ho Chi Minh. President Johnson saw the conflict in these simplistic terms and ordered a major escalation from the relatively indirect support of South Vietnam provided by President Kennedy. Johnson did not want the Pacific to become a "Red Sea." He determined to stop the spread of Communist aggression by a demonstration of power and national will, so that the United States would not make the same mistake that it made in not initially opposing the aggression of Germany and Japan in World War II. Ho Chi Minh's forces responded with guerrilla tactics at first, and then as the U.S. will to resist weakened, escalated their attacks. With their patience and superior strategy they "won" the war and unified Vietnam, but at the cost of devastating their country.

NOTES

[1] Senator Gravel edition, The Pentagon Papers (Boston: Beacon Press, 1971), Volume I, pp. 82-225.

[2] Bernard B. Fall, Ho Chi Minh on Revolution (New York: Frederick A. Praeger, 1967), pp. 326-333, 284-285.

[3] General Giap, Peoples War, Peoples Army (New York: Frederick A. Praeger, 1962), p. 20.

NOTES (cont.)

⁴ J.J. Zasloff, "Origins of the Insurgency in South Vietnam, 1954-1960," Rand, Memorandum RM-5163/2-ISA/ARPA, May, 1968; John C. Donnell, "Vietcong Recruitment: Why and How Men Join," Rand, Memorandum RM-54-86-1-ISA/ARPA, December 1967; W.P. Davison and J.J. Zasloff, "A Profile of Viet Cong Cadres," Memorandum, RM-4983-1-ISA/ARPA, June, 1966. See also: Stanley Karnow, Vietnam: A History (New York: Penguin, 1983), pp. 230-239, 256- 259.

⁵ Dwight D. Eisenhower, Mandate for Change (Garden City, NY: Doubleday, 1913), p. 340.

⁶ New York Times, Pentagon Papers, (New York: Bantam Books, 1971), pp. 126.

⁷ W. W. Rostow, The Diffusion of Power (New York: The Macmillan Company, 1972), pp. 270-272.

⁸ Ibid., pp. 272-279.

⁹ Pentagon Papers, op. cit. pp. 201-232.

¹⁰ New York Times, Pentagon Papers, pp. 127-130.

¹¹ Ibid.

¹² A convincing account of this process is given by David Halberstam's, The Best and the Brightest (Greenwich, Conn: Fawcett Crest, 1972).

¹³ Volume III, pp. 212-215.

¹⁴ Leslie H. Gelb, Richard K. Betts, The Irony of Vietnam: The System Worked (Washington, D.C.: The Brookings Institution, 1979), p. 121. George C. Herring, America's Longest War (New York: John Wiley and Sons, 1979). In my view, these books, plus Peter A. Poole, The United States and Indochina from FDR to Nixon (Hinsdale, IL: The Dryden Press, 1973), the Gravel Edition of the Pentagon Papers, and Halberstam's The Best and the Brightest, give the best accounts of the policymakers' viewpoints of the Vietnam War. Gelb is the editor of the Gravel edition.

¹⁵ Lyndon Johnson, The Vantage Point (New York: Popular Library, 1971), p. 127.

¹⁶ Henry Kissinger, White House Years (Boston: Little, Brown, & Company, 1979), p. 1373.

¹⁷ Far East Economic Review, April 1975, pp. 1-2.

¹⁸ Ibid.

CHAPTER 8

The India-Pakistan War of 1971

The war between India and Pakistan of 1948 over Kashmir and their territorial conflicts of 1965 were closely related to the civil war that was a consequence of the partitioning of India in 1947. The subsequent 1971 war, however, had different causes and, therefore, is evaluated below as an international war. During this war Bangladesh was born, and major world powers were brought into confrontation. We will first look briefly at the underlying causes of the above initial wars between the two Hindu and Moslem nations formed from the colony of India, before examining the causes of the international war of 1971 between India and Pakistan.

The Spread of the Civil War

The most serious religious war of our era occurred between Hindus and Moslems when the British ended their colonial controls over India in 1947. Their religious beliefs were irreconcilable. The Moslems believed in one god while Hindus worshipped many gods. When the Moslems had come to India about 1,000 A.D., they destroyed Hindu temples and sculptures as idolatrous. To the Hindus the cow was sacred and they would not eat beef, while Moslems would eat beef but considered pork as unclean. Moslems considered the rigid caste system of Hinduism as being heartless and leaving millions of untouchables to their tragic fate. Moslems tried to obtain converts to Islam, while the Hindus tended to be passive. There was no intermarriage between devout Moslems and Hindus, and the two groups regarded the other as mortal enemies. The Indian saint, Mahatma Gandhi, devoted his life to trying to reconcile the two hostile groups and to obtaining independence for India. He was not successful in preventing violence, and he was assassinated in 1948 by a Hindu fanatic opposed to Gandhi's doctrine of reconciliation.

During the partition there was a vast amount of violence and bloodshed as about 15 million Hindus and Moslems fled from their homes and settled in Pakistan and India. Pakistan was split into two areas one thousand miles apart. In the west was West Pakistan with the capital and about 40 percent of the population. One thousand miles to the east was East Pakistan with a Bengali population, which was Moslem but which had a different language and cultural background from the West. Aside from weak governmental ties, the only major links between East and West Pakistan were the Islam religion and Pakistan airlines.

After a 1948 conflict over Kashmir, sporadic fighting over the terms of the partition continued between Pakistan and India, breaking out into two small scale wars in 1965. A small conflict broke out in the Rann of Kutch, which during the monsoon was a marshy area in the state of Kutch on the border of India and Pakistan. In January, 1965 border clashes escalated into a major offensive by April by Pakistani troops. The British Government helped arrange a cease-fire and later a hearing by a tribunal, which in 1968 awarded about 90 percent of the area to India and about 10 percent to Pakistan.

A larger scale conflict broke out the same year in Kashmir. The dispute over Kashmir had been simmering since the original cease fire in 1949. Kashmir's prince had decided at the last minute to accede to India to protect his state from Pakistan. Pakistan, believing that most of his Moslem subjects would chose Pakistan, demanded a plebiscite. Fighting broke out in the area, and a U.N. mission managed to arrange a cease-fire in 1950. A permanent U.N. presence was established in the area. Clashes continued and finally in August, 1965 Pakistan crossed the U.N. cease-fire line in an invasion of Kashmir. Indian forces managed to retaliate successfully in an invasion of West Pakistan. U.N. observers and the U.N. Security Council called for a cease-fire. The Soviet Union also offered its good offices, and in January, 1966 mediated an end to the conflict.

The 1971 war between India and Pakistan was in a new dimension involving a confrontation of the superpowers and formation of a new nation. East Pakistan after the partition had come to believe it was neglected by the Pakistan government, which was dominated by West Pakistan interests. East Pakistan was very poor, and its poverty was intensified in 1970 when a violent cyclone from the Bay of Bengal killed about 200,000 persons in the low-lying areas. The government in West Pakistan was slow to aid the devastated areas, adding to the friction between the two parts of Pakistan.

In 1970 President Yahya Khan held three elections to establish a new constitutional system to take over from his military regime. In the elections in East Pakistan the nationalist party, the Awami League, won 167 out of 169 seats. This would have given

it a majority in the new Pakistan parliament, and General Yahya Khan faced the likelihood of the Awami League's delegates establishing a government virtually independent from the West. President Yahya Khan, not wanting to preside at the dismemberment of Pakistan, postponed the convening of the new parliament to an unspecified date. The Awami League saw this as postponing their movement for autonomy and responded with a general strike and a campaign of civil disorder. Talks between Yahya Khan and Sheik Mujibur, the leader of the Awami League and who was known as Mujib, broke down, and he returned to East Pakistan to head up the resistance.

West Pakistan's repression of the rebellion was brutal, marked by killing of civilians, pillage, and rape. A powerful resistance movement sprung up, and the 70,000 West Pakistan soldiers could not pacify the 75 million East Pakistanis. Meanwhile, during the crisis 10 million Bengalis fled from the repressive measures of the West Pakistan troops to eastern India in the area of Calcutta. This also was a Bengali area, but the Bengalis there were mostly Hindu instead of Moslem.

This flood of refugees to India's poorest area severely strained its meagre resources. India sharply criticized the brutal oppression of the Bengalis by the Pakistani troops. By the spring and summer of 1970 there were clashes between Indian and Pakistani border patrols, and India provided arms and training to the resistance movement in East Pakistan. By July, Mrs. Indira Gandhi was making contingency plans for a lightning strike against East Pakistan to permit Bangladesh to obtain its independence. In July, the Indian Institute for Defense Studies and Analysis published a report that the burden of the refugees would be $900 million within a year, which was more than 13 times the cost of the Kashmir War with Pakistan in 1965. This report caused a wave of popular emotion in India in favor of war.[1] At the same time, Mrs. Gandhi was making pleas to the United Nations and to the United States to force Pakistan to settle the problem so that the refugees could return to their homes.

By July there was a growing awareness by Secretary of State Kissinger, U.N. Secretary-General Waldheim and other observers that war between India and Pakistan would occur if the Pakistan refugee problem were not settled. On August 9, 1971 the Soviets signed a friendship treaty with India; Article VIII called for consultation and "appropriate effective measures" if either party were attacked or threatened with attack. With the Soviet Union officially allied with India and with the Chinese allied with Pakistan, the groundwork was laid for big power confrontation. Secretary Kissinger described the treaty as throwing a lighted match into a powder keg.[2]

On August 9 Yahya Khan announced that Mujib, who had been captured by his troops, would be tried in secret for treason. The

United States and others urged reconciliation between East and West Pakistan, and the United States also contacted representatives of the Bangladesh government in exile which was set up in Calcutta. Negotiations between the Bengali government in exile and the West Pakistan government stalled on the issue of a demand of the Bengalis to release Sheik Mujib so that he could carry on the negotiations. U.N. Secretary-General U-Thant in vain tried to mobilize or organize action in the Security Council and the United Nations to head off the impending conflict. By November, a few units of Indian troops had penetrated Pakistan allegedly in retaliation or in self-defense against Pakistan troops' attacks. India was also harboring the government in exile of the Bengalis and providing major equipment and support to the rebellion in East Pakistan.

Tensions between India and Pakistan rose because of open intervention of Indian troops, and India laid plans for a lightning surprise attack against both East and West Pakistan. The major fear of Kissinger and other observers was that the war would escalate into a major war between India and Pakistan to settle accounts remaining after the bloody partition between India and Pakistan. The 1948 partition had left a major area unsettled, that of Kashmir which was predominately Moslem but ruled by a prince who chose to unite with India. War had been waged in 1947, 1948, and also in 1965 over this area. Truces had been arranged by United Nations intervention and mediation but there was no permanent solution of the issue.

At the end of November, 1971 Indira Gandhi, in a last attempt to get U.S. support for her position, visited Washington, but the results of the visit were inconclusive. On December 3, 1971 Yahya Khan, goaded into war by open Indian support of the Bengali rebels in East Pakistan, launched a surprise attack on Indian forces. Observers were in despair, realizing that India and Pakistan were historic enemies and fearing that the war would escalate into an all-out conflict between the two nations and that it would draw in Russia and China. President Nixon and Secretary Kissinger tended to "tilt" towards Pakistan, largely because Yahya Khan was managing a secret visit of Kissinger to China and because the United States was interested in broadening its new relationship with China, which supported Pakistan. The State Department, not knowing about the trip, sympathized with India. Both factions agreed on U.N. mediation.

The United States brought the war before the U.N. Security Council on December 4, 1971. A resolution calling for a cease-fire obtained an 11-2 vote majority but failed to pass with Russia, India's major ally, exercising a veto. The Security Council then passed the question to the General Assembly, and on December 7 it called for a cease-fire by an overwhelming vote of 104-11 with only India, Bhutan, and the Communist Bloc opposing. The debate continued in the United Nations, but on December 16 the West

Pakistan army surrendered to the overwhelming might of the Indian and Bangladesh forces. By that time, the issue was back in the Security Council, and it adopted by a vote of 13 to 0, with Poland and the U.S.S.R. abstaining, a resolution calling for a cease-fire and withdrawal of the armed forces to their respective territories as soon as possible. India complied, having crushed the Pakistan forces in East Pakistan and having left the rebel forces in control of the new state of Bangladesh. On December 6, Mrs. Gandhi officially recognized the independence of Bangladesh.

During the crisis, President Nixon received "completely reliable" reports of Indira Gandhi's cabinet deliberations that indicated India was preparing to attack West Pakistan after the conflict in the East was ended. Completely reliable implies a transcript or audio tape of the cabinet proceedings. This is also confirmed in Kissinger's memoires. These allegations later caused a major political flap in India and were not denied by Mrs. Gandhi.[3] Indira Gandhi's motive for an attack would have been to settle the Kashmir boundary dispute and establish India's predominance in South Asia. Nixon and Kissinger, as a deterrent to a larger war, sent an aircraft carrier to the Bay of Bengal, ostensibly to help evacuate Americans if necesary, but in reality as a signal to India not to attack in the West. At the same time, Kissinger carried out strong diplomatic initiatives with Russia requesting it to ask India to cool it. Kissinger admits in his memoires he was playing from a weak hand. The United States was bogged down in the Vietnam conflict, and no one took seriously the aircraft carrier as a threat for U.S. intervention. The United States' political system would not have supported such intervention. Kissinger finally played one of his last cards by a refusal to carry on further detente with Russia unless it put pressure on India not to widen the war. Whether this weighed much in Russia's decision is doubtful, but, in any event, Russia did ask Indira Gandhi to stop the conflict in East Pakistan.

Probably more important in India's decision was the overwhelming U.N. vote calling for withdrawal of forces and an end to the fighting. As indicated above, the General Assembly vote was 104-11 indicating India would have been left with only Communist countries as friends if it had widened the war. Moreover, China and the United States were lining up in support of Pakistan.

After the war ended, the United Nations performed a remarkable task in assisting resettlement of the 10 million refugees back to their homes in East Pakistan. The U.N. mobilized for the refugees over $1 billion in aid, largely from the United States. Both India and Bangladesh accepted the neutral U.N. presence in the operation, whereas they would have been very reluctant to accept any big-power presence in their country. U.N. organs which assisted the refugee resettlement included the U.N. Relief Operation in Dacca and the U.N. High Commissioner for Refugees (both under the U.N. Secretary-General), as well as U.N.I.C.E.F., the World Health Organization, and other U.N. Specialized Agencies.

Religious and Nationalist Causes

Yayha Khan seems to bear the major responsibility for the crisis with his brutal repression of the Bengalis, which caused 10 million of them to flee to India. This was an unacceptable burden for the Indian government to bear, and it made open, repeated attempts to get the world community and the United States to help correct the situation.

Dr. Kissinger, in his White House Years, takes strong exception to blaming Pakistan. He cites reliable intelligence reports that Indira Gandhi intended to attack West Pakistan and settle the Kashmir problem, in blaming her for the conflict. He notes in detail how he had persuaded Yahya Khan to to spare the life of Mujib and to begin negotiations with the Bengali government in exile. Kissinger expected Bangladesh to achieve virtual independence by March, 1972, and he was attempting to delay the Indian attack. The major issue preventing a peaceful settlement of the dispute was West Pakistan's refusal to release Mujib to take charge of the negotiations for autonomy. Even a last minute visit by Indira Gandhi to President Nixon failed to forestall the war. Kissinger was convinced that Gandhi was engaged in brutal power politics with the aim of establishing predominance in the area.[4]

An interpretation that would embrace both the desire of India to solve the tremendous burden imposed by the refugee flow and its desire for predominance in South Asia as primary motives for Indira Gandhi's action would be that the refugee issue caused the war, and, that India later decided to use her superior position to establish Bangladesh and thereby weaken Pakistan. If India was set on war with Pakistan from the first, why then did India delay a year and why did India make all the public pleas for the international community and the United States to intervene to settle the problem? India's demand that West Pakistan release Mujib seemed reasonable, since otherwise the Bengalis would probably have refused to negotiate. On the other hand, one cannot fail to acknowledge the fact that Yahya Khan did make significant concessions by not executing the leader of the Bengali movement and by indicating willingness to grant considerable measures of autonomy to East Pakistan. Later, the civilian government headed by Bhutto did, in fact, release Mujib, who returned to Bangladesh and became its first President. This was a remarkable act of statesmanship and helped not only ease the way for a reconciliation between West Pakistan and Bangladesh but also to facilitate the establishment of normal relations between India and Pakistan.

There is no consensus, therefore, on who started the war. Pakistan actually launched the surprise attack against Indian forces, but Indian forces had violated the border and were openly supporting a civil war in East Pakistan. I would attribute the blame to India, but the question is so controversial that in Table 1 there is a column for each country as an aggressor in the India-Pakistan War of 1971.

The issue caused great controversy in the United States, initially because the U.S. visit to China was one of the most closely held secrets of the Nixon presidency and people could not understand the White House "tilt" toward Pakistan. State Department officials not "in the know" could not understand the failure of the United States to criticize Yayha Khan for the brutal suppression and deaths caused in the conflict. The Consul General at Dacca resigned in protest, and Kissinger's accounts in his memoires are filled with exasperation over the failure of the State Department to fall in line with the President's orders.

Kissinger, in this crisis, admitted Pakistan acted unwisely, brutally, and immorally, but he said it was a matter within Pakistan's "domestic jurisdiction." The U.S. was working towards self-determination for East Pakistan but not in "plain violation of the rules by which the world must conduct itself if it is to survive."[5] Kissinger's policy aims in the crisis did not violate international law, recognizing that civil war was within domestic jurisdiction, and that countries such as India had no right to commit aggression against Pakistan under a strict interpretation of international law. Nevertheless, the international lawyers probably would have been satisfied with the truce which left the boundaries with India virtually the same and which permitted the Bengalis the right of self-determination. Supporters of U.N. would add that the final outcome was a political solution that did not violate the principles of the U.N. charter.

Perhaps the major lesson is that the U.N. provided a remarkable instrument to help settle a war that could have taken years to unravel. It was a war which found Russia and India, on the one hand, confronting Pakistan and China, and to a less extent, the United States on the other. Credit should also be given to the supportive diplomacy of Kissinger and the Soviet Union in settling this conflict. Kissinger described his strategy as a geopolitical approach, that is, paying attention to the requirements of "equilibrium," and supporting the "rules by which the world must conduct itself if it is to survive." Another way of expressing this would be to say that the world community represented by the U.N. supported principles of international law in the conflict, while leaders of the United States and the Soviet Union also supported these principles with the view of helping to maintain the balance of power in the area and in the world.

There were relatively few misperceptions of leaders in the war. Indira Gandhi used force only after pleas to the world community failed to settle the conflict. If she did have aims of settling accounts with Pakistan, she probably wisely calculated that most of the world was against India and that the costs would be too great for the gains. As in other conflicts, nationalism was the ideology at the root of the conflict. Religious and cultural differences intensified the tensions.

The world was fortunate with the long history of wars in the area that the conflict was settled quickly, and that the United Nations was able to help resettle the 10 million refugees back in Bangladesh. When one considers the terrible problems and world tensions caused by one million Palestine refugees in the Middle East, the successful and peaceful solution by the U.N. of a problem of 10 million refugees in South Asia deserves more credit than it received from most observers of the war.

NOTES

[1] John G. Stoessinger, Why Nations Go to War (New York: St. Martins Press, 1974), p. 163.

[2] Secretary of State Henry Kissinger in his memoires gives a detailed account of the crisis which he calls "perhaps the most complex issue of Nixon's first term." Kissinger, op. cit., pp. 842-913.

[3] Hindustan Times, November 29, 1979, p. 1.

[4] Kissinger, White House Years, op. cit., Chapter XXI.

[5] Ibid., pp. 913-915.

CHAPTER 9

The Cuban Missile Crisis

Most accounts of the Cuban missile crisis of 1962 tend to make President Kennedy a hero. The way in which he faced up to the Russians "eyeball to eyeball" in the game of power politics and forced them to withdraw the missiles was almost like winning the Super Bowl. If we take into account the views of Russians and Cubans, however, the incident was not that simple, and it leaves some troublesome questions. Whose fault was the crisis? How close did we come to nuclear war? What lessons are to be learned from this crisis?

During this confrontation between the United States and the Soviet Union in October, 1962 the world was close to disaster. Secretary of Defense Robert S. McNamara wrote: "The world was faced with what many of us felt then and what since has been generally agreed, was the greatest danger of a catastrophic war since the advent of the nuclear age." He continues, "Prime Minister MacMillan has said that the weeks of the crisis represented the greatest period of strain which he faced in several decades of public service, including the whole of World War II."[1] At another time, McNamara said that during the crisis he was not sure that he would live to see the sun come up the next day. Accounts of the crisis indicate that General Curtis LeMay, the Air Force Chief of Staff, recommended the use of nuclear weapons against Cuba to destroy the missile sites. Before the crisis, on September 11, the Soviets had warned that an attack on Cuba would unleash a nuclear war.

Accounts of the crisis generally agree that President Kennedy did a brilliant job in getting a committee of top officials to come up with options for policies other than a direct attack on the missile sites. After five days of deliberation, he decided to "quarantine" Cuba to prevent further shipments of missiles, which avoided the more forceful options originally proposed. At the same time he mobilized U.S. troops, sending a message to the Russians that the United States was preparing, if necessary, to invade Cuba to destroy the missiles. The fact that these power plays succeeded in getting the Russians to back down helped convince observers that his policy was correct. There was much more involved in the story than the above, however, and a logical place to start is with the abortive attempt at the invasion of Cuba by U.S.-supported Cuban forces.

The Bay of Pigs

Fidel Castro, starting out with a handful of men in the Sierre Madre mountains, within two years promoted a major revolution against Cuba's right-wing dictator, Batista. In 1958 Castro marched on the capital with a small force that expanded to only two or three thousand men. It was an easy revolution with people joining the revolutionary force to overthrow the hated Batista regime. Castro's first announcements indicated that he would establish a left-wing regime, but not a Communist system, and apparently even the Russians did not regard him as a Communist at first.[2] By the end of 1959, however, several of the non-Communist members of his cabinet had either been arrested or had fled to the United States along with about 100,000 other refugees. By this time he was taking over newspapers and establishing a Communist-type regime. He also made arrangements with the Soviet Union for a large-scale import of arms which were scheduled for delivery in the summer of 1961.

On January 3, 1961 Castro ordered the U.S. Embassy staff to be reduced to 11 people in 24 hours. Why did he do this? The U.S. Senate report on assassination plots that was published in 1975 throws light on this question. In August, 1960 the CIA officials in Havana offered $10,000 to a new Cuban contact if he would kill Castro. In line with Washington instructions, the CIA later dropped the matter. On August 16, 1960, however, CIA in Havana received a box of Castro's favorite cigars with a botulism toxin so potent that Castro would die if he put one in his mouth. It was ready on October 7, and presumably the CIA was discussing with some contact in Cuba how to get these cigars to Castro. In October, 1960 a Chicago gangster, Giancana, was bragging that he was arranging with CIA to kill Castro in November. This report was picked up by the FBI, which knew nothing of the CIA plot. Meanwhile, early in 1960, the Eisenhower administration had authorized CIA to begin training and arming of a Cuban Exile Liberation Army in Guatemala. By October 30, 1960 a Guatemala city newspaper broke the story saying that the army was training to invade Cuba, and it hinted at U.S. collusion. In the following months, U.S. periodicals and newspapers picked up the story, and by April there were numerous news stories telling about recruitment in the United States for the invasion efforts. In retrospect, the plotting for Castro's death seemed so widespread and amateurish that it seems likely that Castro received word of it. If he did not, he certainly read the reports about CIA support for the invasion army of Cuban dissidents. Either one of the reports would have warranted Castro's action to severely cut back the U.S. Embassy staff.

President Kennedy at his inauguration in January, 1961 inherited the invasion plot from President Eisenhower. After discussing it with top intelligence and military officials, Kennedy decided to go ahead with it on the condition that the U.S. would not provide direct military support. On April 17, the landing of Cuban exiles was attempted at the Bay of Pigs with disastrous results. About 1,400 Cubans failed to maintain a beachhead. Instead of fading into the jungle as planned, almost all of them were captured by Castro. By the time the fiasco ended, a few U.S. pilots had helped in raids with B-26's, and the U.S. Navy and U.S. aircraft had escorted vessels in the attack.

President Kennedy publicly took full responsibility for the failure. Although the attack did not come close to success, it was clear to Castro that the United States was making determined efforts to attack his regime.

The Russian Missiles

Before judging whether the U.S.-sponsored efforts to attack Cuba and kill Castro led to the decision of Khrushchev to emplace missiles in Cuba, it is useful to review how the crisis unfolded. On the morning of October 16, 1962 President Kennedy was shown pictures of missile sites in Cuba where 16 to 32 intermediate-range Russian ballistic missiles were being emplaced. It was estimated that they would be operational in about two weeks. President Kennedy immediately appointed a committee of top officials to recommend what action the United States should take. This executive committee (EXCOM), which included top officials of Defense, the State Department, CIA, as well as Bobby Kennedy, the Attorney General and brother of the President, initially favored the idea of a quick air strike to destroy the sites of the missiles, which had a range reaching as far as Washington D.C. and other major U.S. cities. The Joint Chiefs of Staff during the following days continued to favor an air strike and invasion to destroy the missile sites. Dean Acheson, former Secretary of State, who was also one of the committee, made a brilliant presentation in favor of this option. Most civilian officials, however, tended to favor other options, particularly as later in the week it became evident that an air strike would require a major effort involving a large loss of U.S. planes and probably many Russian casualties. Bobby Kennedy, who tended to take a leading role in raising question on options, at the beginning raised a moral issue saying that in the last analysis they were advocating a surprise attack by a very large nation against a very small one. He pointed out our struggle against Communism throughout the world was far more than for physical survival-- it had as its essence our heritage and our ideals and that we should not destroy these.[3] Legal issues were also debated, and three of the legal memoranda submitted agreed that emplacement of these missiles in itself did not justify the use of force in self-defense. However, all agreed that the Organization of American States (OAS) could authorize such a response, and that there was an obligation to consult the OAS and the United Nations before taking action. (The United Nations Charter permits actions to remove threats to the peace if duly authorized by regional organizations, such as the OAS, and if such actions are consistent with the Charter.)

During the week after the initial discovery of the missile sites the President carried on business as usual, while the Committee debated various options for action. On Friday, October 20, after listening to the conclusions of EXCOM, the President decided on the limited blockade option to be called a quarantine. During discussion of this option, Adlai Stevenson, U.S. Ambassador to the United Nations, suggested this demand be coupled with an offer to withdraw our nuclear missiles from Turkey. The President replied that some time ago he had asked the State Department to negotiate the removal of these Jupiter missiles since they were obsolete, liquid-fuel missiles, but he was irritated to find that the State Department had not carried out this task. The missiles were tied in to NATO defenses, and the State Department had gone on the assumption that removal required approval from the NATO and Turkish authorities, and this approval had not been forthcoming. The President replied to Stevenson, however, that backing down and withdrawing the missiles from Turkey at this point would undermine the confidence of our European allies and our willingness to help defend them.[4]

Later, at American University, the President explained his choice of strategy as follows: "Above all while defending our own vital interest, nuclear powers must avoid those confrontations which bring an adversary to a choice of either humiliating retreat or a nuclear war." He wanted to leave some options for Khrushchev and some options for saving face that a direct invasion would not permit. Khrushchev, as late as September 11, had indicated that a military invasion of Cuba would unleash a nuclear war. Moreover, the blockade option was pictured as "a quarantine" that would only block shipments of additional missiles and missile components, and it was not a full scale blockade including petroleum and other civilian products.

On Monday, October 22, after consulting with Congressional leaders, President Kennedy announced the quarantine. In reporting to the American people he said that the Soviets' "sudden, clandestine decision to station strategic weapons for the first time outside of Soviet soil, is a deliberately provocative and unjustified change in the status quo which cannot be accepted by this country, if our courage and commitments are ever to be trusted again by either friend or foe." He added that, "The 1930's taught us a clear lesson: aggressive conduct, if allowed to go unchecked and unchallenged, ultimately leads to war." He then outlined the steps that would be taken including the quarantine on shipment on additional missiles and missile parts.[5]

The following week was a period of high tension as the world waited for the Russian response. An important action in the minds of the Executive Committee during that week was the unanimous endorsement of the OAS of the quarantine in a broad, authorizing resolution. The following Thursday and Friday on October 23 and 24, 16 of the 18 Russian ships sailing towards Cuba stopped dead in the water and then turned around. The tension continued, however, because daily U-2 flights over Cuba indicated that the emplacement of the missiles was being rushed, and reports indicated that Russian diplomats in New York were burning their secret messages and getting ready to leave.

On Friday, October 26, President Kennedy received a rambling letter from Khrushchev that the missiles were being emplaced only to defend Cuba, and that if he had assurance that the United States would not attack Cuba, he would withdraw them. The Executive Committee immediately went into session to consider how to reply to this message. On Saturday, October 27, however, another letter arrived from Khrushchev with an added condition that the Jupiter missiles in Turkey should be withdrawn. After intensive consideration with EXCOM, Kennedy decided that the United States would not withdraw the Jupiter missiles under pressure and that he would finesse the second letter by replying only to the first one. In the reply, which was agreed to by the Executive Committee, the President agreed to the conditions set by Khrushchev in his October 26 letter saying that the United States would give a commitment not to invade Cuba if work on the missile sites would cease and if this would be confirmed by U.N. observation. He ignored the question of the Jupiters. Nevertheless, the Joints Chiefs of Staff continued to favor an air strike. One of the Joint Chiefs, probably Air Force General Curtis LeMay, favored a nuclear strike against Cuba.

The next day Khrushchev publicly announced the missiles would be withdrawn since the U.S. had pledged not to invade Cuba. This was the climax of the missile crisis, and most accounts of the missile crisis end with this decision, noting that the missiles were withdrawn as promised by the Russians. Although the U.N. did not supervise their withdrawal because of strong objections by President Fidel Castro, the Cubans did permit daily U-2 flights to moniter the dismantlement of the Russian missiles, and U.S. Navy ships and U-2's from a distance checked on their return shipment as the ships sailed back to Russia.

Most accounts of the missile crisis conclude that Kennedy's actions were a model of forceful and effective diplomacy using the strategic advantage of nuclear and conventional military power to force the Soviets to withdraw their missile threat to the United States. A few note that this crisis did encourage the Soviets to accelerate their own development of nuclear missiles so that within a few years they had achieved rough equality in nuclear strike power through expansion of their intercontinental-range ballistic missiles.

There is little agreement on the motives for the Russian move in the first place. The most obvious conclusion was that it, in one stroke, would have greatly reduced the strategic-missile advantage of the United States. At that time, the United States' arsenal of intercontinental missiles far exceeded that of the Russians by probably a ratio of 5 or 10 to 1. Placing intermediate range missiles in Cuba, which the Russians had in greater numbers, would have reduced the strategic advantage of the U.S. Other reasons seriously considered by Kennedy as being behind the Russian move were: 1. That it was a probe or test of our will. 2. That it was a trap to divert our attention from another power move. 3. That it was designed to defend Cuba against attack. 4. That it was a bargaining move to exchange for a U.S. withdrawal from Berlin. The President tended to lean towards the first, that it was a test of our will, with the defense of Cuba and a move to catch up with us in missile strength as secondary motives.[6]

President Kennedy made a diplomatic move during the crisis that initially escaped the attention of many commentators. After the EXCOM decided not to offer to withdraw the missiles from Turkey, the President sent Bobby Kennedy to discuss the issue with Ambassador Dobrynin. In this discussion, Bobby Kennedy assured Ambassador Dobrynin that the President would remove the missiles from Turkey, but that he could not make such a commitment in public at this time. Bobby also indicated that there was a great deal of pressure being exerted by the U.S. military command for an invasion, but that the President was resisting such pressures. This assurance about the missile sites in Turkey, off the record, did meet the important condition laid down in the second Khrushchev letter and at least added more room for Khrushchev to maneuver.

Before making a final assessment on the causes of the crisis and the lessons to be learned from it, it is helpful to look at it from the point of view of Khrushchev and Fidel Castro. Fortunately, we have Khrushchev's account in his memoires, which gives insight into Russian actions during the crisis.

Khrushchev notes that at the beginning of the revolution he had no idea that Castro would establish a Communist regime, although Khrushchev knew that Raul Castro, his brother, was a Communist and Che Guevara, the leader of his military, was also a good Communist. Then, before the Bay of Pigs invasion, Castro came out with a declaration that Cuba would follow the Communist course. This puzzled Russian leaders, since from a tactical standpoint it did not make sense to invite U.S. opposition. Khrushchev notes that he believed the Bay of Pigs was only a beginning of the assaults against Castro. To Khrushchev, Cuba appeared like a "sausage" that was vulnerable to a U.S. attack.

Khrushchev then asserts that Russia had to confront America with more than words. The logical answer was missiles, and his major motive, he asserted, was to restrain the United States from precipitous actions against Castro. He added, "In addition to protecting Cuba, our missiles would have equalized what the West likes to call "the balance of power." It was high time, he said, that America knew what it felt like to have her own land and her own people threatened. Therefore, Khrushchev decided to install intermediate-range missiles and the medium-range Il-28 bombers, which although they were getting obsolete could reach American cities.

He noted then that the American became frightened, so the Soviets stepped up their shipments to get the missiles in place. Then, he said, Kennedy issued a warning, and Americans began to make a belligerent show of strength including blockading the island. By that time, Khrushchev said, the Russians had installed enough missiles to destroy New York, Chicago, and other huge industrial cities, as well as Washington, D.C. Then President Kennedy, Khrushchev stated, issued an ultimatum about withdrawing the missiles. Robert Kennedy went to see Ambassador Dobrynin, and according to Khrushchev, Robert Kennedy, the President's brother and Attorney General, said that if the situation continued much longer, the President was not sure but that the military would seize power. Later, according to Khrushchev, Robert said, "We don't know how much longer we can hold out against our generals."[7]

Khrushchev spent the night at the Council of Ministers Office, and, upon receiving the President's assurance that there would be no invasion of Cuba by the United States or anyone else and after consultation with his comrades, Khrushchev agreed to remove the missiles. Khrushchev reports that Castro was furious and even refused to receive the Russian Ambassador. Nevertheless, despite the Russian withdrawal of the missiles under pressure from the United States, Khrushchev states in his memoires that he remembers President Kennedy with "deep respect" because he was sober minded and determined to avoid war. Moreover, Khrushchev says, Kennedy left himself a way out of the crisis and showed real wisdom in turning his back on the right-wing forces who were trying to goad him into military action against Cuba. Khrushchev concludes it was a great victory for the Soviets because the Americans probably had to pledge not to invade Cuba. He adds that "the American imperialist beast was forced to swallow a hedgehog, quills and all."[8]

Kennedy conditioned his commitment about not invading Cuba on the U.N.'s supervising the withdrawal of the missiles. However, Castro refused to admit the U.N. officials to supervise dismantling of the missile sites, and as Khrushchev noted, even refused for many days to discuss the matter with Mikoyan, the Russian emissary. Nevertheless, the Soviets destroyed the missile sites and withdrew the missiles with the U.S. monitoring them by U-2 aircraft and close surveillance from Navy ships.

Why We Went to the Brink

Whose fault was the 1962 Missile crisis? Seen from the standpoint of Cuba and the Soviet Union it was not a simple Russian power move to equalize missile strength or to put pressure on the United States. The United States, by attempting to assassinate Castro and by virtually open support for the Cuban exile army that invaded Cuba, "asked for it."

Certainly, as many observers pointed out, President Kennedy managed the crisis well. Even Khrushchev respected Kennedy for his sober-mindedness. The ending could have been quite different, however, if Brezhnev had been Chairman or if another President had accepted the advice of the Joint Chiefs of Staff and attacked Cuba. Khrushchev, himself, about a month before the crisis, had indicated that such an attack could lead to nuclear war.

Many lessons, particularly on the conduct of diplomacy and foreign policy, have been drawn from the Cuban missile crisis. Some observers have noted with approval how Kennedy forced his top advisors to consider a number of options and consequences that would result from taking certain steps. He was skillful in mobilizing public opinion and getting backing of the Organization of American States, which created a framework of international law to support the "quarantine." He did not even call it a blockade, which is an act of war and would have been more provocative. Moreover, answering the first letter from Khrushchev, which did not include the demand for removal of the Turkish missile sites, also gave Khrushchev more room to maneuver. At the same time, Kennedy performed a diplomatic maneuver that has been overlooked by many observers when he sent his brother Robert to Dobrynin. In the conversation Robert offered to withdraw the Turkish missiles, explaining why the President was constrained from doing this publicly. If the Turkish missiles were an important issue to Khrushchev or to his colleagues on the Politburo, this was a face saving device for Khrushchev. Also, Kennedy did not publicly cause Khrushchev to back down but gave him enough maneuverability that allowed him to save face and even come out of the missile crisis with respect for the young president.

A major lesson learned from the crisis was the importance of maintaining communication between the top leaders. Khrushchew had already initiated personal correspondence between the two leaders, and Khrushchev's personal letter of Friday, October 26 was the key to the solution of the crisis. There has been speculation that the October 27 letter, a day later, might have represented Politburo views, while the first letter may have been from Nikita himself. Kennedy was able to answer the first for the record, and only indirectly meet the additional demand of the second on the withdrawal of the missiles from Turkey. In any event, after the crisis was over, the two leaders maintained the exchange of personal letters and formally improved the lines of communication for a crisis by establishing a Hot Line Agreement for electrical communication between top officials of the White House and the Kremlin.

The world was perilously close to a nuclear disaster during the crisis. In view of the history of provocative American actions against Cuba, was the missile issue worth a nuclear confrontation? Robert McNamara, Secretary of Defense, reportedly in initial consideration of the crisis, said it was not, since both sides already had overkill. Certainly the Russians entered into an intensive effort to increase their intercontinental missiles after the Cuban crisis and within only a few years had achieved equality with the United States. By the 1970's the United States was as vulnerable to missiles from Russian submarines and from intercontinental missiles launched from the Soviet Union as it would have been if the intermediate missiles had been placed in Cuba.

Many observers assume that U.S. nuclear superiority was the critical factor that permitted the United States to take a strong stand against the Soviets. However, on the twentieth anniversary of the crisis major participants in the U.S. decisions of 1962 issued a statement indicating that they did not even consider the nuclear balance during the crisis. A much more important factor, they said, was the preponderance of U.S. naval and military strength in the area, which permitted the U.S. to institute the quarantine of Cuba without a serious conventional challenge from the Soviets.[9]

I routinely poll my classes, before describing the outcome of the crisis, on whether President Kennedy should have agreed as part of the bargain to withdraw the "obsolete" missiles from Turkey. The response usually is overwhelmingly no, which is similar to recommendations of the EXCOM group that advised Kennedy. This is the most alarming lesson that I draw from the Cuban missile crisis. It illustrates how public opinion would easily fall in behind a leader who would take a tough, uncompromising stand against the Soviet Union and who would be reluctant to compromise, even on removing some obsolete missiles. Students and the public often see the decision like a bargaining game, and they gamble on not backing down under pressure. They would tend to reject the above compromise proposal even though it may have prevented a nuclear war that could have destroyed civilization.

Fortunately, Kennedy approached the crisis with great care and with open lines of communication to Khrushchev, a leader whom he had met and corresponded with. Kennedy's skillful compromise in dealing with the Russian leader, and luck, saved the world from a war that could have escalated into a nuclear holocaust.

NOTES

[1] Robert F. Kennedy, Thirteen Days (New York: Signet Books, 1969), pp. 13-14.

[2] Nikita Khrushchev, Khrushchev Remembers-The Last Testament (New York: Little Brown, 1974), pp. 580-83.

[3] Robert F. Kennedy, Thirteen Days, op. cit., pp. 38-39.

[4] Theodore Sorenson, Kennedy (London: Pan Books, 1966), p. 770.

[5] Ibid., p. 780.

[6] Sorenson, op. cit., p. 747-49.

[7] Robert Kennedy was probably telling Dobrynin that there was strong pressure from the Pentagon to mount an invasion and air attack against the missile sites and that pressure was building up in the United States for such a move. By the time it was relayed through Ambassador Dobrynin to Moscow, it sounded like a threat for the military to take control of the U.S. Government.

[8] Nikita Khrushchev, Khrushchev Remembers-The Last Testament (New York: Little Brown, 1974), p. 584.

[9] Statement by Dean Rusk, then Secretary of State; Robert McNamara, then Secretary of Defense; George W. Ball, then Under Secretary of State; Roswell L. Gilpartic, then Deputy Secretary of Defense; Theodore Sorensen, then special counsel to the President; and McGeorge Bundy, then special assistant to the President for national security affairs. Time, September 27, 1982, p. 85.

CHAPTER 10

Soviet Invasions of Satellites

After World War II most nations recognized as a fact of international life the Soviet domination of a group of East European states, which the Soviets viewed as a buffer against a revival of German aggression. The world's callousness to this Soviet type of imperialism has prevented many observers from recalling that the Soviet invasions of Hungary in 1956 and Czechslovakia in 1968 amounted to wars against these nations. Both Hungary and Czechoslovakia had been recognized as independent nations and had been admitted to the U.N., even though they were dominated by the Soviet Union.

On the other hand, the Soviet Union's invasion of Afghanistan during the Christmas holidays of 1979 was recognized clearly as an imperialistic war, even though the Soviet Union had already achieved a strong position of influence there. That invasion to some seemed like the first step in a Soviet drive to take over control of the highly strategic Middle East oil fields. To others, the Soviets seemed to be seizing a target of opportunity and trying to consolidate a Communist regime which had had serious troubles in controlling a local rebellion. The following facts on these invasions will help us to see patterns similar to those of other wars.

The Invasion of Hungary

Hungary was one of the East European buffer states occupied by Soviet troops after World War II. Soviet troops brought with them Hungarian Communists who had lived in exile in the Soviet Union, as well as Soviet political experts, to set up a government to replace the pro-Nazi Hungarian government defeated by Soviet troops. The Hungarian Communists and their Russian advisers reestablished the Communist Party and brought together a coalition of other parties dominated by the Communists to form a new government. By 1949, with indirect Soviet assistance, the Hungarian Communist party dominated the political process.

The privileges and high standard of living of high Communist officials in Hungary contrasted with the economic distress of others, and by 1956 opposition to the party leadership developed in intellectual circles. Opposition centered in the Petofi Circle, a Communist debating club, and it supported policies of a former Communist premier, Imre Nagy, who had tried to relax the heavy emphasis on heavy industry and bring about increased production of consumer goods. He had been arrested and imprisoned by Communist leaders who replaced him.

The 1956 Khrushchev speech denouncing Stalin and the success of the Polish Communists in standing up to the Soviet Union and keeping their leadership intact encouraged the Hungarians to press for reforms. In the summer of 1956 the Hungarian Communist Party appointed a new secretary, but public pressure demanded he be replaced by Nagy.

On October 23, 1956 about 200,000 demonstrators marched in Budapest demanding that Nagy take over leadership of the government and carry out basic democratic reforms. At first the Soviet leadership and the Hungarian Communist Party agreed to Nagy's leadership in the hopes that he could stabilize the situation. Soviet troops were brought in at Nagy's request, and on October 29, the Soviets appeared confident enough of Nagy's leadership to make a conciliatory statement and began withdrawing troops. On November 1, however, Nagy overreached himself by not only promising free elections and more private enterprise, but informing the Soviets of Hungary's desire to secede from the Warsaw Pact, to become neutral like Austria, and to have Soviet troops withdraw from Hungary. Nagy, perhaps, reasoned that the Soviets two years earlier had withdrawn troops from Austria, formerly part of Austria-Hungary, and permitted it to be neutral. The Soviets had also backed down in the face of a strong stand by Prime Minister Gomulka against Soviet military intervention in Poland a few weeks earlier. Nagy's gamble failed. After much debate in the Kremlin and after consultation with other Communist leaders, Khrushchev on November 1 ordered Soviet troops to oust Nagy and establish order in Hungary.

Prime Minister Nagy denounced the invasion on November 1 by the Soviet troops and appealed to the United Nations for assistance. The U.N. by this time, however, was diverted from the Hungarian problem by a major Middle East crisis in which Israel, in league with Britain and France, had attacked Egypt in the Suez Canal area. The Soviet troops quickly crushed their opposition in Budapest and placed Janos Kadar, a previous deputy prime minister, who during the crisis had sought sanctuary with the Russians, in control.

The U.N. Security Council was blocked by a Soviet veto, but by November 4 an emergency special session of the General Assembly met and adopted a resolution calling on the Soviet Union to withdraw its troops without delay. The resolution called on the Secretary-General to investigate and for the Hungarian Government to admit U.N. observers. On November 7, however, Janos Kadar, backed by Soviet troops, as First Secretary of the Communist Party informed the U.N. Secretary-General that all communications from former Premier Nagy were invalid.

In the succeeding months the General Assembly repeatedly condemned the Soviet's violation of the U.N. Charter in depriving Hungary of its independence. On December 12, 1958 the U.N. denounced Hungary's execution of Imre Nagy and his associates. The U.N. discussed the issue until 1962, deploring the Soviet action in numerous resolutions. However, there was no support for sanctions because the U.N. members feared a Soviet withdrawal from the U.N. would fatally weaken it.

The Soviet version of events was that it would have been "inexcusable" if it did not "help the working class of Hungary in its struggle against the counterrevolution."[1] The controlled press and radio of Eastern Europe joined the Soviet press in praising the Red Army's suppression of "counter- revolutionary terror" in Hungary. Noting the demonstrations in Poland and the possible reverberations of a successful challenge to the Communist regime in Hungary, the Russian leadership feared that the whole Eastern bloc would be destabilized. The Hungarian revolt demonstrated that the Eastern European Communist regimes "rest nakedly on the presence or proximity of the Red Army."[2]

The 1968 Invasion of Czechoslovakia

The sad history of Czechoslovakia since 1938 arises from its strategic location. Hitler's massive and successful intimidation of England and France to permit him to take over that country in 1938 paved the way for World War II. After World War II Czechoslovakia lay in the heart of the Soviet East European empire, separating Poland from the rest of the East European bloc. Czechoslovakia's northwest border stretched along the Federal Republic of Germany's southern flank, and Soviet mobilization of its divisions there could threaten NATO's main forces in Germany. It is not surprising, therefore, that the Soviets strongly supported Communist domination of the government after World War II, and moved in on Czechoslovakia in 1968 when it threatened to change drastically its Communist system.

The Communists got off to a strong start in Czechoslovakia after World War II because of Czech gratitude to the Soviets for liberating them, and Czechoslovakia's distrust of France and Britain because of their sell-out of Czechoslovakia at Munich in

1938. For a brief period Czechoslovakia started to revive democracy, but in 1948 the Communist Party engineered a coup with its Communist-controlled police force. The police raided the headquarters of non-Communist parties, and the Communists generated street demonstrations against the government. Russian forces looked on with approval. During this crisis President Benes resigned, and one of the strongest anti-Communist ministers, Jan Masaryk, was murdered.

Czechoslovakia settled down into the Communist economic and political mold until 1965 when deteriorating economic conditions stimulated the government to decentralize and relax economic controls. These changes were accompanied by a political liberalization including elections, reestablishing a parliament, and giving workers a stronger voice in management.

In January, 1968 Dubcek, who supported these liberal reforms, took over as leader of the Party. To allay Soviet fears he immediately visited Moscow and proclaimed the solidarity of Czechoslovakia with the Soviet Union. Nevertheless, the Soviets beefed up their Warsaw Pact maneuvers as a warning to the Czechs and called a meeting of their East European allies, except for Romania, to coordinate action to oppose the reforms. In the middle of July, 1968 the Soviets, Hungary, Poland, East Germany and Bulgaria sent a letter to Prague warning it that hostile forces there had created a "threat of weaning away Czechoslovakia from the socialist community." It stated that the strength of that community "depends on the internal strength of the socialist system in each of our fraternal countries."[3] The Czechs, wishing to reassure the Soviets, argued they had not the slightest desire to opt out of their obligations under the Warsaw Pact.

The Soviets then called a meeting of their satellites in the easternmost corner of Czechoslovakia at Cierna near the Soviet border. General Svoboda, the President, and Prime Minister Dubcek held firm there in opposition to Soviet demands to station troops in Czechoslovakia. At the same time the Soviets and their satellites insisted on a reversal of Czechoslovakia's liberalization and a muffling of criticism of the Soviets that was appearing in the Czechoslovakian press, which by this time was virtually unbridled.

On August 20 the Soviet troops aided by East German, Polish, Hungarian and Bulgarian forces suddenly invaded Czechoslovakia. President Svoboda denounced the invasion, and before the Soviets could throttle the radio, TV, and other communications, the Czechoslovakian representative appealed to the U.N. Security Council. At this meeting Jan Musik, acting head of the Czech delegation, said he had been instructed by his foreign minister to protest the illegal occupation of his country, and he demanded the withdrawal of the Soviet forces.

Czechoslovakian TV showed two tanks set on fire by civilian resistance, but the Czech government ordered its armed forces not to resist, and armed resistance was minimal, although the people openly jeered at the invaders. Dubcek and Svoboda were then taken to Moscow and after two sleepless nights returned to Czechoslovakia to read speeches calling for cooperation with Moscow. Czech officials instituted a passive non-cooperation policy, Soviet tanks were pulled back from Prague, but within a few months Dubcek had been removed from office and expelled from the party. In October the Soviets signed a treaty with Czechoslovakia providing for Soviet troops to be stationed in Czechoslovakia.

The Soviet invasion was too quick and effective to generate a conventional war, but it was vigorously opposed by the Czech government and people, and they made a plea for assistance to the United Nations. From the Soviet point of view it was a highly successful military operation with few or no deaths, accomplishing its objective of removing Dubcek and reversing liberal reforms of the Communist system. The invasion, however, was denounced by almost all the Western European Communist parties and by China. Peking claimed that the Soviet motive was to block a chain reaction of reform movements in Eastern Europe which would threaten Soviet hegemony in the area. The Brezhnev doctrine proclaimed during the crisis asserted the right of the Soviets to intervene if the cause of "socialism" was in danger. The invasion demonstrated Soviet control over its East European empire, and as of 1985 none of the East European satellites had succeeded in breaking away from military and political domination by Russia.

The Soviet Invasion of Afghanistan

The basis for the Soviet move into Afghanistan was an April, 1978 coup which brought the Communists to power. The Communist Party of Afghanistan in the guise of the Democratic Party of the Masses was formed in 1965. Nur Mohammed Taraki was selected to be general secretary and publisher of the party newspaper Khalq, which means "masses;" the Party is commonly called Khalq. Taraki was born in Afghanistan. One of his first jobs was with a fruit company, which sent him to Bombay, India, where he became interested in Marxism. He later spent a short time in Washington, D.C. as a press attache for the Afghan Government, and for a time worked for the United States Overseas Mission in Kabul. Khalq's articles and the Party followed a Marxist-Leninist line and supported the Soviet model of development. Khalq split into two groups largely along ethnic lines with a seceding group publishing its own newspaper Percham (flag). This latter group was led by Babrak Karmal, who later was established as president by Soviet troops in the December, 1979 invasion. The two Communist groups cooperated in overthrowing the monarchy in 1973 and establishing a non-Communist, Mohammad Daud, as President. Daud at first cooperated with his Communist allies, but after he consolidated his pos-

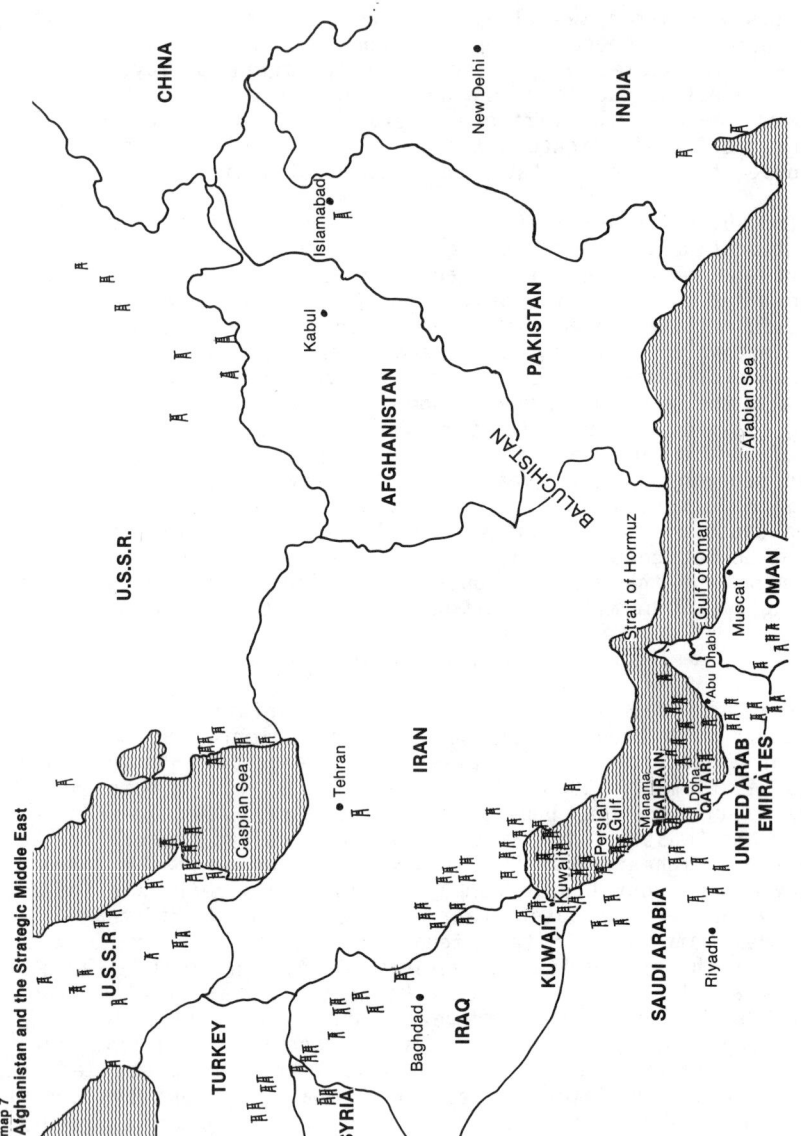

map 7
Afghanistan and the Strategic Middle East

ition, he weakened Afghanistan's ties with Russia, improved relations with Pakistan and Iran, and arrested the leaders of the leftist organizations that had brought him to power. At this point the two Communist factions united again and mounted the April, 1978 coup against Daud.

Taraki became president and Karmal vice president, but Karmal was soon sent to Czechoslovakia as ambassador to get him out of the country. Taraki then dismissed him, and Karmal and other Perchami leaders formed a group in exile in Eastern Europe. The Soviets brought them to Moscow in preparation for the 1979 invasion.

The success of the Khalq and Perchami factions in the 1973 and 1978 coups was based in part on the close ties of Afghanistan's military to the Soviet Union. Although Afghanistan authorities had requested military aid from the United States, the U.S. was more interested in aiding their rival, Pakistan; this helped persuade the Afghanistan Government to seek military aid from the Soviet Union. The Soviets helped construct airfields and train about 200 Afghanistan officers every year in the Soviet Union. This, of course, gave the Soviets a chance to influence these officers ideologically and provide recruits for Khalq. The Soviets' program of modernization of Central Asia was impressive to these young officers, who had come from the primitive areas of Afghanistan. Also, Daud lost the support of the Muslim Brotherhood, which distrusted him because of his past association with the Communists, who had helped manage the 1973 coup. The anti-religious bias of Communism is at the root of the present conflict between the Moslems of Afghanistan and their Communist rulers.

Although there was speculation that the Soviets played a part in the 1978 coup which brought Communists to power, there has been no direct proof of this. If the Soviets did play a role, it was so discreet that it was hardly noticed in the United States at that time. It was a violent coup with 2,000 to 10,000 killed and with major support from the armed forces. American authorities in Afghanistan initially claimed that coup leaders were not Communists, and U.S. observers generally overlooked the significance of extending Communist rule in this strategic region.

After the 1978 coup the new Communist government soon showed its true colors, changing the flag to a Soviet red, enthusiastically supporting the Soviet Union in its international policies, and instituting a mandatory course in Marxism for students and government officials. Reportedly the regime imprisoned and executed many thousands of opponents, and within a few months the regime was faced with a major civil war. Army morale collapsed, and Soviet officers took increasing command of the war. At the beginning of 1979 there were 7,000 Soviet military advisers in Afghanistan. In 1979 there were an estimated 200,000 casualties in the civil war and even a greater number of refugees fleeing to Pakistan and Iran. Opposition centered in the Muslim clergy and their followers who were the major targets of the regime's reforms. The Afghan tribesmen, who make up most of the population, have a long history of resistance to foreigners and they waged the civil war with ferocity. The armed forces came close to disintegrating as officers and soldiers defected to the freedom fighters. Many Soviet soldiers were killed in the fighting, some of them brutally beheaded.[5]

This rebellion and chaos set the stage for a September, 1979 Afghanistan coup and the subsequent Soviet invasion a few months later. Apparently the Soviets backed President Taraki, because of his loyalty, hoping to make his Prime Minister Amin the scapegoat for the rebellion. Amin beat Taraki to the punch, however, and in a shootout in September killed Taraki and took over the government. Amin then intensified the Khalqi feud with the Perchamis, and the military defections and refugees increased. A team of Soviet generals visited Afghanistan in the fall of 1979 and apparently recommended replacement of Amin. Amin, during this period, apparently not trusting the Soviets, demanded that Puzanov, the Soviet Ambassador to Kabul, be recalled.

Over the Christmas holidays of 1979 the Soviet forces made their move. Fifty thousand Soviet troops advanced suddenly into key areas of Afghanistan, and by the beginning of 1980 there were 90,000 to 100,000 Soviet troops in place. Initially, the Soviet authorities persuaded or forced President Amin to move to the outskirts of Kabul. They then attacked his headquarters and killed him. In his place they installed as President his old rival, Babrak Karmal, the leader of the rival Communist faction.

The Soviet invasion was so quick and so ruthless that there was no opportunity for the Afghanistan government to appeal for help. In fact, the first announcement of Amin's overthrow, ostensibly broadcast by Kabul Radio, reportedly came from a transmitter in the Soviet Union.[6]

The most common explanation for the Soviet invasion was that they saw Amin as an ineffective ruler and they wanted to establish a stronger and more reliable Communist government. According to this theory, the Soviets could not stand idly by while the Communist regime was being fatally weakened and while Soviet advisors were being murdered.

The above hypothesis is supported by the fact that after the invasion Soviet advisors came to dominate the regime. Russians acted as security guards for Karmal. Soviet officials reportedly occupied all senior positions in Afghan ministries except for the foreign ministry. After the invasion dependents of Soviet military personnel were brought into the country and permanent military installations were constructed.[7] In short, Afghanistan became a Soviet satellite. (See Map 7.)

Other observers emphasize the strategic importance of Afghanistan. The Soviets, if they succeeded in pacifying the country, would be closer to the Persian Gulf and the world's major source of petroleum. During this period Iran was threatened by insurgent movements and by the political instability following the overthrow of the Shah. It had lost the support of the United States through its defiance of international law when it refused to release the diplomatic hostages taken by a radical group of students. Iran also at the end of 1979 was being threatened by an attack from Iraq, a Soviet ally, and later the following year war did break out between the two countries. In this context, it is easy to picture the Russian's move as part of a great pincer move designed to exploit Afghanistan's and Iran's weakness and aimed at eventually controlling the Persian Gulf and the strategic oil fields of the Middle East. There was also the possibility of Russia's exploiting the separatist sentiment of the Baluchistans of Pakistan who are situated on the Persian Gulf.

A less convincing reason was that the Soviets were troubled by militant Islam movements and wanted somehow to end the infection by stabilizing the situation in Afghanistan, a predominately Islam state. There is an Islamic community in that southern part of the Soviet Union that is united by faith with the Islam community of the Middle Eastern countries. This is not a convincing reason, however, because by attacking Afghanistan, an Islamic nation, Russia alienated the other Moslem nations in the region.

A few have suggested economic motives, but they are not convincing. Although the Soviets were quick to absorb imports of Afghanistan's extra natural gas production at a low price, the total value of this natural gas was less than $10 million, which is a very small prize in the game of power politics.

The world was shocked by the brutal Soviet invasion, and the United States took the lead in retaliatory action. The U.S. helped sponsor the Security Council resolution of January 7, 1980 calling for the immediate withdrawal of foreign troops from Afghanistan. The vote was 12 - 2 with five non-aligned nations joining in the vote and with only Russia's East German satellite opposing. After the Russian veto of the Security Council resolution, the Council sent the issue to the General Assembly, which overwhelmingly by a vote of 104 - 18 called for the withdrawal of foreign troops from Afghanistan. Only a few close allies of the Soviet Union plus most East European nations joined the Soviets in the vote.[8] The new Afghanistan representative appointed by the Karmal government joined with the Soviets in the vote. Romania had the courage to abstain. Cuba, by voting with the Soviet Union, lost its chance for a Security Council seat; for months Cuba had been trying to muster the necessary two-thirds vote. After it voted with the Soviet Union on the Afghanistan issue, Cuba realized its candidacy was hopeless and withdrew it, leaving Mexico to take the seat.

The major United States' moves to show its disapproval of the Soviet aggression and flouting of the "rules of the game" were to limit exports of grain to the levels set by the long-term agreement with the Soviet Union, which was about half the amount the Soviets wanted to buy. It cut back further on exports of high-technology goods and mounted a boycott of the Moscow Olympic games as a political gesture of disapproval. About 65 nations refused to participate in the Moscow Olympics the following summer, and another 15 participants refused to raise their national flags at the Moscow ceremonies. The U.S. also withdrew consideration of the SALT Treaty by the Senate.

Why the Empire Strikes Again

The Soviet Communist imperialism in Eastern Europe was a form of extreme nationalism. Soviet leaders believed the security requirements for the Soviet Union justified establishing a protective ring of subservient governments in Eastern Europe after their forces liberated these countries from the Nazis after World War II. These governments not only were forced to place their military forces in the Warsaw Pact under Soviet military leadership, but the governments had to maintain a strict Communist system.

Soviet poitical advisors and East European Communists established the Communist systems in these states. Soviet forces stood ready to enforce Soviet policy on these satellites, particularly those in the strategic areas of central Europe, if they showed signs of loosening their ties with the Warsaw Pact or liberalizing their political systems.

Some of the Russian intervention was indirect or was not classified as an international war. Local Communist organizations did the dirty work in Czechoslovakia in 1948 and in Poland in 1981. Soviet occupation forces put down a rebellion in occupied East Germany in 1953. However, Soviet troops invaded Hungary in 1956 and Czechoslovakia in 1968, which was the equivalent of war. These latter invasions were condemned overwhelmingly in the U.N., but members did not impose sanctions and try to force a Soviet withdrawal, which would have undermined the U.N.

The arrogant Soviet policy placed its perceived national security interests above any rights of neighbors to self-determination. This was easy for the confirmed Communists because their doctrine pictured most of the rest of the world as being controlled by capitalist circles. They believed these circles controlled other governments by force, and that the United States and other world powers sent troops to other countries to maintain the capitalist-democratic system. For example the Soviets pictured the United States and U.N. defense of South Korea as capitalist imperialism against the forces of national liberation.

By the 1970s most other world Communist movements were not so taken in by Communist doctrine. The Chinese Communists and West European Communist parties condemned the Soviet invasions of Czechoslovakia, and later of Afghanistan, as Soviet hegemonism and imperialism.

The Soviet imperialism in Eastern Europe was accepted as a fact of life by most countries, but most were outraged when the Soviets extended their rule over Afghanistan, which was not a part of the East European system. This was blatant imperialism, and Soviet claims its attack was defensive were not credible. This Communist form of imperialism saw Soviet security as requiring stable regimes along its border organized in the image of the Soviet Communist system. The invasion of Afghanistan may have had an additional element of greed in taking over a target of opportunity on the road toward the control of the highly strategic Middle East oil fields.

The Soviets probably expected the world eventually to accept Afghanistan as a satellite, just as most countries had accepted the countries of Eastern Europe as Soviet satellites. After all, most of the world community had quickly forgiven or forgotten Russia's invasion of Czechoslovakia in 1968, Hungary in 1956, and East Germany in 1953. The Soviets correctly reasoned that the United States and other countries would not give troop support to Afghanistan resistance to the invasion. In Russian eyes Afghanistan had already entered the Communist orbit without important objections from the West. Why, then, would the United States and its allies object to trying to end the civil war and to bring order out of chaos? Perhaps Soviet leaders realized they were breaking the rules of the game, i.e., international law which forbids attacks against another state, but they were willing to pay a temporary price of world condemnation in order to achieve domination of Afghanistan.

The Moslem nations, China, and of course the United States led the world in condemning the Russian invasion. The Russians may have expected this, but they did not anticipate the fierce Afghanistani resistance. The U.N. Security Council initiated peace talks between Pakistan, informally representing refugees and the resistance, and the Soviet-dominated regime in Kabul. In September, 1987 the Kabul regime asked to resume the talks, giving rise to speculation Russia might compromise on the major issue--how soon Soviet troops would withdraw. This would be joined with a commitment of the United States and others, not to supply arms after the withdrawal began. However, observers were pessimistic because the Kabul regime depended on Soviet military backing.

A tentative lesson might well be drawn from the conflict that the embarassment of the Soviet Union caused by the Olympic boycott plus the severity of the economic retaliation led by President Carter probably had an impact on Soviet leaders. Although as of

1985 they had not withdrawn their forces from Afghanistan, they may have been greatly impressed by the world's reaction, and this may have deterred further moves of this nature. They did not intervene in Poland later in 1980 when the Solidarity Union challenged the Communist system of Poland by establishing a new center of political and economic power. The Soviets blustered and threatened to intervene, but the unfortunate experience in Afghanistan where the rebel forces taxed Soviet occupation troops, joined with the overwhelming condemnation of the world community of the Soviet's action, perhaps caused them to refrain from ordering an invasion of Poland. At the end of the 1981 Polish Communist leaders did their dirty work for them, when General Jaruzelski arrested Solidarity leaders, stifled opposition, and installed a strict military dictatorship.

The Russian action in Afghanistan brought an end to detente and brought back the Cold War climate of the 1950's. This contributed to greatly increased defense expenditures in the United States and tough rhetoric from the new Reagan Administration.

The overwhelming condemnation of the Soviet invasion in United Nations bodies showed that the world by and large supported in principle the anti-aggression provisions of the U.N. Charter. How significant such U.N. actions and attitudes are in opposing aggression and establishing peace are issues addressed in the final chapters.

NOTES

[1] Edward Crankshaw and Strobe Talbott (Editors and translator), Khrushchev Remembers (Boston: Little Brown, 1970), p. 417.

[2] London Economist, November 10, 1956, p. 485.

[3] London Economist, August 3, 1968.

[4] London Economist, August 24, 1982, pp. 13-17.

[5] Zalmay Khalilzad, "Afghanistan and the Crisis in American Foreign Policy," Survival (International Institute for Strategic Studies, July/August 1980). p. 152.

[6] U.S. Department of State, "Soviet Invasion of Afghanistan," Special Report #70, April, 1980.

[7] U.S. Department of State, "Soviet Dilemmas in Afghanistan," June, 1980.

[8] The Soviets have three votes in the General Assembly.

Notes (cont.)

[9] Authoritative accounts of the invasion can be found in Lord Saint Brides, "Afghanistan: The Empire Plays to Win," Orbis, Fall 1980, pp. 533-540; Zalmay Khalilzad, "Afghanistan and the Crisis in American Foreign Policy," Survival, July-August, 1980, pp. 151-159; William E. Griffith, "The Implications of Afghanistan," Survival, pp. 146-151; Hannah Negeran (pseudonym), "The Afghan Coup of April 1978: Revolution and International Security," Orbis, Spring 1979, pp. 93-113; and Asian Yearbook 1980 (Hong Kong), pp. 96-99.

CHAPTER 11

Other Recent Wars

Six other recent wars warrant attention, although at the end of 1985 they were not ripe for the detailed analysis applied to the other major wars. The first two conflicts were spin-offs of the Vietnam War--Vietnam's invasion of Kampuchea (Cambodia), which had not ended, and the Chinese "punishment" of Vietnam for that invasion. Another was Iraq's war against Iran in 1980, which was also continuing through 1985. The others are the Cyprus war, Great Britain's successful military campaign to regain the Falkland Islands, and the U.S. invasion of Grenada in 1984. A preliminary examination of these wars indicates some familiar patterns.

Vietnam's Attack on Kampuchea and China's Retaliation

The Vietnam war ended with a dramatic victory of the North Vietnamese forces, which were battle-hardened by their fight with the powerful American forces and well supplied with modern American weapons captured during the long war. Many observers were uneasy that the Vietnamese troops might press on into other countries of Southeast Asia, particularly Thailand, which had provided bases for the air attacks against Vietnam during the war. One military observer remarked that the only real barrier to Vietnam's tanks in Thailand was the afternoon traffic in Bangkok. This, of course, was an insult to the American-equipped Thai troops, but it was clear they would have been no match for the powerful Vietnamese forces.

Both North and South Vietnam were devastated by the long wars, and initially North Vietnam's Communist regime devoted its major efforts to digesting its conquest of the South. Meanwhile, the pro-U.S. Lon Nol Government of Cambodia was toppled by Communist forces under the leadership of Pol Pot in the same month that

Vietnam won its war. On March 20, 1975 "elections" were held with Communist cadres reading off the candidates before crowds of assembled voters, who vocally approved them. Prince Sihanouk announced his retirement as chief-of-state, and a fanatical group of Communist revolutionaries, the Khmer Rouge, took over the government.

Kampuchea was then forced into the dark ages with the Khmer Rouge army forcing the people of the capital to evacuate the city completely and to try to grow food under the direction of the collective leadership of party cadres. Foreign missions and reporters were forced to leave the country, and horror stories of the refugees indicated that a million or perhaps several millions of its people perished in the countryside during the next few years. Since Cambodia started with only about 8 million people, the effects were catastrophic.

Kampuchea's agony was not over, however, since it was subjected to an invasion from Vietnam in 1978. The origins of the invasion are still cloudy. On December 31, 1977 Cambodia announced the severance of ties with Vietnam. Vietnam charged Cambodia with repeated border incursions and called for a ceasefire and a 10 kilometer demilitarized zone. During 1978, however, border clashes continued, and pro-Vietnamese elements planted in the Cambodia Communist party tried to wrest control from Pol Pot.[1] Each side blamed the other for border clashes during that year. The hostility between the two Communist nations intensified as China backed Kampuchea and the Soviet Union backed Vietnam.

At the end of December, 1978, about 120,000 Vietnamese troops invaded Kampuchea and within a few days surrounded Phnom Penh, the capital. A few days later Vietnam established a puppet regime, headed by Heng Samrin, a defector from the Khmer Rouge. Hanoi in a transparent ploy justified its action by saying that 19 Khmer Rouge divisions had been massed for aggression along the border of Vietnam, and that Vietnam had acted in self-defense. The attack of the Vietnamese army, it continued, allowed Kampuchean "patriots" to seize power in Phnom Penh. On February 18, 1979 Vietnam established a post facto legal facade for the intervention by a 25 year treaty of peace, friendship and cooperation providing for all necessary Vietnamese assistance upon request by the Government of Kampuchia for its defense. The new Vietnamese representative to the U.N. in March, 1979 said the Kampuchean people had faced extinction by the "monstrous neo-colonialist regime (of Pol Pot) imposed by Peking" and that the Vietnamese people did not "have the heart to refuse the aid and assistance demanded of them" by the Kampuchean people.

The Vietnamese invasion opened a narrow window into what had happened to Kampuchea between 1975 and 1978. Vietnam occupied a wasteland. Photographs released to the news media revealed evidence of large scale executions and torture. International relief officials who were permitted to visit the country in 1979 found that hospitals, schools, water supplies, and sanitary systems had been demolished by the Khmer Rouge to eliminate vestiges of Western society. Only 40 physicians of the 500 who had existed in 1975 had survived; the remainder were presumably killed during and after the evacuation from the cities.[2] Signs of modern civilization had been destroyed. The Vietnamese invaders in effect took over the leadership of the country, and Kampuchea became a Vietnamese satellite.

However, the bulk of the Khmer Rouge forces eluded the invading Vietnamese forces and began a campaign of terrorist opposition to the invaders. China continued to supply the Khmer Rouge forces, while Vietnam consolidated its position in the cities and strengthened its alliance with the Soviet Union, which provided large-scale deliveries of modern weapons. In November, 1978 Vietnam signed a treaty of friendship with the Soviet Union. China then confronted a hostile Vietnam on the south linked to the Soviet Union on the north.

The Vietnam-Cambodian war threatened to escalate out of control on February 17, 1979 when Chinese forces invaded Vietnam's northern provinces. In a 17-day war about 250,000 Chinese troops drove as far as 25 miles inside Vietnam causing extensive damage and probably tens of thousands of casualties. The Chinese announced that their troops were sent "to teach a lesson" to the Vietnamese for their invasion of Kampuchea and to end Vietnam's "wanton incursions into Chinese territory"— the Chinese contended that Vietnam held 38 square miles of Chinese territory. An important factor precipitating the invasion was Vietnam's action against the ethnic Chinese in its country.[3] Like other Southeast Asian countries, ethnic Chinese had controlled the commerce of Vietnam. Hanoi, apparently frustrated by them in its attempt to build a new socialist system in the south, had ordered their stores closed and nationalized most of their shops. By early summer, 1978 over 170,000 Chinese had fled, resulting in China's decision to close its borders. A large share of the hundreds of thousands of "boatpeople" who later fled from Vietnam were Chinese, and this added to the hatreds and resentment that exploded in the 1979 war.

After 17 days of bitter fighting and surprisingly strong resistance by Vietnam against the Chinese invaders, China announced that its mission was completed and it withdrew from North Vietnam. Some military observers suggested the fight was a draw in view of the high Chinese casualties. The war, however, caused a heavy economic burden on Vietnam, already bogged down in the civil war in Kampuchia, and further delayed its recovery from the extensive destruction caused during the Vietnam War.

The Soviet Union in the first week of the new war made threatening statements against China calling attention to the Soviets' obligations under the friendship treaty with Vietnam, which were vague as to the type of support the Soviets were committed to provide. Six days after the Chinese invasion started, Moscow started to airlift supplies, and it dispatched a naval task force toward the South China Sea. China, on the other hand, indicated its objectives were limited and that they did not include a full-scale drive to Hanoi. By March 5, China announced that its objectives had been achieved and that it would withdraw, and the operation was completed by March 16, 1979.

It is difficult to unravel the threads of motives of leaders in closed Communist societies such as that of Vietnam, but certain evidence stands out. The Indochinese Communist Party from its founding supported the idea of a federation of the three French colonies--Vietnam, Cambodia, and Laos. The Vietnamese would naturally dominate any such federation because of their size, population, and development. After the 1954 Geneva agreement, which recognized North Vietnam, the Vietnamese dominated the Khmer Communist party. The Party split on strategy in the 1960s with Pol Pot, the Party's First Secretary, advocating armed struggle against Sihanouk's regime, while the other wing advocated cooperation. This militant line found a sympathetic audience in Mao's China. Thus, when Pol Pot's regime succeeded in its coup in 1975, China was his natural ally against Vietnamese-trained Cambodian cadres who opposed him. There was a short period of cooperation between Kampuchea and Vietnam after the end of the war, but by the end of 1975 Kampuchea was rapidly gravitating toward China while Vietnam was drifting toward the Soviet Union.[4]

Kampuchea, after the devastation wreaked by Pol Pot's radical Communism, became a pawn of the great powers--Vietnam, China, and the Soviet Union. Vietnam, with military and political support from the Soviet Union, succeded in ousting the Pol Pot government, while China supported the remnants of Pol Pot's forces in their fight against the Vietnamese aggressors.

Vietnam's aggression was a Communist invasion of another Communist country. It was not spreading a proletarian revolution but carrying out a traditional, imperialistic type of policy, which was called hegemonism by Chinese Communist critics. Kampuchean nationalists resented such foreign domination. Prince Sihanouk, while indicating his distaste for the Pol Pot forces, still supported them politically in their resistance to Vietnam's invasion. Thus, we have the familiar thread of hegemonism or imperialism as a cause of the war which generated strong nationalist opposition.

China's punishment of North Vietnam seemed to be aimed at weakening Vietnam and at shaking its fist at the Soviet Union. At the same time, elements of racism and economics entered the picture when Vietnam's massive uprooting of Chinese merchants heightened the tension between Vietnam and China. China's attack was classic realpolitik--limited use of armed forces to try to force

Vietnam to withdraw its forces from Kampuchea or to weaken the alliance with the Soviet Union. If this were its aim, beyond "punishing" Vietnam for its actions, China did not succeed. It had the sense, however, to end its invasion before the conflict escalated out of control.

Most of the world watched in amazement as the former Communist allies fought and quarreled among themselves. China drew closer to the United States and later supported Thailand to help protect it from the threat of Vietnam, while press reports indicated Thailand permitted China to supply the Pol Pot forces through Thailand.

It is too early to push the analysis much further. Communist leaders seldom write memoirs or give frank interviews to the news media. The record indicates the action was dominated by Vietnam's imperialism (hegemonism), power politics, and racism, and China's self-assumed role as a world policeman in Southeast Asia. Communist ideology was a factor to the extent it supports force in politics and eschews moral restraints on action. The Soviets increased their support to Vietnam during the invasion of Kampuchea, and seemed relieved that the Chinese-Vietnam War was contained.

The Cyprus Wars

Cyprus occupies a highly strategic position, at the eastern end of the Mediterranean near the Suez Canal. For that reason the United Kingdom has valued its bases on these islands highly. After World War II, with the growth there of the desire for independence and under pressure from the U.N. General Assembly, the British agreed in 1960 that Cyprus should become independent. They retained two limited bases on the islands.

Cyprus in its past history had been controlled both by Turkey and Greece, and as a result there have been conflicts between the Turkish and the Greek communities on Cyprus. This has caused friction between Turkey and Greece despite their common alliance in NATO. On December 26, 1963 after fighting broke out Cyprus called on the U.N. Security Council to help establish order, since Turkish troops already on the island were supporting the Turkish community. On March 4th the Security Council unanimously recommended the creation of a peace keeping force in Cyprus ("UNFICYP"). This force grew to 6,234 military personnel by June, 1964. In addition, the U.N. Secretary General appointed a mediator to try to settle the dispute. Conflicts continued, culminating in a minor war in 1974.

On July 15, 1974 a coup d'etat was launched by the Cyprus National Guard, which was controlled secretly by Greek military intelligence forces. The coup came close to capturing President Makarios, who was evacuated at the last minute by British helicopter from its base on the island. On July 20, Turkish troops landed from the mainland and began to take over control of part of the island for the Turkish communities.

Within a few days a more moderate government was formed in Cyprus, while the military government of Greece fell and was replaced by a democratic one. A U.N. Security Council resolution of July 20th had called on Greece, Turkey, and the United Kingdom to enter negotiations without delay to restore peace and a constitutional government on Cyprus. Fighting broke out again for a few days, but by August 16th Turkey and Greece had accepted a cease-fire. Meanwhile, the northern Turkish part of the island proclaimed independence, and the U.N. High Commissioner for Refugees began to assist the 2,000 refugees displaced by the war.

Although the Soviet Union and the United States were not in direct confrontation on this issue, the Soviets were glad to see serious friction between Greece and Turkey, the southern anchor of the NATO alliance. On the other hand, the fact that this fracas was between two NATO allies made it easier for the United States and Britain to turn it over to a neutral umpire, the United Nations. Other members of the United Nations reacted, as expected, to support cease-fires and the ending of hostility. Even the Soviets joined in trying to end the conflict. As a result the U.N. was able to agree on peacekeeping forces.

The peacekeeping force suffered a large number of casualties while it tried to mediate the conflict. On the whole, however, the mediation effort was cost-effective, costing only about $20 million a year between 1964 and 1978. The Secretary-General took an active role in trying to mediate differences between the Greek and Turkish communities, and a precarious cease-fire has been maintained since 1974. It was a classic case of competing nationalisms starting and escalating a conflict.

The Iran-Iraq War

Border skirmishes between Iran and Iraq escalated into a war in September, 1980. In the middle of the month Iraqi troops took two small strips of land from Iran, which Iraq claimed under a 1975 treaty. Iraq then two days later renounced the 1975 treaty, claimed the entire Shatt al-Arab waterway, which carried most of the oil traffic and commerce of the two states, and invaded Iran in several places along their common border. There had been a long dispute over this waterway and over a few small Persian Gulf islands. Iraq had inherited the waterway from Turkey when the Ottoman Empire was broken up after World War I, but Iran retained navigation rights up and down the waterway. The arrangements were disputed by Iran, and finally in 1975 Iraq under pressure from the Shah, who at that time was supporting Kurd rebels in Iraq, agreed to a treaty which fixed the boundary at the center line of the river for the entire length of the Shatt al-Arab. President

Saddam Hussein, at that time vice premier, signed the treaty for Iraq. On September 7, 1980, just before the attack on Iran, President Hussein denounced the treaty.[5] Observers were puzzled at Iraq's going to war over this issue, since dividing the waterway down the middle appeared to have given Iraq adequate rights to access to the Gulf. True, Iran could have cut it off by force, but this was also true for Iraq, and the waterway was as vital to Iran as it was to Iraq. (See Map.)

There had been other major issues between the governments that prepared the way to war. The first was long standing religious differences based on the fact that Iraq's rulers, who were mostly Sunni Moslems, felt threatened by Iranian appeals to Shiites of Iraq. Shiites made up a majority of Iraq's population, and some of them followed the Shiite religious leadership of Iran. When the Ayatollah Khomeini took over control of the Iranian Government after the revolution of February, 1979, the religious differences with Iraq came to a head. The Ayatollah had fled to Iraq in 1964 after being expelled by the Shah, and in October, 1978, the Iraqi Government also expelled him at the request of the Shah. Khomeini, the Shite leader, after he returned to Iran and assumed power in a revolution, called on Muslims of the world to "wake up and liberate Islam and Islamic countries from the yoke of imperialists and their supporters." His speeches made it plain he was referring to Iraq as well as conservative Arab regimes and kings friendly to the United States such as Saudi Arabia, Egypt, and Oman.[6]

In October, 1979 there were violent Shiite demonstrations for Khomeini in Saudi Arabia, Bahrain and Kuwait. President Hussein of Iraq warned that "Iraq's capabilities can be used against any side which tries to violate the sovereignty of Kuwait or Bahrain," and that this warning applies to the entire Gulf. This was followed by Iranian Revolutionary Guard attacks on the embassy of Iraq and its consulates in Iran, and by an escalation of border incidents.[7]

In 1980 there were disturbances and terrorist acts by Shiites in Iraq, and the Iraq government expelled to Iran 35,000 Shiites reportedly of Iranian descent. President Hussein pointedly couched his propaganda attacks against Iran in terms of "Arabs" against the "Persian" menace to counteract the Ayatollah's religious appeals to Shiite Moslems in Iraq.[8]

The third factor that played a part in Iraq's hatred of the Iranian Government was the long-standing problems of the Kurds. The most recent conflict had begun in 1974 when Iraq nationalized its Kirkuk oil fields and evacuated the Kurds to an autonomous zone. Major fighting broke out, and the Kurds received financial and military assistance from neighboring Iran. The Kurdish leader even appealed to the UN, but he was not successful, and the Kurdish forces were forced to retreat to the Iranian border, where regular Iranian forces provided support. In March, 1975 an unexpected agreement was reached in which Iran agreed to this assistance to the Kurds in return for Iraqi territorial concessions. Part of the concessions included settlement of the Shatt al-Arab dispute, noted above, ending Iraq's claims to its east bank.[9]

With these long-standing conflicts with Iran, President Hussein probably decided that in the fall of 1980 the situation would never be more favorable for a strike against the Khomeini regime. Khomeini's government was isolated diplomatically by its radical call for revolution throughout the Middle East, and by its unprecedented challenge to the world's diplomats by holding 51 American diplomatic personnel as hostages. The Iranian Government had been condemned by unanimous votes in the UN General Assembly, the Security Council, and the World Court for holding diplomats as hostages. The United States had cut off supplies of spare parts to the Iranian military forces, and had frozen about $13 billion of its foreign exchange assets. Unemployment was soaring, and the Iranian government was in disarray with political conflicts between President Bani-Sadr and the militant radicals of the Islamic Republic Party. Although Iraq's population was only 13 million in comparison with the 39 million of Iran, their armed forces were approximately the same size. Also, Iran was extremely vulnerable to a surprise attack in the southeast since it, too, depended for the great bulk of its oil traffic on the Shatt al-Arab waterway, which bordered the two countries. Moreover, Iran's richest oil province, Khuzestan, which has a large Arab minority on the border of Iraq, was penetrated in the initial attack. Some observers suggested this province, too, was an objective of Hussein, even though he denied it and offered to withdraw from it if his objectives in Shatt al-Arab were recognized.

Another, perhaps principal factor, entered into President Hussein's calculations. Until his death in 1970, President Gamal Abdel Nasser was the unchallenged leader of the Arab nations. His successor, President Anwar Sadat, although a statesman of world stature, was not able to achieve the popularity of Nasser among the Arab nations, and after the Camp David peace agreements with Israel, Sadat was politically isolated by almost all the Arab leaders. Hussein tried to move into the gap by vigorous diplomatic activity among Arab and third world nations. Iraq's oil and financial resources potentially are second only to Saudi Arabia's in the Arab world, and its military strength was greater. He picked up the banner of the Palestine cause against Israel, which also made him popular among the Arabs. In a major speech on April 16, 1980 he declared that "Iraq always had a unique historical position within the Arab nation" and that "the Iraqi army will remain strong to defend the honor of all Arabs fighting foreign forces." In 1980 more than 30 heads of state and prime ministers visited Iraq, and his government transferred about $500 million to Third World countries to help them in their economic problems of purchasing high-priced petroleum.[10]

Perhaps Hussein's grand strategy to assume leadership of the Arab cause was revealed in his nuclear reactor program. France had supplied Iraq with a large nuclear research reactor and ample supplies of enriched uranium. Brazil supplied further uranium and nuclear technology, while Italy provided a "hot cell" that could be used for extracting plutonium suitable for nuclear weapons. Iraq used nuclear materials within the framework of the International Atomic Energy Agency safeguards, and the IAEA inspectors reported that Iraq had not diverted any of it for weapons production. However, at the beginning of June, 1981 Israel in a surprise bombing raid completely destroyed Iraq's atomic research facility claiming it had evidence Iraq planned to use it to help build nuclear weapons. There was strong circumstantial evidence Iraq ultimately intended to build such a weapon, even though it had continued to abide by the IAEA safeguards. Iraq's research reactor was unusually large and could be converted to producing weapons material. Iraq did not need nuclear energy for economic reasons since it had a surplus of oil. Moreover, the nuclear technology and materials it was acquiring would have permitted it at some future date to withdraw from IAEC controls and move toward weapons production. Finally, in response to the Israeli raid President Hussein said that "all peace-loving nations of the world" should help the Arabs "to acquire the atomic bomb to face the real Israeli atomic bombs."[11] All these factors indicate Hussein may have aspired to exercise a leading military role among the Arab states of the Middle East.

One last possible factor in President Hussein's calculations demands comment. Some observers have seen Iraq's move against Iran as part of the Soviet strategy to take over the Mideast. It is true that Iraq had long standing and close political-military ties with the Soviet Union, and that its armed forces were mostly based on Soviet equipment. However, in recent years Iraq has been moving out of the Soviet orbit. The Soviet's share of Iraq's military imports fell from 95 percent in 1972 to 63 percent in 1979. In subsequent years the Iraqi government turned to France for Mirage aircraft, AMX tanks and other basic equipment at the rate of over $1 billion a year. It also purchased military hardware from other countries including Italy and the United States.

On the diplomatic level, Iraq condemned the Soviet invasion of Afghanistan at the Islamic Summit in late January, 1980, and criticized Soviet actions in certain other Arab countries. At about the same time the Iraqi government instituted wholesale purges and arrest of Communists in the armed forces and drove them underground. In February, 1980 President Hussein called them "a rotten, atheistic, yellow storm which has plagued Iraq."[12] The Soviets cut down on supplies of military equipment from Iraq, after the war with Iran started, and opened up a major supply route to Iran through its northern border. Iraq's move away from the Soviets strengthened Iraq's developing ties with the moderates of the Arab world such as Saudi Arabia and Jordan.

The Iraqi attack was a move of power politics to control a strategic waterway, eliminate a potential political and religious rival, and to assume the mantle of Arab political leadership. In the mid-80s Iran and Iraq began attacking each others' oil tankers and installations. In the summer of 1987 the U.S. Navy intervened to escort newly American-flagged tankers to pressure Iran to stop the attacks. Meanwhile, the United States was working through the Security Council to get a cease-fire, and, failing this, an arms embargo on Iran. Iran's Khomeini, angered at Iraq's aggression, refused to bow to pressure and stop the war. As this edition went to press in October, 1987, the U.S. Navy had attacked Iranian gunboats, and there was a threat of escalation.

The War in the Falkland Islands

The Falkland Islands War was a test-tube war, remote from complications of superpower rivalries and major stragetic interests. These islands begin about 400 miles off the coast of Argentina and stretch about 1200 miles to Antarctica. The weather there is harsh, there are few trees, and only a few miles of roads. When they were invaded by Argentina on April 2, 1982, they supported only 1,800 British subjects and 800,000 sheep.

Argentina had claimed the islands since 1834 when Britain forced out a few Argentinians and successfully established its rule. Before that there had been claims by both Spain and Argentina. Argentina managed to get approval of the UN General Assembly in the 1960s for negotiations with Britain, although the General Assembly did not accept Argentina's claim. Britain at that time did not seem to be greatly interested in the islands. In 1980, after a British Foreign Office minister held talks with the Argentinian Government, the British Government floated the idea that sovereignty should be transferred to Argentina with the islands leased to Britain over a long term, similar to its arrangements for Hong Kong. When this was proposed to parliament in December, 1980, the idea was savagely attacked by Tory and Labor members of parliament, forcing the Government to pledge that the Falkland islanders would have the last word through a referendum or general election.[13] Both the islanders and the Argentinians opposed that solution.

Argentina was clearly taken off balance by the vigor of the British reaction to Argentina's 1982 invasion. Britain mobilized its fleet, whose power was only a shadow of former days, but which was adequate to meet the Argentine challenge. With the aid of its submarines Britain isolated the 15,000 Argentine landing force, and by June, 1982 had forced its surrender by amphibious and air operations that progressively hemmed in the attacking force.

Nationalism stimulated by economic problems were major causes of war. Argentina had never acknowledged the British taking over of what Argentina called the Malvinas. Britain showed no signs of making significant concessions in the negotiations over the islands. Before Argentina's attack, it faced an inflation of over 100 percent a year, a collapse of the value of the peso, and severe unemployment. After the invasion, instead of demonstrations protesting General Galtieri's dictatorship, a crowd of 10,000 assembled in front of the presidential palace to cheer him. Ardent demonstrations of popular support continued, but they were replaced by large demonstrations of despair and demands for Galtieri's resignation when the British forced the Argentine troops to surrender.

The resurrection of British naval power, which steamed majestically into battle, and successes of the amphibious and air arms of the British fleet generated a wave of popular enthusiasm for the Thatcher Government, which had been sinking lower in the polls.

Thus, the essence of the war was a conflict between Argentine and British nationalisms. Argentina was the aggressor and its nationalism bears the major blame for the war. General Galtieri seems to have been motivated by a desire to rejuvinate Argentina's economic and political situation, just as Anwar Sadat and Nasser in Egypt had tried to use war for the same purpose. Although there were hints of superpower involvement, with the United States passing on intelligence information to Britain and the Soviets doing the same for Argentina, the superpowers and the rest of the world stood back as Argentina and Britain thrust and parried for victory. British airpower and submarines cut off supplies to the Argentine invaders, and a British relief force made short work of the Argentine forces on the islands.

The Invasion of Grenada

On October 25, 1983, President Reagan surprised his own nation and most of the world by ordering an invasion of Grenada, a small nation of less than 100,000 people at the eastern entrance of the Caribbean. A few months earlier he had expressed public concern about Cuban and Russian Communist influence over Grenada's Marxist-oriented government, but even critics of Reagan were surprised at his flouting of international law. Reagan had expressed concern that the construction of a large airport posed a threat to the eastern Caribbean, but others noted that it was a justified commercial project for tourism just like seven other airports of the same size on the other Caribbean islands.

The announced reason for the initial invasion by 1,900 U.S. troops joined by very small contingents from small neighboring islands was to protect American medical students threatened in the aftermath of a coup by a rival Marxist military commander. There was little resistance to U.S. forces aside from that by a few Grenadian troops and Cuban construction workers. Many of the

American students expressed gratitude for their rescue after the operation was concluded, but prior to that they appeared unconcerned about their safety.

The official U.S. justification for the invasion, that the small neighboring nations had asked for U.S. intervention, did not convince the Organization of American States and the United Nations, which passed resolutions condemning the invasion and demanding U.S. withdrawal. Even the strong-willed Thatcher Government of Britian was miffed that the U.S. did not consult it before invading a small Commonwealth nation. The hardline London <u>Economist</u> in an assessment of invasion joined the critics to the extent of noting that the prime motive of the invasion was not to save American lives and that Grenada was not a Cuban military stronghold. Reagan, it concluded, "invaded Grenada for reasons of cold-blooded Realpolitik."[14]

However, in the United States there was little criticism by Congressmen and U.S. commentators. This was submerged in the pride of most observers and of the U.S. public. U.S. casualties were small--18 servicemen killed--and the U.S. had asserted its strength in overthrowing a small Marxist government in this hemisphere. Most Grenadians welcomed the overthrow of the Marxist Government. In December, 1984, the New National party lead by a middle-of-the-roader Herbert Blaize in a free election won 14 of the assembly's 15 seats. The rump of the revolutionary pro-Cuban Party that had ruled Grenada before the invasion received only 5 percent of the votes. Its criticism of the remaining 300 U.S. policemen and troops and of the 435-person Caribbean force did not strike a responsive cord among the voters, who were glad to get rid of the Marxist dicatorship. The Commonwealth nations and the United Nations still demonstrated disapproval of U.S. flouting of international law by not sending observers to the election.[15]

It is possible to make some broad generalizations about the Grenada invasion, the two Vietnamese-Kampuchean-Chinese wars, the Cyprus War and the Iran-Iraq War before trying in the next chapter to generalize about all the wars we have studied. All these wars were wars of nationalistic hegemonism in which aggressive leaders tried to expand the power and influence of their nations. In all except the Grenada invasion the victims put up a stronger fight for their national independence than was probably anticipated. In the Grenada invasion the United States quickly withdrew almost all of its forces after capturing the Marxist leaders and setting up arrangements for an election.

In each case the United Nations, at least initially, was not able to end the wars, although it did provide a forum for other nations to express their disapproval. In the next chapter we will examine more closely the patterns of these wars in the context of the other wars we have already analyzed.

NOTES

[1] Far East Economic Review, Asia 1979 Yearbook, pp. 160-166; FEER, Asia 1980 Yearbook, pp. 205-208; Gareth Porter, "The Sino-Vietnamese Conflict in Southeast Asia," Current History, December, 1978, pp. 193-195.

[2] Sheldon W. Simon, "Kampuchea: Vietnam's Vietnam," Current History, December, 1979, pp. 197-198.

[3] FEER, Asia 1980 Yearbook, pp. 43-47.

[4] Gareth Porter, "The Sino-Vietnamese Conflict in Southeast Asia," Current History, December, 1978, pp. 193-196.

[5] Charles Maechling Jr., "At Stake in the War," Washington Post, October 14, 1980, editorial page.

[6] Consulate General of the Islamic Republic of Iran (San Francisco), "Ayatollah Khomeini: On Issues Related to the Struggle of the Muslim People of Iran," "Imam Khomeini's Message to Liberation Movements," November 27, 1979; and Embassy of the Islamic Republic of Iran," "Iman's Message Marks Mobilization Week," February 22, 1980; Washington Post, November 13, 1979; "How to Lose Arab Friends and Madden Almost Everybody," The Economist, April 12, 1980, pp. 23-24; and Washington Post, April 9, 1980, p. A18.

[7] Claudia Wright, "Implications of the Iraq-Iran War," Foreign Affairs, Winter, 1980-81, p. 278.

[8] Adeed I. Dawisha, "Iraq: the West's Opportunity," Foreign Policy Winter, 1981, p. 134-153.

[9] Robert Lyle Butterworth, Managing Interstate Conflict, 1945-74: Data with Synopses (University of Pittsburgh, 1976).

[10] Dawisha, op. cit., p. 140.

[11] Associated Press, June 25, 1981. He repeated the substance of this statement in an interview on "Issues and Answers" on June 29, 1981.

[12] Dawisha, op. cit., p. 140.

[13] The Economist, "The Islanders - Lessons of History," April 10, 1982, p. 27.

[14] The Economist, December 8, 1984, pp. 31-32.

[15] Paul Seabury and Walter McDougall (eds.), The Grenada Papers, San Francisco: Institute for Contemporary Studies 1984).

CHAPTER 12

The Causes of War Since 1914

The above analysis has highlighted the actions and ideas of leaders and their societies, as listed in Table 1, that caused major wars of this century. Leaders making the crucial decisions were influenced by these powerful ideas and used them to start the wars. In most cases these ideas helped leaders to obtain enthusiastic support of their peoples.

Tables 8A and B summarize the analysis, listing the principal ideas and actions of Table 1, and types of societies of Table 2 that were associated with most wars.* The ideology that stands out as the most dangerous type of idea that caused war is nationalism. Nationalism seems to be a permanent fact of life in today's world, and in itself does not cause war. Extreme nationalism, however, that glorifies the state and supports force in contests for control and influence played a part in all the wars.

Niebuhr's insights about nationalism that were cited at the beginning of this book are worth reviewing. He noted how people's love of their countryside and the familiar scenes of their youth are converted to a patriotism that gives a blank check to their nations' leaders in a time of crisis. Peoples' instincts for survival are expanded to a "will to power" that requires an unreasonable position of national dominance or security. Since there is no sharp line between the means of defense and aggression, unscrupulous leaders can lead a nation into aggression. People lose their identity in the nation during a crisis and support violence at a national level that would appall them on a personal level. This sense of national pride and identity with the nation causes men enthusiastically to enlist for war and sacrifice their lives in battle. Leaders can distort reality and exploit patriotism to get their soldiers to fight in wars of aggression.

Nationalism, when aroused, not only triggered wars but added years to the length of wars and millions to the casualty lists. It played a particularly strong role in World War I, the Korean War, the Vietnam War, and the Arab-Israeli wars. An extreme form of imperialist nationalism was behind the Russian invasion of Afghanistan. Russia's leaders' imperialistic nationalism was demonstrated when they extended their controls over Afghanistan to make Russian border areas more secure. The Afghan's nationalistic resistance to the Russians not only helped trigger the invasion but prolonged the battle against heavy odds and caused high casualty lists. On the other hand, the India-Pakistan War of 1971 was brought to a quick halt before the conflicting nationalisms and religious beliefs of Indians and Pakistanis got out of control. Before the Indian intervention, however, the Bengali nationalism provoked a civil war, where West Pakistan forces attacked and caused hundreds of thousands of deaths.

Other dangerous ideologies have often joined with the nationalist ideology to plunge nations into war. These include fascism and Communism.[1] Hitler, allied with fascist Italy, led Germany into World War II. Hitler's nationalistic and racist fascism and its atrocities still profoundly disturb philosophers and others who would count on the innate goodness of man.

Communism joined with nationalism played a major part in the Korean War of 1950 and in the Vietnam War. In both cases, the aggressive leaders were Communists who wanted to unify their country and promote the Communist form of government. They were supported politically and economically by Communist allies. Communism in natural alliance with power politics also played a major role in Vietnam's invasion of Kampuchea, as well as in Russian invasions to restore Communist control and Soviet domination of Hungary and Czechoslovakia.

Religious ideologies were not the primary cause of wars we studied, although religion contributed to the nationalism that caused wars between the Arab nations and Israel, the Iran-Iraq War beginning in 1980, and the conflict of Hindu and Moslem nations in the India-Pakistan war of 1971. A racist ideology was an integral part of the aggressive Nazi fascist doctrine. The Japanese fascists to some extent in World War II also demonstrated a racist belief in their superiority over other nations.

In the realm of strategies, the extreme nationalist leaders naturally use the strategies of power politics. The imperialistic Axis leaders used power politics in their attempt to dominate the world. The four Communist wars were a form of Communist imperialism, while the 1956 Mideast war also fits a definition of imperialism. This imperialism can also be called hegemonism. Our analysis of World War I, however, indicates Germany initiated war essentially with a balance-of-power strategy of power politics rather than an imperialistic one. None of the wars was started by a nation guided by an internationalist strategy, which is on the opposite side of the spectrum. (Table 3) By definition an internationalist would support international law, which rejects aggressive wars.

These above threads lead us to another pattern that emerged in the analysis. Almost all the wars were started by authoritarian and totalitarian governments. The three authoritarian emperors, Franz Joseph, Kaiser Wilhelm, and Czar Nicholas, authorized the decisions that led their nations into World War I. The decisions of these inept and blundering rulers were not limited by parliaments. These leaders were not well informed during the crisis, but they had the authority to question or overrule their military and diplomatic officials. The hawks under the emperors manipulated them, urging war in order to preserve their empires or to maintain a strategic advantage. Nevertheless, the crucial decisions for war were made by these emperors and would not have been carried out without their authorization. Authoritarian military governments started the Iraq-Iran War, the Falkland Islands War, and the 1967 and 1973 Arab-Israel wars.

The fascist and Communist ideologies have promoted totalitarian rule where a few leaders dominate a state. The German fascism and Russian Communism were expansionist, using force to achieve their aims. Hitler's totalitarian Germany, allied with Italy and Japan, led the German people into a series of aggressive wars, and the totalitarian Japanese military leaders obtained the tacit approval of the Emperor of Japan to strike against the United States,which was opposing their expansion into China. Communist totalitarian leaders initiated wars against South Korea, Afghanistan, and Kampuchea, and the Soviets used force to take over territory and consolidate their empire in Eastern Europe.

Authoritarian and totalitarian leaders with dominant power over governments are easily corrupted by their power to use the same strong-arm methods in international politics that they used to achieve and maintain power domestically. They can use powerful instruments of propaganda, that they control, to exaggerate threats from abroad and to justify an aggressive policy. Soviet leaders have been corrupted by their power, and they have not been restrained by their own people in projecting Soviet power into Eastern Europe and into Afghanistan to achieve buffer zones, which are justified as necessary for security.

The warlike, expansive ideologies of fascism, Communism, and racism are generally not associated with the democratic form of government, and these ideologies have not led democracies into war. Democracy does not provide fertile ground for aggressive ideologies because it is based on the ideal of allowing different values and ideas to compete peacefully. Thus, true democrats do not support aggressive, totalitarian, fascist, racist, Communist, or religious ideologies asserting supremacy and aimed at sup-

TABLE 8-A
IDEOLOGIES, STRATEGIES, AND TYPES
OF GOVERNMENT HELPING CAUSE MAJOR WARS   1914-1985

				Ideologies		Strategy	Government
1.	World War I						
	a. Austria-Hungary vs. Serbia	June 1914	EN			PP	A
	b. Germany vs. France	Aug 1914	EN			PP	A
	c. Germany vs. United States	Mar 1917	--			PP	A
2.	Japan vs. China	1931-1942	EN			PP	A
3.	Italy vs. Ethiopia	1936	EN	F		PP	T
4.	World War II						
	a. Germany vs. Poland, etc.	1939-1945	EN	F	Ra	PP	T
	b. Japan vs. U.S., etc.	1941-1945	EN	F	Ra	PP	T
5.	North Korea vs. South Korea	1950-1954	EN	C		PP	T
6.	N. Vietnam vs. South Vietnam	1959-1975	EN	C		PP	T
7.	Arab Israeli Wars						
	a. Arabs vs. Israel	1948	EN	Re		PP	A
	b. Fr., Eng., Israel, vs. Egypt	1956	EN			PP	D
	c. Egypt vs. Israel	1967	EN			PP	A
	d. Egypt vs. Israel	1973	EN			PP	A
	e. The War in Lebanon	1982	EN			PP	D
8.	India vs. Pakistan	1972	EN	Re		PP	D
9.	Russian Attacks on Satellites						
	a. Hungary	1956	EN	C		PP	T
	b. Czechoslovakia	1968	EN	C		PP	T
	c. Afghanistan	1979-	EN	C		PP	T
10.	Vietnam vs. Kampuchea	1978-	EN	C		PP	T
	China vs. Vietnam					PP	T
11.	Turkey vs. Cyprus	1974-	EN			PP	A
12.	Iraq vs. Iran	1979-	EN	Re		PP	A
13.	Falklands War	1982	EN			PP	A
14.	The Grenada Invasion	1983	EN			PP	D

EN Extreme Nationalism   PP Power Politics   D   Democracy
F   Fascism   A   Authoritarianism   RE Religious
C   Communism   T   Totalitarianism   RA Rascism

Note: See Table 8-B for explanation of markings. See also Tables 1, 2, and 3.

TABLE 8-B
SUMMARY RATIONALE FOR MARKINGS OF TABLE 8
(For further details see Table 1 and individual chapters)
EN, F, C

1. World War I
   a. The emperor of Austria-Hungary was urged by extreme nationalist leaders to declare war against Serbia to punish it for the assassination of Archduke Ferdinand, even though there was no proof the Serbian government was responsible. Their aim was to preserve the Austro-Hungarian empire as a nation.

   b. The Russian leaders mobilized their troops to support fellow Slavs in Serbia against Austria-Hungary. This mobilization also threatened Germany, Austria-Hungary's ally, and triggered a decision of German leaders to overrun Belgium and Luxemburg to attack France, which was Russia's ally. The aim of the German leaders, who ignored the rights of these two small nations, was to preserve the favorable military position of Germany against the Franco-Russian alliance. The German people enthusiastically supported their government's decision.

   c. German submarines attacked U.S. ships with the aim of improving the German military position in World War II. This brought the U.S. into the war. The move was primarily strategic and not nationalistic in character.

2. Japan vs. China
   Japan's extreme nationalist military leaders attacked China with aim of expanding the Japanese empire (Greater East Asia Co-prosperity Sphere). The military were not controlled in the early 1930s by the civilian cabinet, so the government was not considered as fascist in 1931. Ten years later it had become a regimented, fascist-type government. (See below.)

3. Italy vs. Ethiopia (Abbyssinia)
   Italian fascists (extreme nationalists) attacked Ethiopia to expand Italy's empire.

4. World War II
   a. German fascists (extreme nationalists) attacked Poland to expand Germany's empire. They saw themselves as a superior German race.

   b. Japanese extreme nationalist leaders attacked the United States at Pearl Harbor because of U.S. economic pressure against their attempt to expand the Japanese empire (Greater East Asia Co-prosperity Sphere) in China. Many saw themselves as a superior race destined to dominate a new empire.

5. North Korea vs. South Korea. North Korean Communist leaders attacked South Korea with the major aim of creating a united Korea under a Communist political system.

6. North Vietnam vs. South Vietnam
North Vietnamese Communist leaders supported an insurgency and later openly attacked South Vietnam with the major aim of creating a united Vietnam under a Communist political system.

7. Arab-Israeli Wars
   a. Arab leaders refused to accept a U.N. compromise plan for a Jewish state in Palestine and attacked the Jews in Israel to prevent them from establishing a state on what Arabs saw as Arab land.

   b. France initiated a war with help of Britain and Israel to regain control of the Suez Canal. The French democracy, as indicated in public opinion polls, and the French government supported the Suez war, and parliament gave the government a vote of confidence on the issue. They saw Nasser as a chief supporter of the Algerian revolution as a threat to their oil lifeline. The British parliament and press was split, with the opposition to the war making the most noise. The opposition was instrumental in forcing Eden to step down, ostensibly for health reasons.

   c. Egyptian President Nasser started the war by blockading Israel to reinforce support for Egypt as the leader of the Arab nationalist movement against Israel.

   d. Egyptian President Sadat attacked Israel to get back Egyptian land lost in the 1967 war and to strengthen Egypt's economic and political position.

   e. Israel attacked the PLO in Lebanon to destroy its capacity to attack Israel.

8. India vs. Pakistan
India attacked Pakistan with the major aim to permit 10 million Pakistani refugees who had fled from East Pakistan to return home. The secondary aim was to weaken a historic enemy, Pakistan. Much of the press and people welcomed a chance to attack their traditional enemy, Pakistan. It is a marginal decision whether to call this war one caused by "extreme" nationalism.

9. Russian Attacks on Satellites
   a. In order to preserve a Communist buffer against what Russian leaders saw as a threat from the West, they attacked and suppressed a revolutionary Hungarian government, which had announced a desire to be free from a Russian alliance and a desire to create a non-Communist form of society.

    b. Russian leaders, in order to preserve a Communist buffer against what they saw as a threat from the West, suppressed a Czechoslovakian move to create a non-Communist form of government.

    c. Russian troops took over control of an Afghanistan Communist government which did not submit to Russian domination and which was not able to suppress violent acts against Russian military advisors.

10. Vietnam vs. Kampuchea
The Vietnam Communist government at the end of 1978 attacked the Communist government of Kampuchea to establish a government subordinate to Vietnam. This was consistent with the historic aim of Vietnamese Communists to keep the Kampuchean Communist Party in a subordinate position and to create a Communist empire under Vietnam control with the same boundaries as the previous French Indochina empire. About a year later China in a limited war to punish Vietnam for invading Kampuchea attacked Vietnam for 17 days and then withdrew.

11. Turkey vs. Cyprus
Turkey initiated the invasion of Cyprus in 1964 to take the Turkish community there under its wing and to prevent a faction dominated by Greece from taking over the government.

12. Iraq vs. Iran
The Iraqi president ordered an attack on Iran to reassert Iraq's control of the Shatt-al-Arab waterway between the two countries and to strengthen Iraq's prestige in the Arab world.

13. The Falkland Islands War
Britain expelled Argentine invaders who claimed the islands for nationalist reasons.

14. The Grenada Invasion.
In October, 1983 the United States invaded Grenada with the announced purpose of protecting Americans from a Marxist regime that had taken over in a coup. Most observers outside the United States recognized the action as hardline power politics designed to oust a Communist Government from this hemisphere.

Definitions:

PP
    Power politics is defined as a nation advancing its perceived interests by coercion. War is the ultimate form of power politics, but all wars need not be for <u>national</u> interests. For example leaders might start wars for religious or other reasons.

Definitions (cont.)

A, T, C, D

An authoritarian government is one based on obedience to authority or recognized power, as opposed to one based on the principle of individual liberty.

A totalitarian government is a highly centralized authoritarian government under the control of a political group which allows no opposition of independent political parties.

A Communist government is totalitarian because it is dominated by one party which permits no opposition and which controls most areas of society.

A democratic government is one in which the supreme power is vested in the people and exercised directly or indirectly through a system of representation involving periodically held free elections. Such a system implies the right of an opposition party to organize free from government coercion along with free speech and a free press.

pressing dissent. This suggests democracies generally would not chose leaders committed to war. For example the inept emperors of World War I would not have been chosen by the ballot. Hitler probably could not have been elected in a fair election.

Anti-Communism, which is associated with democracy, did lead to the U.S. support of Cuban insurgents in the Bay of Pigs invasion, as shown in Table 1. Singling out this support to Cuban nationalists would distort the overall picture, however, since Communists have supported dozens of insurrections in many countries since World War II, and these efforts were not analyzed in this study.

Some observers have blamed United States democratic leaders for the Vietnam War because they escalated the fighting in trying to protect South Vietnam from the North. As indicated in Chapter VII, however, the Communist leaders of North Vietnam, a totalitarian society, were the aggressors who mounted the attack on the Republic of Vietnam. Many observers still blame Diem's authoritarian government for escalating the civil conflict and inviting attacks from the North because of his suppression of villagers and former Communist cadres. Defenders of Diem point out that the Communists during the same period mounted a systematic program of assassination of government officials and that Diem was trying to establish order. It is not necessary to apportion the blame between the Communists and the Diem government for this initial civil conflict to note that, in fact, by 1959 North Vietnam was directing and supplying the Communist forces opposing the Republic of South Vietnam. The conflict escalated into an international war during the 1960's and particularly after 1965 when the United States sent hundreds of thousands of troops to protect South Vietnam. By this time it was clear that North Vietnam was supplying manpower and equipment to the war against South Vietnam. The war was ended in 1975, after the United States withdrew almost all its forces, by North Vietnam's conventional military invasion of the South. About 17 out of its 19 regular divisions won the short, conclusive campaign. I would not agree with those who call that conflict a civil war since most nations of the world recognized South Vietnam as an independent nation when it was under attack. This is a logical way to distinguish international wars from civil wars. Many helped South Vietnam. No matter how we label the war, however, North Vietnam, a totalitarian nation, won the final victory with a conventional-type war.

Democracies started a war in the 1956 colonial-type war of England and France against Egypt, in the 1971 war between India and Pakistan, in the 1982 Israeli invasion of Lebanon, and the 1983 Grenada War. The 1956 war against Egypt was quickly brought to a halt, however, by democratic processes in Britain and with support of other democracies led by the United States in the U.N. Casualties were relatively low. Who started the India-Pakistan war of 1971 is a close call. India, a democracy, bears most of the blame for starting that war by its attacks in East Pakistan.

This war was a limited war quickly brought to an end. The above 1982 and 1983 wars also were quickly ended. The wars started by authoritarian and totalitarian rulers, on the other hand, were much more serious. World War I, World War II including wars against Ethiopia and China, and the Korean and Vietnamese Wars were major conflicts lasting years, and they caused millions of deaths. (See Figure 1) As noted above, democracies in the period since World War I have been less susceptible to the aggressive war virus than the totalitarian and authoritarian governments. Some historians and observers would not agree with this, because since the era of democracies wars have involved entire societies and have become more destructive. These observers tend to confuse popular support for war with the causes of wars. However, popular enthusiasm for fighting World War I, which was started by authoritarian governments, soon turned to horror at its destructiveness. The resulting pacifism and aversion to armaments in Europe and the United States left a vulnerability in democracies that totalitarian governments exploited by rearming and threatening the world with their conquests.

World War II was even more terrible in its destructiveness, particularly to civilian populations, and it gave birth to a pacifism in the Japanese democracy and in Western European democracies, which suffered more than the United States in World War II. The Korean War and Vietnam War, which involved principally the United States, engendered an aversion to war, particularly when TV brought the horrors of the Vietnam War to American living rooms every evening.

The active projection of U.S. power around the globe and the invasion of Grenada are minor exceptions to the above trends. However, the slogans of U.S. power politics are collective security and deterrence, not aggression. These slogans are used to support its arms budgets, which are seen as insurance against attack. Many U.S. leaders believe the Soviet Union potentially presents the same type of threat as the fascist aggressors before World War II, and U.S. policies are aimed at deterring the Communist threat. The Grenada invasion was an extreme manifestation of this view. It was so quick and relatively painless it did not engender anti-war opposition. Nevertheless, the memories of Vietnam in Congress caused it then to restrain President Reagan from escalation of troop involvement in the Central American crises of his administration.

The beleagured Israeli democracy, which has engaged in defensive and offensive wars, is a special case. Before 1967 that democracy seemed content with the status quo, although it had a long and vulnerable border with the West Bank. After the 1967 war, which was started by Egypt, the Israeli democracy has been willing to fight to preserve its expanded borders and the West Bank buffer, and to strike out aggressively at the P.L.O. threat from Lebanon. Israel did not embark on the 1967 war with an aim of territorial aggression, but after it was blockaded and threatened with aggression, it struck out and took the Sinai, West Bank, Golan Heights and Gaza strip. It gave up the Sinai only after receiving iron-clad guarantees against aggression, and it still retains the other territories as a buffer.

All countries beginning the wars claimed a right to wage war and asserted their determination to protect their rights. It would be more correct to call their perceived rights as vital interests, however, since international law does not recognize that a nation has a "right" to initiate a war. The only right is self-defense, while vital interest can be used to cover any national aim leaders think is important.

"Hatred of another nation" was an important factor in all the wars. This, however, is another way of saying there were underlying historic differences and conflicts. These specific causes of war have been summarized in each of the chapters.

As we noted in the introduction, Geoffrey Blainey stressed false images and false ideas of rivals as factors causing wars. As we can see in Table 1, many of these false conceptions were prevalent among the leaders who led their nations into wars we have studied. The rulers of the nations starting the war almost by definition were aggressive. Most were overoptimistic about their own strength and did not accurately estimate the reactions of their opponents. The exceptions to this overoptimism and misjudgment of their rivals were the wars actually won by the aggressors--the Vietnam War, the Indian leaders in their war against Pakistan, and the Grenada War. Also in the 1973 war, President Sadat apparently had no illusions about being able to defeat Israel, and he claims persuasively that his major aim was to show that the Arabs could fight and regain some of their territory. If this was his aim, he succeeded.

The "overreaction to a perceived threat" was a major factor in World War I, particularly when Germany struck out against France, because Germany feared France would help Russia against Germany. The Japanese attack at Pearl Harbor perhaps also was an overreaction to the threat their leaders perceived in the U.S. cutting back on oil exports and trade. At the same time, the Japanese would be called realistic because they rightly believed the United States was determined not to accept or recognize the Japanese invasion and attempt to control China.

Some authors have tried to psychoanalyze leaders such as Hitler to divine what motivated them. For many of the wars we analyzed, however, it is difficult to get reliable personal histories of who made the critical decisions and particularly in the Communist countries a personal, psychological profile is out of the question. There are volumes of their speeches which have been analyzed, however, and this data, showing what they said to influence their colleagues and people, did have a major impact. With this data we can see that without exception they were nationalists, and most of them extreme nationalists, and willing to go to war and use other instruments of power politics to strengthen their nations. They appeared to believe in their ideologies. These elements helped them overestimate their strength and misjudge their victims.

It may be that with the explosion of information in the news media that it is more difficult for leaders today to have misperceptions about threats than it was in the World War I era. Related to this is the existence of a forum for all major powers, the UN, which did not exist before World War II, where issues involved in disputes are often aired. However, we certainly have not come near to the millenium, when there are no misperceptions, as indicated by the fact that in the middle of the 1980's there were three major international wars in process (Iraq-Iran, Russia-Afghanistan, and Vietnam-Kampuchea), plus a number of conflicts that threatened to become international. It was obvious in many of the wars after World War II that the aggressors were overconfident and surprised at the strong reaction of their victims.

We then have as the principal pattern for wars of our era authoritarian leaders of governments, which include the totalitarian regimes, who are influenced by extreme nationalism and use policies of power politics. Included in this aggressive pattern were fascist, Communist, racist, and extreme religious ideologies. These leaders imprisoned by their ideologies had serious misperceptions about their opponents.

Quincy Wright in his classical study of war explained the above process as follows. Totalitarian and authoritarian leaders making decisions at the top inculcate policies and their related values into their peoples. These leaders build up the armed forces to achieve their aims. Powerful religious values and other peaceful values are abandoned and subordinated to national policy. In such a state it is easy for leaders to make a foreign enemy a scapegoat for frustrations. Belligerency generates an arms race and each side assumes the worst about an opponent.²

The wars we have studied, however, have not sprouted like seeds as implied by the above. These wars usually occurred by the leaders' designs. These leaders used the above process to get the support they need to fight a war successfully. Since World War I this means that arms races in themselves have not appeared to have caused wars, although arms races have been associated with war. Naturally an aggressor will build up arms, and the nation threatened will respond. But usually the victim is too weak to deter or quickly repel an aggressor. It is easier to see where weakness or perceived weakness, rather than an arms race, has caused a war-- e.g. World War II, the Korean War, the Vietnam War, the Arab-Israel wars, and the India-Pakistan, Russia-Afghanistan, and

Vietnam-Kampuchea wars. This could imply the world is a jungle of power politics, as pictured by Morgenthau and other philosophers of power politics. It should be remembered, however, that in comparison with the dozen or so aggressors in our study of wars since World War II, there were about 140 nations which were not aggressors.

Many observers assume wars often are caused by economic problems and also that soldiers often lead nations into wars. Table 2, however, indicates that only in the last two Arab-Israeli wars, in the Falkland Islands War, and in the 1971 India-Pakistan war were economic causes important. Sadat's memoires indicate Nasser in 1967 and Sadat in 1973 were striking out at Israel in frustration at Egypt's deteriorating economic situation and loss of prestige in the Arab world. The India-Pakistan conflict was started in part because the Bengalis in East Pakistan were convinced the West was exploiting them, and not interested in their plight after the 1970 cyclone struck. Also, Indian leaders believed India could not bear the cost of support of 10 million refugees in one of the poorest areas of India near the border with West Pakistan. General Galtieri launched the Falklands Islands attack probably to help gain political support in the face of a deteriorating economic situation. Although Table 1 indicates that economic arguments were part of the imperialistic arguments of Germany and Japan in starting World War II--they believed they needed additional resources and living space for their nations--their remarkable economic expansion since World War II without an empire indicates their prewar, imperialistic arguments were fallacious.

In regard to the question of military leadership, in the cases of Japans attack at Pearl Harbor, the Arab-Israel 1967 and 1973 wars, the Iraq-Iran war, the Falkland Islands war, and the 1982 war in Lebanon, military men were at the helm. However, the two Egyptian leaders, Nasser and Sadat, were politicians as much as they were military commanders. Thus, in most cases conventional military dictators did not start the wars. Military leaders, however, helped persuade their leaders to precipitate World War I, and probably that is where the military earned a reputation for belligerence.

Part II of Table 1 flags danger signals for aggressive wars. Rigid mobilization schedules and the arms race do not figure in many wars. This would be no consolation, however, if a future nuclear war would be triggered by nuclear alerts or a nuclear arms race. Wars are unique events, and so much is at stake that we should not discard the lessons of World War I. The rigid mobilization schedule for the German Army was an important factor causing the German General Staff to decide to attack France first and then Russia. Today, alert schedules for nuclear weapons are in minutes, not weeks. Careless talk about the advantages of a first strike could persuade a partly insane ruler to strike first in a crisis in order to preserve nuclear forces from a first strike by an opponent. World War I, unfortunately, may still have lessons for us.

Similarly, most of the wars were preceded with military mobilizations, terrorism, probes, and clashes. Such danger signals, which are common in crisis areas today, certainly should be regarded as a very serious matter by the world community.

To sum up, in reviewing the spectrum of ideas through actions as causes of major international wars of this century, shown in Table 1, we find extreme nationalism and ideas associating with it as the major causes. Also, most wars were started by totalitarian societies, and authoritarian societies. Fascism was the most aggressive totalitarianism (Manchuria, Ethiopia and World War II). The Communist ideology, which still dominates much of the world, also has joined with a form of extreme nationalism to start six of the wars we have studied in Korea, Vietnam, Hungary, Czechoslovakia, Kampuchea, and Afghanistan. Moreover, the Soviet Union encouraged Egypt to start the 1967 war.

This is not to conclude all Communist societies are aggressive. Communist China and Yugoslavia, for example, have not started aggressive wars. Communist China has strongly opposed the hegemonism of Vietnam and the Soviet Union, to the extent of making a punishing attack on Vietnam. It also criticizes the hegemonistic actions of the United States in Central America. Nevertheless, Communism as an ideology associated with a totalitarian form of government, extreme nationalism, and power politics that caused war.

The next chapter will suggest ways of discouraging and containing aggressive ideas and actions and will propose an agenda for achieving peace.

NOTES

[1] As indicated previously, I use the dictionary definition of fascism which designates it as a political philosophy, movement or regime that exalts nation and race above individual and that stands for a centralized, autocratic government headed by dictatorial leaders who support economic and social regimentation and suppress opposition.

[2] Quincy Wright, "The Nature of Conflict," Western Political Quarterly, June, 1951, pp. 193-209.

* This paragraph (page 195) has been clarified to answer John F. Murphy's question of how the analysis of this chapter relates to chapters 1 and 2. (John F. Murphy's review of World Politics and War, American Journal of International Law, July, 1987, pp. 822-824.)

CHAPTER 13

The Prevention of War

Diplomats in their contemplative moments often call for establishing a system, a structure, or an international organization to help maintain peace. Sir Edward Grey, the British Foreign Secretary, after the outbreak of World War I proposed a future "league of nations" to help maintain the peace. Secretary of State Hull, President Roosevelt, Prime Minister Churchill, and Premier Stalin helped found the United Nations Organization to maintain peace. President Truman worked through the U.N. to repel aggression in the Korean War. Truman and three other presidents (Eisenhower, Johnson and Nixon) used the U.N. along with tactics of power politics to help bring about truces in the major Mideast conflicts.

Secretary of State Henry Kissinger, who used naked power politics in the Vietnam War and rejected an important role for the U.N., advocated creating an "equilibrium" through a "network of relationships" among "several balances of power."[1] He centered his diplomacy on strengthening the NATO alliance and using U.S. military and economic power to support his policies. Secretary of State Haig aimed to coerce the Soviets and other countries into playing the "rules of the game," or international law, which is based on non-aggression and respect for state sovereignty. He proposed to achieve this aim through increasing the military power of the United States and its NATO allies, rather than through the United Nations.

Thus, the above leaders like other world leaders have oscillated between two philosophies for avoiding war--the one emphasizing support for the United Nations, and the other utilizing power politics with a major use of alliances.

Alliances as an Instrument to Deter War

Alliances are the traditional approach to deterring or containing war. Throughout history nations have relied principally on their own strength and that of their allies to deter war and discourage an aggressor. We will first review the major wars to see how the power brokers have tried to use alliances to deter wars, and then examine the experience of the internationalists who have tried to work within the framework of the United Nations.

World War I. Alliances played a part in almost all the wars we have studied, but they played a particularly prominent role in World War I. German leaders were dragged into that war by their determination to support their major ally, Austria-Hungary of the Dual Alliance. Historians and the media sometimes focus attention on the Triple Alliance, which also included Italy as it "confronted" the Triple Entente, which embraced the Franco-Russian alliance and the Franco-British understanding on colonial issues and naval cooperation. Italy, however, left the Triple Alliance at the outbreak of World War I, and Britain was drawn into the conflict by its guarantee of Belgian neutrality, not by understandings with France as part of the Triple Entente. The key alliances in the crises were the German alliance of 1879 with Austria-Hungary and the Franco-Russian alliance of 1894. Germany and Austria-Hungary believed themselves to be threatened by France and Russia, and German leaders were determined to back Austria-Hungary as their only dependable ally. Germany, therefore, backed Austria-Hungary in its conflict with Serbia, to the extent of issuing the famous "blank check." Then, as Russia supported Serbia, Russia's mobilization of forces also threatened the German border. Germany then decided on a preemptive strike on France, fully expecting France to fight with Russia in a war, which Germany then saw as inevitable. Ironically, the wording of the opposing alliances was defensive in nature, but they were perceived, at least by German and Austro-Hungarian leaders, as commitments to support their ally even in an offensive war. The phrase "entangling alliances" was coined to show how these alliances drew the major European powers into World War I.

World War II. This war was caused by opposite problems, weak alliances and alliances used for aggression. Hitler was able to pick off countries one by one, because they were not prepared to honor alliances and agreements. Particularly in the case of Czechoslovakia, France failed to honor its alliance, and Hitler took over the country with the aid of Czechoslovakia's former friends, France and Britain. They hoped to appease Hitler by ceding to Germany ethnic German areas of Czechoslovakia.

After Hitler absorbed all of Czechoslovakia, he concluded an alliance with Russia to neutralize it as he threatened to invade Poland. England then concluded a guarantee to Poland while it came under increasing German threats. The guarantee was iron-clad. It stated that in the event of any action which clearly threatened Poland and which was resisted by Polish forces, Britain would lend the Polish government all support in Britain's power. Hitler ignored this guarantee and denounced his non-aggression treaty with Poland. As he invaded Poland, Britain and France declared war on Germany. Russia took over border areas of eastern Poland during the German invasion. Then after months of a "phony war" along the German-French border, Hitler swept through France in a matter of weeks. Hitler's alliance with Russia protected Germany's backside while it invaded France.

England tried to support France against Hitler, but England's small contingent of troops was lucky to get out of Europe through Dunkirk without being totally wiped out.

Hitler then in 1941 turned on the Soviet Union invading it and shattering the new Russo-German Alliance. Britain, and later the United States after Pearl Harbor, without the benefit of a formal alliance then joined Russia in a fight to the death. Their commitment of demanding unconditional surrender demonstrated the binding nature of their "non-alliance."

Hitler in his aggressive designs was backed by the Axis alliance. First in preparation for his move into Austria in October 1936 Hitler concluded the first part of the Axis agreement with Italy. In November, 1937 Hitler concluded the German-Italian--Japanese anti-Comintern pact completing the Axis. Hitler's commitment to his alliance with Japan caused his government to declare war on the United States after Japan's attack on Pearl Harbor, formally triggering World War II, as far as the United States was concerned. I say formally, because the U.S. Congress was in the process of declaring war on Germany, which beat the U.S. Congress to the punch.

To sum up, in the World War II era alliances were ineffective, or discarded, or were used to support aggression. As the war spread, alliances were overshadowed by effective non-alliance arrangements.

NATO and the Warsaw Pact. The major post-World-War-II alliances of the superpowers grew out of actions of Russian leaders to control a buffer of East European states to insure Germany would not again threaten the Soviet Union. After World War II Soviet troops were occupying Eastern Europe, and the Soviets installed friendly Communist leaders to control these states.

The Soviets hoped that the Western Allies in an extension of their World War II cooperation would remain committed to four-power control of Germany, which would allow the Soviets to veto moves to restore German independence and power. The allies after two years of occupation determined not to keep the German economy permanently suppressed and to allow it to recover independently from Russian control over financial, economic, and political matters. Russia's Communist ideology made it suspicious of these Allied moves to promote German recovery. When the Allies gave Germans responsibility for financial matters by a new currency independent of East German and Russian control, the Russians retaliated with the Berlin blockade. About the same time a Communist coup in Czechoslovakia overthrew the government. The Russian blockade of Berlin and the Communist coup in Czechoslovakia stimulated the United States' leaders to form the NATO alliance to protect Western Europe, and they were strongly supported by the U.S. Congress. When Germany joined, Russia responded with the Warsaw Pact patterned after NATO. By 1955, the two superpowers and their new alliances confronted each other in Europe in the Cold War.

Although the wording of the NATO alliance is ambiguous, it is a strong alliance supported by a joint command structure, now not including France. Many assert it has prevented war in Europe, and there are few critics, particularly in Western Europe. Although NATO is one of the most closely-knit alliances in the world, it does not extend outside the North Atlantic area, and it has been of little value in crises outside that area.

The Far Eastern Alliances. The NATO alliance provided a model for the system of alliances built by the United States in the Far East from 1950 to 1955. Table 9 shows the similarity of wording of key provisions. They are ambiguously worded because of constitutional provisions giving Congress power to declare war. Even the Warsaw Pact had provisions patterned after the NATO alliance, and one provision provides for its disbanding if the NATO alliance is disbanded. Apparently, there are no secret provisions of these pacts, which like other international agreements after World War II are registered with the United Nations. Many make reference to the U.N. Charter, and all are defensive in wording.

In 1950 North Korea, a satellite of Russia, began the Korean war with a massive attack on the Republic of Korea (South Korea), a nation recognized by the U.N.. Historians generally point to a statement of Secretary of State Acheson noting that the Republic of Korea was outside the U.S. defense perimeter as encouraging the North Korean leadership to mount the attack, although there is no direct evidence to support this. Acheson's statement, which repeated a previous statement of General MacArthur, did note that South Korea could rely on the U.N. for its protection. The Communist powers were undoubtedly amazed at the strength of U.S. reaction, under the U.N. framework, to the aggression of the North Korean forces. When the U.N. troops pushed back the North Korean invaders close to the borders of China, Chinese "volunteers" entered the war in masses. Communist China had protected its backside the previous year by amending its treaty with Russia, so that if China were attacked by an ally of Japan (the United States), Russia would be committed to help China. Also by calling the Chinese forces volunteers, China avoided a direct war confronta-

TABLE 9
OPERATIVE PHRASES OF U.S. COLLECTIVE DEFENSE TREATIES

NORTH ATLANTIC TREATY. (15 Nations). Signed April 4, 1948. "The Parties agree that an armed attack against one or more of them on Europe or North America shall be considered an attack against them all; and...each of them...will assist...the attacked by taking forthwith individually and in concert with other Parties such action as it deems necessary including the use of armed force...."

RIO TREATY. (21 Latin American Nations). Signed 1947. The Parties agree that an armed attack against any American States "shall be considered as an attack against all the American States and...each one...undertakes to assist in meeting the attack ...."

ANZUS. (Australia, New Zealand, United States). Signed September 1, 1951. Each of the parties "recognizes that an armed attack in the Pacific Area on any of the Parties would be dangerous to its own peace and safety and declares that it would act to meet the common danger in accordance with its constitutional processes."

PHILIPPINE TREATY. (Bilateral). Signed August 30, 1951. The parties recognize "that an armed attack in the Pacific Area on either of the Parties would be dangerous to its own peace and safety" and each Party agrees that it will act "to meet the common dangers in accordance with its constitutional processes."

JAPANESE TREATY. (Bilateral). Signed September 8, 1951. Japan on a provisional basis requests and the United States agrees to "maintain certain of its armed forces in and about Japan...so as to deter armed attack upon Japan."

REPUBLIC OF KOREA TREATY. (Bilateral). Signed October 1, 1953. Each Party "recognizes that an armed attack in the Pacific area on either of the Parties...would be dangerous to its own peace and safety" and that each Party "would act to meet the common danger in accordance with its constitutional processes."

SOUTHEAST ASIA TREATY (SEATO). (8 Nations). Each Party "recognizes that aggression by means of armed attack in the treaty area against any of the Parties...would endanger its own peace and safety and each will in that event act to meet the common danger in accordance with its constitutional process."

REPUBLIC OF CHINA TREATY. (Bilateral). Signed December 2, 1954. Terminated January 1, 1980. Each of the Parties "recognizes that an armed attack in the West Pacific Area directed against the territories of either of the Parties would be dangerous to its own peace and safety" and each "would act to meet the common danger in accordance with its constitutional process." The territory of the Republic of China was defined as Taiwan and the Pescadores.

tion with the U.N. forces under the command of General MacArthur. A truce was finally negotiated between the U.N. forces and North Korea and the Chinese "volunteers" after years of fighting, although there is still no peace along the 38th parallel.

The Korean War gave an impetus to the American alliance system for the Far East. During the war the United States concluded an alliance with Japan as part of its treaty arrangements returning sovereignty to Japan after its defeat in World War II. Other Far East nations readily accepted an offer of a U.S. alliance to help protect them against what was seen as a growing threat of Communist expansion in Asia. The United States made bilateral alliances with Korea, Taiwan, and the Philippines. The U.S. concluded multilateral alliances with Australia and New Zealand and the South East Asian Treaty (SEATO) with the United Kingdom, France, Australia, the Philippines, Thailand, Pakistan, and New Zealand. This latter alliance also pledged protection to South Vietnam and Laos, without their participation in its SEATO command structure.

The SEATO alliance was worth little more than a piece of paper in the Vietnam war. France and Britain did not give any important assistance to defend South Vietnam, even though they were committed by the SEATO treaty. Australia, New Zealand, and Thailand did give limited support under the Treaty, but the fighting was dominated by U.S. forces. There was no pretense that a SEATO command was waging the war. The United States used the SEATO Treaty as an excuse to intervene, but it did not wage war under a SEATO flag. In 1975 the United States and its ally, South Vietnam, suffered a humiliating defeat.

The U.S. bilateral pact with Japan is useful for defensive and deterrent reasons. The Japanese Government is so confident of its provisions that it spends only about 1 percent of its GNP on defense, one of the lowest expenditures in the world. This reliance on the U.S. partner has helped the Japanese economy to achieve one of the best records of economic development in history. The U.S. values the Japanese alliance primarily for political reasons. China with its sensitivity to a long history of Japanese aggression in China would find it difficult to maintain detente with two powerful capitalist allies, Japan and the United States, if Japan's rearmament threatened China. The United States still remembers Pearl Harbor, and a major Japanese rearmament program would probably still disturb many American officials. To be blunt, the U.S.-Japanese alliance is helpful in preserving peace because it helps discourage a major Japanese arms build-up of offensive weapons and makes possible a U.S.-China detente. The Soviet Union and China have not demonstrated aggressive designs toward Japan; perhaps the alliance has deterred such threats.

The SEATO alliance combined with U.S. assurances probably is reassuring to Thailand, which faces the Vietnamese armed forces, which are now the fourth largest in the world. However, the essence of the alliance is the U.S. commitment, and Thailand would count on little help from the other five partners. On the other hand the ASEAN treaty between Thailand, Malaysia, Singapore, Indonesia and the Philippines is explicitly not a military alliance, but it has provided an informal framework for close consultation on threats to the security of the region posed by the Vietnam-Kampuchea war. Here again is an example of a non-alliance being relatively effective in comparison with a formal alliance.

Communist Alliances. The U.S. alliances are essentially defensive in nature. The Communist alliances are another matter. The Soviet Union with its alliance and supplies of military equipment to North Korea encouraged it to launch the Korean War. The Russian and Chinese alliances and support to Vietnam helped it to win a victory over South Vietnam and the United States, although Russia and China did not commit troops to the conflict. The Soviet Union's alliance with Egypt and supply of arms encouraged it to begin the 1967 and 1973 wars against Israel. The Soviet alliance with Iraq may have emboldened it to attack Iran with Russian equipment supplied under the alliance. The Soviet alliance played a part in encouraging India to attack East Pakistan since India was assured of Soviet support if China came to Pakistan's defense. The Warsaw Pact was used as a cover for Soviet intervention in Hungary in 1956 to crush a revolt and to mobilize East European forces to restore order in Czechoslovakia in 1968.

The alliance between the Soviets and Afghanistan provided Russia with a cover to attack Afghanistan at the end of 1979 with the excuse of defending it. There were no important alliances in the 1980's for oil-rich Iran, whose army and government were greatly weakened by internal strife. Statements by the United States and its allies and their power moves in the Persian Gulf, rather than alliances in that area, were major deterrents discouraging Russia from further direct moves toward the oil riches of the Middle East.

Other Alliances. The alliance system also was of no use in containing the Arab-Israel wars. In 1956, in the U.N. the United States took action against its NATO allies, France and England, in their colonial war against Egypt to recover the Suez Canal. The U.S. was joined in the UN by Russia, the enemy of the NATO alliance. The U.S. opposition to France and England plus the uproar the war caused among members of the opposition in Britain's House of Commons who were opposed to Britain's colonial adventure, helped bring the war to a quick end. The most effective arrangement in this Mideast crisis was the U.S. non-alliance with Israel. In the Arab-Israel crises the U.S. often was Israel's only effective supporter, and Israel probably could not have survived without its non-alliance with the U.S.

In the 1971 war India was allied with the Soviet Union, and Pakistan with China. Secretary of State Kissinger in describing events leading to that war, asserts that Russia in concluding the 1971 treaty of friendship and alliance with India "threw a lighted match into a powder keg."[2] Whether or not this is true, that war was not deterred by the alliances with the superpowers, and alliances had no direct part in bringing about a settlement, although Russia, India's alliance partner, probably put pressure on India to cool it. Perhaps someday Prime Minister Gandhi will reveal what factors really influenced her to stop the war against Pakistan, but from our present viewpoint it appears that the overwhelming U.N. resolution calling for a withdrawal of Indian forces plus pressure from the United States and the Soviet Union were major factors.

To sum up, we have little evidence of alliances deterring war. However, we have alliances used as instruments of aggression, alliances ignored, non-alliances being most effective in fighting aggressions, and non-alliances allowing a stalemate in a war. We are forced to conclude that alliance systems as such are not useful in solving the problem of war. Like weapons--they can be used defensively or offensively, or not used at all. Requirements that alliances be registered under the League of Nations and the U.N. have not prevented their use for offensive purposes. Perhaps, however, the process has removed unreasonable fears of alliances like those that contributed to World War I. We will now examine to what extent the U.N. System and its support of international law have deterred war.

The U.N. System and Peacemaking

World War I convinced many leaders and their people that the old system of power politics and alliances should be replaced with a world organization to maintain peace. We will briefly evaluate the experience of the League of Nations after World War I, since its experience is useful in evaluating the U.N. We will then review the U.N.'s peacemaking efforts in the wars we have examined. Since the basis of U.N. actions in war crises is negotiation and not enforcement, we will also look at the negotiation of arms limitation treaties as a part of the process of preventing war. Finally, in conclusion we will suggest a possible agenda for preventing war.

Those who designed the United Nations attempted to create an organization to prevent war which could survive the types of strains that caused the demise of the League of Nations. Examining the origin of the League and its work in major crises of the 1930s helps us understand the design for the U.N. peacemaking process.

During the 19th century many of the colonial and other international crises were settled by the Concert of Europe, which was the name given to the conferences called by the great powers.

These were ad hoc meetings, and there was no permanent secretariat or organization. This diplomatic system with the balance of power idea as its guide was credited with the era of relative peace between the Napoleonic wars and the beginning of the 20th century.

Britain's Foreign Secretary, Sir Edward Grey, was not able to activate the Concert in the weeks before Europe plunged into World War I. As war started and the "lights went out in Europe," he vowed to created an organization to prevent a future catastrophe of this nature. He, if anyone, was the father of the League of Nations, and soon after the outbreak of war he started corresponding with Colonel House, President Wilson's foreign policy advisor, about the issues of war and peace. The "pearl of wisdom" that Sir Edward proposed was that after the war there should be a "league of nations that would be relied on to insist that disputes between any two nations must be settled by arbitration, mediation, or conference of others."[3] Ray Stannard Baker, Wilson's foremost biographer, is convinced that this letter stimulated President Wilson to begin his crusade that established the League of Nations as part of the Versailles peace settlement.[4]

President Wilson's health collapsed during his speeches advocating the League to the American people and to the United States Senate. His effort was not in vain, however, despite the subsequent failure of the United States to join the League. A young salesman, Harry Truman, was impressed by Wilson's efforts to sell the League, and about 25 years later, as president of the United States, Truman brought the United States into the United Nations with the overwhelming support of the United States Senate. Truman was determined not to repeat the mistakes of failing to get great power support for the world organization, and he authorized the compromises needed to get the Soviet Union to participate. He then helped convince the United States Senate to ratify the Charter. The full participation of the two superpowers has provided the two pillars that have strengthened the United Nations through the many political crises that it has faced, many of them involving confrontation of these superpowers.

The failure of the League of Nations was due to more than the absence of the United States. The League was essentially a forum for great powers to meet, and it depended, therefore, on the will of its members. During the 1930's they were not willing to take the risks of confronting the totalitarian aggressors--Japan, Italy, and Germany. The United States, which informally participated in many League activities, did persuade the League Council not to recognize Japan's aggression in Manchuria and the puppet state that Japan established. This was not an empty gesture, since after World War II the world community endorsed the peace treaty with Japan which returned Manchuria to China.

In 1936 the League rallied to stop Italy's aggression against one of its members, Ethiopia, by arranging an oil embargo, but the foreign ministers of Britain and France, Hoare and Laval, at the last minute pulled the rug on this effort in a secret compromise with Italy. Hoare and Laval were hoping by this maneuver of sacrificing territory in Ethiopia to get Mussolini on their side to oppose Hitler. Mussolini in the Axis alliance beat them at their own game, by joining with Germany and Japan in an imperialistic design to take control of Europe and Asia.

Later, Hitler cynically exploited divisions among the European powers and the bad conscience of some of its leaders, who regretted imposing such harsh peace terms on Germany after World War I, by picking off European countries one by one. When European leaders finally realized what was happening, Hitler's armies dominated Western Europe. The point is that it was not just the League which failed, but that its members failed by refusing to use the League forum to join together to stop these aggressors.

President Roosevelt, Prime Minister Churchill, and General Stalin, the leaders of the World War II alliance against the Axis, were determined to form a strong international organization to keep the peace and act against future aggressors such as Hitler. At first they favored a system based on regional alliances to keep the peace, in which each of the great powers would be a leader, but Secretary of State Cordell Hull insisted on a universal organization more like the League of Nations model. (Hull, too, had been strongly influenced by President Wilson.) After extensive lobbying with Congress and the public, and exploring the idea with other nations, the Department of State prepared a first draft of the organization that later became the U.N. This draft was revised at Dumbarton Oaks in 1944, and in about a year it had received the approval of delegates of 50 nations cooperating in the war against the Axis. Five weeks after the Charter draft was signed in San Francisco, the U.S. Senate approved the Charter by a vote of 89 to 2, and on October 24, 1945 the United Nations was formally established.

Fundamental commitments of U.N. members related to war and peace are spelled out in Article 2. This states that all members should settle their disputes by peaceful means, and that they should refrain in their international relations from the threat or use of force against the territorial integrity or political independence of any state. Furthermore they are obliged to fulfill in good faith the obligations of the Charter, which include supporting the peacekeeping processes described below.

The major organ of the U.N. charged with acting to maintain the peace is the Security Council. Under the Charter each of the five major world powers (the United States, Russia, the United Kingdom, France, and China) have the so-called veto right to block actions of the Security Council, other than votes on procedural issues and measures for the peaceful settlement of disputes. This provides an incentive for the great powers to stay in the U.N. to protect their interests when crises involve them or their close allies. As we will see, the Korean War crisis showed that the Charter also granted considerable power to the General Assembly, which represents all the U.N. members, to act without a veto on security issues.

The original idea of the three leaders of the Western alliance that the great powers should manage world peace was reflected in Article 47 of the Charter. This provides for a Military Staff Committee composed of representatives of the five permanent members of the Security Council to direct armed forces placed at the disposal of the Security Council. The Cold War broke out soon after the end of World War II, and the major powers could not agree on forming the military enforcement units, although lightly-armed U.N. "peacekeeping" and observer units have been established outside the above framework.

The failure to form a U.N. army did not cripple the U.N., and in fact Chapter IV of the U.N. Charter calls for many types of political devices as the first steps in settling disputes, including negotiation, mediation, judicial settlement and resort to regional agencies, before considering the use of armed force.

Article 51 is a key article that provides additional flexibility to the U.N. peacemaking process. It states that

> Nothing in the Charter shall impair the inherent right of individual or collective self-defense if an armed attack occurs against a Member of the United Nations, until the Security Council has taken measures necessary to maintain international peace and security.

This article encourages friendly nations and allies to assist a member attacked by another nation, even if Security Council action is blocked by a veto of one of the permanent members. This does not authorize, however, intervention in civil wars, and Article 2 states nothing in the Charter shall authorize the United Nations "to intervene in matters which are essentially within the domestic jurisdiction of any state." The General Assembly in 1974 in order to prevent aggression under the cover of a civil war approved a definition of aggression which included prohibiting a state from sending armed bands across a border to attack another state. The above ideas of not using force against the territorial integrity or political independence of another state are a fundamental part of international law or the "rules of the game." As we have seen, like all laws they are not always observed.

To briefly review the success of the U.N. in its major task of keeping the peace we will focus only on its role in the major wars we have studied since World War II. Nevertheless, we should note that the U.N. has been involved in almost every world crisis since that war, and that it has helped settle a majority of the disputes. Some have been settled without war or conflicts--in other cases the U.N. has brought about cease-fires before the conflicts escalated into a major war. Supporters of the U.N. process point to how it has facilitated diplomacy and used pressure to bring about agreement between adversaries, which is the only sure basis for peace. Countries of the world are not prepared at the present time to submit to a supra-national police authority, and the only alternative for peaceful settlement, then, is for agreement among the adversaries. Critics point out that the United Nations is weak and not able to enforce a peace against those who do not want to stop fighting, particularly if they are great powers. Few, if any, of those critics, if pressed, offer an alternative, since they realize nations would not accept a world police organization able to enforce its will on sovereign nations.

The Korean War was a major test of the U.N. System. (See also Chapter 5). At the close of World War II the United States and the Soviet Union were not able to agree on unifying their occupation zones in Korea, so the United States submitted the problem to the General Assembly. In line with the recommendations of a temporary commission set up by the General Assembly, the United States permitted elections with U.N. observers in August, 1948 to set up a South Korean Government, and the General Assembly recognized it on December 12, 1948 as the only lawful government in Korea. Russia did not permit such elections in North Korea, and that government was not recognized by the U.N.

When North Korea attacked the South, there were U.N. observers there to confirm that North Korea was the aggressor. The United States brought the issue immediately to the U.N. Security Council, which that same day voted 9 to 1 that the attack was a breach of the peace and that the North Korean forces should be withdrawn. The United States immediately provided military help under Article 51 while the Security Council was acting. Within two days and after a further report from the U.N. observers in Korea, the Security Council called for support to South Korea by all U.N. members. The Soviet Union probably thought its absence from the Security Council would prevent such action, since the Charter apparently required Russian assent to such Security Council action. However, the other Security Council members acted without the presence of the Soviet Union's representative, relying largely on the general intent of the Charter to be used to repel aggression. When the Soviet representative did appear two months later, the Security Council in a procedural action under the "uniting for peace" procedure shifted decisions on the war to the General Assembly. The Soviet Union could not block such a procedural vote in the Security Council.

The General Assembly by overwhelming votes continued to oversee actions of sixteen nations that provided military aid to help defend South Korea. Technically, the United Nations was not in command of the forces, but it recommended that members provide assistance to a unified command under the United States, and the Security Council authorized the use of the U.N. flag for this command. The Unified Command, with the United States providing most of the manpower and funds, repelled the attack of the North Korean aggressors and of the Chinese "volunteers" and negotiated a truce. The U.N. command still exists along the 38th parallel and has not been able to negotiate a final peace between North Korea and South Korea, but there has been no outbreak of war since the 1954 truce.

The United Nations was not asked by the belligerents to settle the Vietnam War, until the United States made a belated effort in 1966 long after the war had escalated to a major conflict. (See also Chapter 7.) Secretary-General U-Thant's repeated efforts to settle the war were not successful largely because they were virtually ignored by the belligerents. China, which was deeply involved in supporting the North Korean aggression, was not even a member of the United Nations at that time, as noted by the Secretary-General. Secretary-General Kurt Waldheim offered his good offices to settle the conflict in April, 1972, but the offer was not accepted. He was invited, however, to attend the 1973 peace conference to guarantee the end of the war. This did not prevent North Vietnam's spring offensive in 1975, which shattered the agreements. After that war ended in 1975, the General Assembly invited both the Democratic Republic of Vietnam and the Republic of South Vietnam to be admitted to membership, even though the D.R.V. controlled all of Vietnam. This was vetoed by the United States in the Security Council. Later when the two areas were formally unified under North Vietnam, it was admitted to the United Nations in 1977 without a U.S. veto. To sum up, the Vietnam War was an exercise in power politics with virtually no U.N. involvement.

The United Nations was saddled with the Arab-Israeli conflicts from the beginning since it inherited from the League of Nations responsiblity for supervising the Palestine mandate, which was turned over to the U.N. by Great Britain. (See Chapter 6.) On May 15, 1947 at the close of a special session on the issue, the General Assembly established the United Nations Special Committee on Palestine consisting of Australia, Canada, Czechoslovakia, Guatemala, India, Iran, the Netherlands, Peru, Sweden, Uruguay, and Yugoslavia. A majority of the committee proposed the partition of Palestine into two independent states--a Jewish state and an Arab state with the city of Jerusalem under an international trusteeship administered by the U.N. The General Assembly adopted the plan on November 29, 1947 by a vote of 33 to 13 with 10 abstentions. The Arab nations refused to accept this settlement and attacked the Jewish communities, which established the State of Israel on May 14, 1948. The Security Council established a truce commission and, after several cease-fires which were broken, managed to negotiate truces with the belligerents early in 1949. As a result of the war, Israel ended up with an area almost twice the size originally granted by the U.N. partition plan. In this war U.N. action precipitated the conflict and then brought it quickly to an end.

On October 29, 1956 Israeli forces attacked Egypt in the Sinai, and a few days later, British and French forces used this as an excuse to try to take over the Suez Canal Zone. French and British vetoes prevented the Security Council from acting on the matter. Under the "uniting for peace" procedures, the Security Council by majority vote, including that of Russia and the U.S., referred the matter to the General Assembly which met in an emergency session from November 1 to 10. The General Assembly called for a cease-fire and established the United Nations Emergency Force (UNEF) to secure and supervise cessation of hostilities. The UNEF, which was the first United Nations "peacekeeping" force, soon obtained a cease-fire and the U.N. backed by U.S. pressure persuaded the French and British forces to withdraw by December 22. The withdrawal of Israeli forces was completed by March, 1957. U.N. action was the key to ending this war. Russian threats came only after fighting had stopped.

In the 1967 war, which was initiated by aggressive action of Egypt, the Security Council obtained a cease-fire on June 10, five days after the war started. By that time, however, Israel had occupied Sinai, the Gaza Strip, the West Bank of the Jordan, including East Jerusalem, and Syria's Golan Heights. Subsequently on November 22, 1967 the Security Council unanimously adopted Resolution 242 which defined the framework for a peaceful settlement in the Middle East. This resolution later was the basis for the Camp David agreements of 1978 and the Egyptian-Israeli peace treaty of March 26, 1979.

On October 6, 1973 war broke out again when Egyptian forces attacked in the Suez Canal sector and Syrian forces attacked in the Golan Heights. By October 22, the Security Council approved a resolution calling on the parties to cease fire and to implement Resolution 242. The prompt arrival of UNEF in the Egypt-Israeli sector helped Kissinger negotiate a final cease fire by October 25. As noted above, the subsequent Camp David agreements and the Egypt-Israel peace treaty of 1979 negotiated by President Carter, brought about peace between Egypt and Israel. The UNEF commander also negotiated a complicated series of withdrawal agreements in various buffer zones. The media gave a great deal of attention to

Secretary of State Kissinger and later President Carter in settling the 1973 conflict, but the U.N. also played a major role. There has been no formal peace between Israel and Syria, and the cease fire is still supervised by the U.N. Disengagement Observer Force (UNDOF), which was established in May, 1974. Another U.N. force, the United Nations Interim Force in Lebanon (UNIFIL) was established in March, 1973 to try to prevent clashes between the PLO and Israel along the Israel-Lebanon border.

UNIFIL was not strong enough to prevent periodic PLO shelling from Lebanon of Israeli settlements, and Israeli military retaliation and attacks against the PLO. When the Israelis mounted a major attack against the PLO in Lebanon in the summer of 1982, the U.N. Security Council was hamstrung by differences between the United States, Lebanon, France, and the PLO on the conditions for a truce.[5] The crux of the matter was whether the PLO would be allowed to stay in Lebanon and keep its arms. Not only Israel and the United States favored disarming the PLO to the extent of permitting Lebanon to regain its sovereignty, but Arab nations appeared to be split on the issue, although they vocally supported the PLO. Some of the more conservative Arab nations felt threatened by the radical ideology of certain factions of the PLO, and its close alliance with the radical Islamic ideology of Iran. The major negotiating action centered on the U.S. special envoy to the Middle East, Philip Habib, who negotiated an evacuation of the PLO from Beirut, after the Israeli forces surrounded the last major elements of PLO forces. The United States went outside the U.N. in trying to stabilize the situation with a multinational force of U.S., French, Italian and British troops. As the situation deteriorated, with major terrorist attacks, the multinational forces withdrew, and Syria and its Druze and Moslem allies gained the upper hand at the beginning of 1984.

To sum up, the United Nations helped bring about relatively quick cease fires between Israel and its Arab enemies in 1948 and in the wars of 1956, 1967, and 1973. In addition it provided peacekeeping forces and care for one million Palestinian refugees after the 1948 war, and provided a neutral instrument for reopening the Suez Canal after the 1956 war. Although Israel and Egypt reached a peace settlement in 1978 and 1979, there is still no peace between Israel and its other Arab neighbors. The major problem, as noted in Chapter 6, is establishing some form of Palestinian self-government on the West Bank and the Gaza Strip, and reaching agreement on the issues of Jerusalem and the Golan Heights.

Arab critics and some others blame the United Nations for its original intervention on the Palestine issue and for creating the state of Israel. However, the U.N. did not create the problem. The issue which demanded a solution arose out of a flood of Jewish immigration to Palestine after World War II to escape the memories of the Holocaust. Perhaps no solution was possible without a war, because the Arabs claimed the territory in which the new Jewish state was established. The Camp David agreements and the Egyptian-Israeli treaty look to an ultimate solution of these problems on the basis of U.N. Resolution 242 and the principle of establishing a self-governing authority of Palestinians on the West Bank. In 1984 no final peace settlement was in sight, but the above indicates any future settlement would probably involve the U.N.

U.N. mediation was a key element in bringing about the containment of the India-Pakistan War of 1972 along with diplomatic pressures by Russia, China, and the United States. The General Assembly's overwhelming call for a cease fire and for withdrawal of Indian troops from East Pakistan played an important role by registering views of the world community on the issue. The General Assembly took action because the issue had been blocked by a Russian veto in the Security Council. After the General Assembly action, which was supported by other diplomatic pressure, India withdrew its forces and the new state of Bangladesh was established. The U.N. then mobilized over $1 billion to help return the 10 million refugees who had fled to India during the conflict. Secretary of State Kissinger was at center stage, but again, the U.N. deserves a major share of the credit along with assistance from the great powers.

The United Nations played a relatively minor role in the settlement of the settlement of the Cuban missile crisis of 1962. However, President Kennedy brought the matter before the U.N. Security Council and acted within the framework of international law and the U.N. Charter. Political support to the U.S. action was provided by the Organization of American States, which is a regional organization of the type recognized by the U.N. Charter. Kennedy's diplomatic management of the missile crisis involved a threat of escalating beyond the "quarantine" action, and helped bring about a resolution of that crisis without a war. Nevertheless, his actions were within the bounds of international law and procedures of the U.N.

The Afghanistan War, which began in December, 1979, had not ended as of the writing of this book. The overwhelming condemnation of Soviet aggression by the U.N. Security Council and the General Assembly had not by the end of 1985 had a noticeable effect on Soviet determination to make Afghanistan a satellite. It can be argued, however, that the strong condemnation of the action by the United Nations, joined with power-politics pressure led by the United States, deterred the Soviets from further aggressive moves in the area. The memory of these actions may have caused the Soviets to refrain from attacking Poland a year later to suppress the growing power of the trade unions there, which challenged the basic Soviet concept of Communism. If Russian forces do not press on in the Middle East or attack Poland, the political pressure of nations condemning Russian violation in Afghanistan of the U.N. charter can be credited as a deterrent.

The United Nations, of course, is not a world government that can enforce the peace. It is principally a forum where nations can meet to resolve disputes, and it provides machinery to make reports, mediate, and monitor settlements. The U.N. procedures do not capture the attention of the media or the affection of U.S. public like dramatic moves of world leaders who mediate disputes or pressure nations to stop fighting. U.N. procedures involve meetings, rhetoric, and often negotiation behind closed doors. Only in the case of Korea has there been prolonged fighting with high casualties in an international war where the U.N. played a major role. U.N. measures on the whole have been surprisingly effective, particularly when compared to the disastrous failures of U.S. power politics in the Vietnam War and in Lebanon in the 1980s.

At the beginning of the 80's the U.N. had failed to get the Soviet Union to withdraw from Afghanistan, to get Vietnam to withdraw its forces from Cambodia, and to get Iran and Iraq to cease fighting. To enforce U.N. resolutions in the case of Afghanistan was not feasible. Major steps by the U.N. to retaliate against the Soviets would have probably shattered the U.N. by causing the withdrawal of the Soviet Union and its allies from the organization. Enforcing a peace in that area would also have required conventional war, which is impractical because there would be few volunteers for such a move in that area where Soviet forces dominate. The U.N. as a political organization recognized the facts of life by not trying to fight that windmill.

In the case of the Vietnam invasion of Kampuchea many members regarded it as a fight between two outlaws and did not propose forceful intervention. U.N. members from Southeast Asia and Western Europe, however, did bring the matter before the General Assembly and obtained resolutions in 1980 and 1981 calling for the withdrawal of foreign forces and assistance to the many refugees fleeing from the fighting. The Secretary General attempted to mediate, but as of the beginning of 1985 had no success. The U.N. coordinated a large-scale relief effort in Thailand and Kampuchea for the victims of that war.

Similarly, the Iran-Iraq War was a war between two outlaws. Iraq seriously violated the U.N. Charter by starting the aggression. At the time of the attack Iran had ignored resolutions of the Security Council, the General Assembly, and the World Court calling on it to release diplomatic hostages of the United States. After its Prime Minister visited the U.N. and found overwhelming disapproval of its action on the hostages, Iran's negotiations for the release of the hostages moved forward. The United Nations, in line with the Charter, turned over the problem of mediating the Iran-Iraq war to the Islamic Council of forty Islamic nations. As of the end of 1985 the war had been contained, and the Islamic Council was continuing efforts to bring an end to the conflict.

Although the U.N. has seldom acted as the world's policeman, it has been much more than a forum for settling disputes. Its activities have ranged from exerting political pressure of condemning aggressors and calling for cease-fires, up to providing conventional military forces under a unified command. It would be a mistake to conclude, however, that the U.N. process excludes the collateral use of power politics. There have been many cases where strong bilateral diplomacy and even alliances have assisted U.N. peacemaking efforts. The U.N. is always ready when a stalemate occurs and the parties grow tired of fighting to offer to assist with its peacemaking. In short, the U.N. Charter has proven to be a flexible and effective instrument for peace when the nations of world want to use it and are willing to back it with diplomacy and various types of pressure.

The U.N. and Arms Limitation Agreements

There are about a dozen important arms limitation agreements negotiated within the U.N. framework by the superpowers and other nations. We will briefly look at the major agreements, not with the aim of judging how they have succeeded in limiting arms, but in how they contribute to the U.N. processes of preventing war. The media and other observers tend to judge these agreements too narrowly because they have not noticably reduced the burden of defense expenditures. Also, the media have been impressed by critics' attacks on the SALT II agreement, which was not ratified by the U.S. Senate. We will see, however, that even the SALT agreements have contributed to a negotiating process of preventing war.

First, the arms limitation agreements, and particularly the SALT agreements, are useful in drawing attention to the terrors of a nuclear war and the insanity of resorting to nuclear weapons. The dimensions of the nuclear threat are awesome. The Soviet Union with one big warhead could cause "near total destrucion" of Washington D.C. and most of its suburbs. One U.S. submarine with its missiles has enough explosive power to devastate every city in the Soviet Union with a population of over 150,000.[6] The present stocks of the superpowers' warheads, even assuming many missiles miss their target, could in a surprise attack immediately destroy most of the population of the other superpower many times over.

Even if the leaders engaged in a theoretical chess game and attacked only prime military targets, the fallout would eventually kill tens of millions and invite escalation into a holocaust. Some scientists say an all-out nuclear war could fatally contaminate the northern hemisphere and kill the inhabitants or even fatally upset the world's environmental balance.

Public abhorrence of nuclear weapons acts as a deterrent to their use. Continuing to negotiate to limit these weapons is a part of the international process of reinforcing this abhorrence.

In line with a U.N. resolution, over 100 nations formally agreed to the Nuclear Non-Proliferation Treaty (NPT) of 1970 not to build or use nuclear weapons. Article 6 commits Russia, the United States and other signatories to pursue negotiations to end the nuclear arms race.

The SALT I agreement included ceilings on intercontinental ballistic missiles (ICBMs) and submarine-launched ballistic missiles (SLBMs). The Anti-Ballistic Missile Treaty (ABM) was joined with SALT I and limited ABM complexes to one each for Russia and the United States. Under this treaty each country was at the mercy of the other in the event of a nuclear war. Another agreement, the Hot Line Agreement, provides for instant communication between the leaders of the two superpowers to eliminate misunderstandings that might lead to war. Finally, a 1973 agreement committed the two superpowers to avoid threats to use force.

The SALT II treaty negotiated by the Carter Administration was withdrawn from Senate consideration after the Russians attacked Afghanistan. The treaty added ceilings on bombers. The SALT II ceilings were observed until Reagan announced at the end of 1986 that the United States would not honor them. The SALT agreement had provided for satellite verification and a Standing Consultative Commission to discuss problems arising from the agreements.

Other agreements, which were under the United Nations, were the 1963 partial-test-ban treaty, and a treaty limiting underground nuclear tests to 150 kilotons, which although not ratified was observed by Russia and the United States. These prevented the testing of new larger weapons of nuclear destruction, and therefore prevented their development. The Antarctic Treaty of 1963 demilitarized Antarctica and provided for full inspection of all installations there. The treaties on outer space and the seabeds, both originating in the U.N. General Assembly, prohibit nuclear weapons in those environments. In the fall of 1987 there was a breakthrough when Chairman Gorbachev made major concessions on issues of controlling medium-range and tactical nuclear missiles in Europe. In essence he accepted the "double-zero" proposal of President Reagan to eliminate these from Europe and Asia. A summit meeting was scheduled for November 1987, after which the treaty would be presented to the Senate for approval. This would be the first major nuclear arms agreement of the Reagan Administration.

The above network of treaties, which originated directly or indirectly from U.N. initiatives, are all designed to prevent nuclear war and to further the process of negotiation rather than confrontation. This body of international law designed for peace with minor exceptions is being observed. It is buttressed by national means of verification and by conferences to help ensure that provisions are being observed.

Wars have occurred since these agreements have been negotiated, but there has been no major nuclear confrontation since the first of the above agreements was concluded. In a world of sovereign nations, peace depends on leaders of nations rejecting war. Nations under these agreements have agreed to reject aggressive nuclear war. Perhaps an international consensus can grow also to reject other forms of war and lessen the danger of escalation to a nuclear war.

Agenda to Eliminate War

Some might say that it is a tautology to suggest that strengthening the United Nations and the rule of international law is the answer to the problem of war since the U.N. Charter and international law prohibit war. Obviously, nation states, some of which have nuclear weapons, are much more powerful and set in their ways than individuals, so that it has not been possible for the international society to enforce international law. Thus, the major question remains unanswered--how to bring about the voluntary acceptance of the rule of international law in a world community?

Internationalists would reply that establishing such a goal at least gives policymakers something to work toward and use in promoting ideas of peace. John Stoessinger, in <u>Why Nations Go to War</u>, notes that thousands of years ago human beings ate each other, and only one hundred years ago, slavery was the accepted way of life. He hopes, "like slavery and cannibalism, war too can be eliminated from mankind's arsenal of horrors."[7]   Colonel House, President Wilson's close adviser, in a quotation at the beginning of this book stated:

> I believe the most viable element in bringing
> about a world-wide reign of peace is to have the
> same stigma rest upon the acts of nations as upon
> the acts of individuals. When the people of a
> country are held up to scorn and condemnation of
> the world because of the dishonorable acts of
> their representatives, they will no longer tolerate such acts.

President Truman carried in his wallet a poem by Tennyson, "Locksley Hall," which reads:

> Till the war drum throbbed no longer and the
> battle flags were furled
>
> In the parliament of Man, the Federation
> of the world."

Can progress toward these long-range goals be achieved? They sound utopian in today's world with nations at war and the two superpowers snarling at each other. However, in 1987 they moved toward a medium-range nuclear arms agreement, and they were cooperating in the United Nations to try to bring an end to the Iran-Iraq war. Following are long-term proposals for ending war.

1. Public Opinion. Ultimately if humans are to prevent war, they must promote a climate of world opinion for peace. Those who support international law and diplomacy for settling disputes, therefore, should speak out. It takes more than words, however. World War II demonstrated the dangers of letting Hitler take advantage of pacifism and weakness. Nevertheless, thousands of years of history have shown that reliance on force and power politics cannot bring about peace. Is there another road? The U.N. experience described above shows that there is a climate of world opinion in U.N. forums that registers opposition to aggression. This suggests that a powerful nation like the United States could take the lead there in promoting wider observance of international law on issues of war and peace. However, power politics is the standard language for U.S. foreign policy today. Among presidential candidates in 1987 only Jesse Jackson and Michael Dukakis spoke out clearly for international law as a standard for foreign policy. Congress was persuaded to give support to the Contras to put pressure on Nicaragua. Politicians garnered support by a tough posture indicating they were ready to play "hard ball" against the threat of Communism. This contrasts with the situation after World War II when presidents spoke out for the United Nations and turned issues over to the Security Council and General Assembly to get international support to settle disputes. Now their language is that of power with words like deterrence, strength, demonstration of will, and bargaining chips, while words like compromise and cooperation are avoided. However, despite hard-line rhetoric, in 1987 there was negotiation of a medium-range nuclear arms agreement and use of the United Nations to try to end the Iran-Iraq war.

2. Education. Closely related to the above is the role of education as a foundation of peace. We have seen how national leaders are often corrupted by the power of their position, and tend to overreact to imagined threats. Their actions reflect their educational background and public pressures. Education of future leaders is a long-range process of encouraging peaceful responses to crises. Teachers should not be Pollyannas, and they should teach about the dangers of the real world. On the other hand, cynicism about international issues and cynicism about the potential of international law and the United Nations are likely to be self-perpetuating. There is a surprising amount of peaceful education in other nations, including Communist states like China and Yugoslavia. The ultimate responsibility for war and peace may rest on the shoulders of teachers and reporters who interpret events and influence future leaders and voters of our societies.

figure 3
The U.S. Defense Budget Compared to the Total Budgets of the United Nations and of Specialized Agencies (U.N. System)

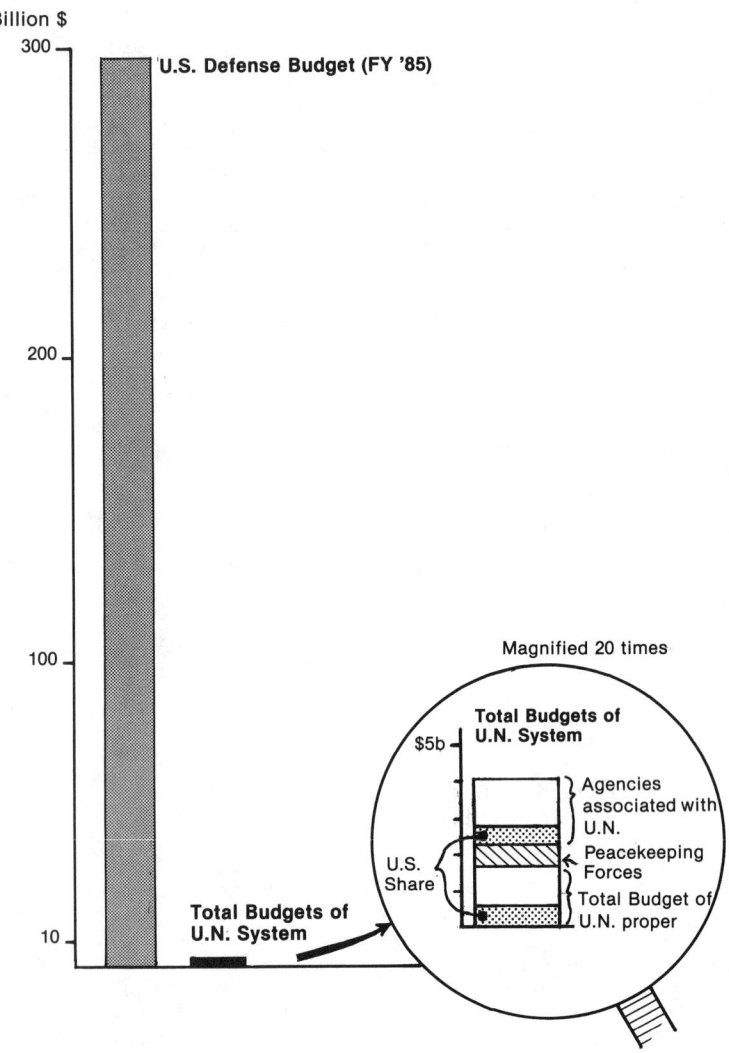

1. The budgets of the specialized agencies associated with the UN in the U.N. System include the Food and Agricultural Organization, the International Maritime Organization, the International Atomic Energy Organization, the International Civil Aviation Organization, the International Telecommunication Union, the Universal Postal Union, the World Health Organization, the World Intellectual Property Organization, and the World Meteorological Organization.

The financial transactions of the World Bank and the International Monetary Fund are not included.

3. Support for U.N. procedures. Actions are more important than words. The U.S. has a powerful position in the U.N., and U.S. leaders could profitably put more emphasis on U.N. diplomacy. The U.S. could also refrain from bitter attacks on the U.N. when U.N. voting on rhetorical resolutions goes against the United States and its friends. Congressmen do not attack the institution of Congress when they are defeated on votes.

The United States could also stop quibbling over financial support to the U.N. There is no harm in supporting economy and efficiency, but in recent years the U.S. has been one of the few countries to vote against the U.N. budget and to attack it as extravagant. Figure 3 compares expenditures under the U.S. Defense budget with total contributions of the United States and all countries for the U.N. system. The U.S. share of the total regular U.N. budget is so small it must be magnified in order to see it at the bottom of the chart. The total budgets of the entire U.N. System, including those of the Specialized Agencies, are about $4 billion. The U.S. share is about 25 percent. The U.S. could increase its economic and political support of these institutions for peace at only a miscroscopic fraction of the cost of U.S. defense spending for weapons of war.

4. Minimal use of power politics. The other side of the coin is to refrain from using power politics to settle disputes except within the framework of international law and the United Nations. U.S. support for U.N. peacekeeping and observer forces in the Middle East is an example of how legal use of power can reinforce U.N. policies in settling crises.

5. Constructive news coverage. The news media tend to concentrate on the crises and drama of international politics and overlook the good news of less dramatic moves toward peace. This is natural since the news media want excitement for their customers. Government control of the media is unacceptable in democratic societies, but world leaders could help correct the media's neglect of the U.N. and media bias toward bad news by more efforts to give credit to cooperative efforts among nations. The media are sensitive and sometimes responsive to criticism, and pressure by academic and other critics could encourage the media to give more attention to constructive developments of peace.

The history of major wars of this century shows that power politics and alliances have not prevented war. The U.N. on the other hand, has been helpful in settling many international disputes, in containing conflicts, and in mobilizing world opinion to deter potential aggressors.

Some of the wars we have studied have indicated, moreover, that nations can use their power effectively within the limits of international law to contain wars. Their leaders have also made agreements to contain power within an international law framework, as in the case of the nuclear arms limitation treaties. On the other hand, there have been some catastrophic failures of aggressive power politics. "Victories" of aggressors such as in Vietnam are extremely costly to them in lives and resources. Unfortunately, reckless power politics and confrontations are still part of today's world, even though such policies could escalate to a nuclear catastrophe. The logical way to work for peace is for leaders to strengthen peacemaking under the United Nations and international law to try to contain sparks of conflicts before they break out in flames.

NOTES

[1] Address at the Pacem in Terris Conference, October 8, 1973, Sheraton Park Hotel, Washington, D.C.

[2] Kissinger, op. cit., p. 867.

[3] See page II-28.

[4] Ray Stannard Baker, Woodrow Wilson: Life and Letters (New York: 1937), p. 126.

[5] Washington Post, June 26, 1982. p. 1.

[6] US Department of State, The SALT Process (Pub. 8947, June, 1978), p. 1.

[7] Stoessinger, op. cit., p. 218.

INDEX

ABM (Anti-ballistic Missile Treaty)-227
Abraham-101
Abdullah-105
Acheson, Dean-74, 84, 90-92, 96, 99, 100
Adamthwarte, A.-85
Afghanistan-171-177, 167, 190, 196, 197-198, 201, 206, 224, 225
Aggressiveness-11, 12, 14
Alexander, King-30
Alliances-2, 23, 24, 49, 76-77, 99, 100, 209, 216
Albertini, Luigi-52
Alsace-Lorraine-2
Amer, General-112, 114, 115
Amin-174-176
Anti-Communism-80, 203, 211
Anti-Semitism-56, 81
ANZUS Treaty-213
Apis (See Dimitrijevic)
Arab-Israel Wars-101, 122, 196-198, 200, 204-207, 215, 221
Arab League-105, 118
Arafat-120
Archduke Ferdinand-27-34, 198, 200, 203,
Argentina-191-193
Arms Race-17, 18, 206
ASEAN (Association of Southeast Asian Nations)-215
Aswan Dam-106
Atlee-97, 98
Attitudes-9, 18
Australia-104, 214, 221
Austria-63, 64, 65, 68, 81, 91, 168
Austria-Hungary-27-34, 46-48, 80, 199, 210
Authoritarian Governments-13, 51, 79, 82, 197, 198, 201, 204, 206
Awami League-150
Azzam Pasha-105
Bagdad Pact-106
Bahrain-188
Baker, Ray-217, 232
Balance of Power-9, 22, 50
Balfour Declaration-101

Balkans-2, 28
Ball, George-135, 166
Bangledesh-152
Bani-Sadr-189
Bao Dai-125, 130
Bay of Bengal-148, 152,
Baynes-84
Bay of Pigs-116, 159
Beer, Francis-10, 14, 15, 18, 24, 25, 52, 53
Beer Hall Putsch-57
Begin, Menachim-102, 119, 120
Belgium-38, 39, 42
Benes-67, 170
Bengalis-148, 150, 151, 153, 196
Ben Gurion-105, 106
Berchtold, Leopold von-33, 34, 47
Berlin Blockade-212
Bernadotte-104, 105
Bernstorff-43-46
Bethmann-Hollweg-38, 42, 44,
Betts, R.-146
Black Hand-29-34
Black September-118
Blainey, Geoffrey-11, 24, 205
Blank Check-34, 210
Blockade-42
Blomberg-65
Bolby-12
Borah, William-72
Bosnia-Herzegovina-27-33
Brezhnev-100, 171
Brides-179
Britain-See United Kingdom
Brodie, Bernard-25
Bruning-61
Buddhists-133
Bulgaria-170
Bunche, Ralph-106
Bundy, McGeorge-135, 138, 166
Burtness-84
Butterworth, L-194
Butterworth, Robert-10

Cambodia-131, 140, 181-185,
  196-198, 201, 206, 207, 225
Camp David-222, 224
Canada-59, 104, 108, 221
Capitalism-17, 18, 20
Carter, Jimmy-119, 177, 223
Castro, Fidel-158-166
Castro, Raul-162
Catholic Center-61, 79
Cecil, Lord Robert-16
CENTO Alliance-107
Central America-204, 208
Central Intelligence Agency-
  see CIA
Chamberlain, Neville-58, 67-70
Chiang Kai-shek-73-76, 94, 95,
  98, 99
China-57, 71-73, 79, 151, 183-
  185, 198-199, 201, 212, 221,
  229
China (Taiwan)-See Taiwan
China, People's Republic of-
  23, 92-98, 99, 106, 116, 125,
  143, 154, 171, 181-185, 204
  214-216, 219, 224
Chou En-lai-95-96, 177, 208
Churchill, Winston-37, 61, 65,
  67, 68, 70, 84, 209
CIA (Central Intelligence Agency)
  158, 159
Ciganovic-30
Cold War-212, 219
Collective Security-99
Collins, Larry-122
Colonialism-87, 125, 130, 134
Comintern-125
Commission of Responsibility of
  the Authours of the War-46
Communism and Communists-1, 5,
  17, 19-21, 56, 58, 61, 62, 69
  79, 81, 92, 99, 123-146, 132,
  134, 157-166, 167-179, 181-185
  19, 195, 196-198, 201-203, 206
  208, 212, 214, 229
Concert of Europe-216
Congress of Berlin-27-29
Cooper-Church Amendment-140
Crankshaw, E.-179
Cuba and the Cuban Missile
  Crisis-157-166, 175, 193-
  198, 224
Cyprus-185-186, 198, 201

Czar of Russia-35-42, 47,
  49, 197
Czechoslavakia-58, 63, 65,
  67, 68, 81, 91, 104, 169-
  171, 176-177, 196, 198,
  210, 212
Darwin-15
Daud-171-172
Davison, W.P.-146
Dawes Plan-60
Dawisha-14, 194
Dayan, Moshe-107, 113, 114
  117, 122
Democracy-5, 19-21, 51, 82,
  83, 197, 198, 203, 204
Denmark-46
Depression-50, 60, 63
Dicatatorship-See Authori-
  tarian
Diem, Ngo Dinh-124, 125,
  128, 133, 134, 143, 203
Dien Bien Phu-123, 125,
  130, 131
Dimetrijevic-29-34
Disease-13
Divale, W. T.-25
Dobrynin-163, 164
Dollfuss, Chancellor-64
Domino Theory-131, 132
Donnell, John-146
Dubcek-170, 171
Dulles, John Foster-92,
  106, 108, 131, 144
Durbin-12, 24
Dutch East Indies-74
East Germany-170, 176, 177
Eastern Europe-20, 23, 167-
  179
East Pakistan-147-156
Economic Factors-17, 50,
  116
Eden, Anthony-107, 108, 109
Education-224
Egypt-102, 105-121, 168,
  198-204, 207, 215, 222,
  224
Eibl and Eibelsfeldt-24
Eisenhower, Dwight D.-17,
  25, 108-110, 130, 132,
  146, 158-159, 209
Estonia-69

Ethiopia-60, 63, 70-71, 91, 199, 204
Executive Committee (EXCOM)-159-162, 165
Falk, Richard A.-24
Falklands War-2, 191-193, 197-198, 201, 207
Fall, Bernard-145
Farouk-105
Fascism-1, 5, 19-21, 72, 79, 81, 196-199, 206, 208
Ferdinand-See Archduke Ferdinand
Fields, S.-24
Finland-69
Fish Hook Area-140
Ford, Gerald-142, 145
Formosa-See Taiwan
Fourteen Points-51
France-33-35, 38, 40-42, 48-49, 57, 61, 64, 65, 67-71, 106-110, 119-120, 124-125, 130-131, 143, 169, 190, 198, 205, 210-212, 215, 219, 222, 223
Franz Joseph-29-34, 47, 49, 52, 197
Freeman, W.H.-10
Freud, Sigmund-12, 24
Galilee-115
Galtieri-192, 209
Gandhi, Indira-150-152, 154, 212
Gandhi, Mahatma-147
Gaza-106, 118, 120, 205, 222
Gelb, L.-146
Genesis-101
Geneva Agreement-123, 125, 128-130, 184
Geneva Conference on Indo-China-125
George, Lloyd-51
German Workers Party-56
Germany-2, 32, 33-42, 42-46, 55-70, 74-83, 87, 99, 102, 169, 196-198, 205, 207, 210
Giancana-158
Giap, Vo Nguyen-127, 145
Gillispie, John V.-10
Gilpatrick-166
Glubb, Pasha-107, 122
Goering, Hermann-62
Golan Heights-118, 120, 205

Goldwater-137
Gomulka-168
Gravel, M-135, 145, 146
Greater East Asia Co-Proserity Sphere-72, 73, 75, 77, 80, 199
Greed-17, 50 177
Grenada-193-195, 198, 201, 203-205
Grew, Joseph-75
Grey, Sir Edward-37, 38, 41, 47, 48, 209, 217
Griffith-179
Guatemala-104, 158, 221
Guevara, Che-162
Gulf of Tonkin-135-136
Habib, Philip-119, 223
Haganah-105
Haig-209
Hague Convention of 1907-46
Haj Amin Husseini-102, 104, 105
Halberstam, David-146
Herring, George C.-146
Herzl-101
Hindenburg, von-44, 61, 62, 78-79
Hindu-147, 196
Hindustan Times-156
Hirohito-77-79
Hiroshima-87
Hitler, Adolf-2, 15, 50-52, 55-70, 76-83, 92, 101, 102, 196-198, 203, 205, 211
Hoare, Samuel-71
Ho Chi Minh-123-146
Holocaust-101
Holsti, O.R.-52
Hooker, T.-122
Hoopes-122
Hoover, Herbert-61
Hotzendorf, Conrad-33, 38, 47
House, Colonel-16, 43-46, 48, 217, 228
Hull, Cordell-73-76, 78, 84
Human Nature-11
Hungary-52, 108-110, 167-169, 170, 177, 196,198, 200, 215
Hussain-102
Hussein, King-113
Hussein, Saddam-188-189, 190

235

IAEA-See International Atomic Energy Authority
ICBM (Intercontinental Ballistic Missile)-226-227
Ideologies-9, 18, 20, 81, 195-208
Imperialism-2, 22, 72, 127, 130, 133, 134, 144, 176, 177, 185, 207
Inchon-97
India-59, 147-156, 200, 203, 215, 224
Indian Institute for Defense Studies-150
India-Pakistan War-147-156, 196, 198, 200, 203, 205-207, 215, 216, 224
Indochina (See also Vietnam)-74-76, 123-124
International Atomic Energy Authority-190
International Bank-82, 110
International Commission of Control-141
International Law-16, 42-46, 59, 80, 81, 108, 130, 131, 154, 160, 177, 192, 197, 209, 220-232
International Monetary Fund-82
Internationalism-21-22
Iran-91, 121, 175, 177, 186-191, 198, 201, 207, 215, 221, 223, 225
Iran-Iraq War-121, 186-191, 197, 201, 206, 215
Iraq-104, 105, 111, 113, 118, 121, 186-191, 198, 201, 207, 215, 225
Irgun-102
Islam (See Moslem)
Islamic Summit-190, 225
Ismail Pasha-105
Israel-5, 91, 101-102, 189, 190, 200, 203-207, 215, 222-224
Italy-37, 49, 57, 64, 70-71, 190, 196, 197, 210, 211, 228
Jackson, Jesse-229
Janis, Irving-16, 25
Janushkevich-37, 40
Japan-60, 71-76, 92, 94, 99, 134, 197, 199, 204, 205, 207, 211, 213, 214, 215, 217

Jaruzelski-177
Jerusalem-104, 105, 114, 222
Jews (See also Israel and Anti-Semitism)-56, 60, 61, 101-122, 200, 221
Johnson, Lyndon B.-18, 114, 124, 131, 134, 136, 137, 138, 143, 145, 146, 204
Joint Chiefs of Staff-159, 161, 164
Jordan-104-107, 111, 113, 114, 117, 121, 190
Jordan River-114
Kadar, Janos-168-169
Kaiser Wilhelm-2, 33-42, 49, 197
Kampuchea (See Cambodia)
Kapp, Wolfgang-56
Karmal, B.-171-176
Karnow-146
Kashmir-147, 152
Kennedy, John-131, 134, 144, 145, 157-166, 224
Kennedy, Robert-159, 162, 163, 164, 166
Keynes, John Maynard-17
Khaled, King-121
Khalizad-179
Khalq-171-176
Khmer Rouge-182-183
Khomeni, Ayatollah-188, 189, 194
Khrushchev, Nikita-88-90, 100, 132, 159-166, 168-169, 179
Kim Il-sumg-88-100
Kim, Samuel-24
Kindelberger, C.P.-84
Kissinger, Henry-117, 122, 140, 141, 145, 146, 150, 151, 153, 154, 156, 216, 223, 232
Konoye-75, 84
Korea-77, 212, 215
Korea (North)-87-100, 197, 198, 200, 206, 212, 215
Korea, Republic of (South)-87-100, 176, 197-198, 200, 204, 212, 213, 215, 219
Korean War-87-100, 196-198, 200, 204, 206, 219, 220
Kurds-188-189
Kuwait-189

Lansing-44
Laos-131, 214
Lapierre, D.-122
Latin America-21
Latvia-69
Laval-71
League of Nations-48, 50, 63,
  67, 70, 72-73, 77, 91, 104,
  216
Lebanon-106, 111, 118, 119, 198,
  200, 203, 204, 207, 224
Lebensraum-57, 59, 69
Le Duc Tho-140
LeMay, Curtis-157, 161
Lend-Lease Act-73, 82
Lenin-127, 133
Libya-120
Lithuania-69
Litvinov-69
Lon Nol-181-182
Lorenz, Konrad-15
Lovett-98
Ludendorff-44
Lusitania-43
Luxembourg-42
Lytton, Lord-72
MacArthur, General Douglas-90,
  92, 94, 95
MacMillan-157
Maddox-136
Maechling, C-194
Makarios-185
Manchuria-60, 71-73, 77, 79, 88,
  91, 99, 208, 217
Mao Tse-Tung (Zedong)-90, 99,
  132, 133
Marshall Plan-82
Martin, Graham-142, 143
Marx-133
Marxism-Lennism (See Communism)
  Masaryk-170
McCarthy, E-138
McDougall-194
McGowan-10
McMahan Correspondence-102
McNamara, Robert-135, 157, 165,
  166
Mein Kampf-56, 57, 63
Mexico-175
Middle East-18
Military-41-42, 49, 75-78, 83,
  165, 194, 207, 231

Military-Industrial Complex
  15, 17
Mobilization-35-36, 40, 48,
  81, 208
Mollet, Guy-106
Molotov-69
Moltke-38, 40, 41
Monnet, Jean-82
Monroe Doctrine-21
Morality-7-8, 50
Morgenthau, Hans-9, 10, 48,
  50, 53, 207
Moslems-31, 102, 118, 119,
  147, 148, 196, 223
Mubarik, Hosni-121
Mujibur, Sheikh-150, 151,
  153
Musik-170
Munich-67, 68, 169
Muslim (See Moslem)
Muslim Brotherhood-173
Mussolini-60, 63, 71, 92
Nagy-108, 169-170
Naroll, R.-25
Nasser, Gamal Abdel-106, 108,
  109, 110, 112-115, 116, 189,
  200, 207
National Council (Vietnam)-141
National Security Council
  (NSC)-123
Nationalism-9, 14-15, 19, 21,
  27-33, 50, 77, 79, 80, 119,
  144, 176, 184, 191-192, 193,
  206, 208
NATO (North Atlantic Treaty
  Organization)-83, 99, 100,
  160, 169, 185, 209, 211,
  212, 213,
Nazis-55-70
Nazi-Soviet Pact-69
Negarin-179
Netherlands-104
Neutral Rights-44-46
Neutrality Acts-55
New Hampshire-140
New Zealand-214
News Media-231
Nicholas (See Czar Nicholas)
Niebuhr, Reinhold-14, 24, 195
Nixon, Richard-117, 140, 141,
  144, 151, 152, 209
Nomura K.-73-74

North Vietnam (See Vietnam, North)
Norway-46
NPT (Nuclear Non-Proliferation Treaty)-227
NSC (See National Security Council)
Nuclear Non-Proliferation Treaty (See NPT)
Nuclear Weapons-18, 91, 97-98, 117, 157-166, 190, 207
Nuri-Said-105
Nye Committee-50
Ober, W.-84
Oil-18, 74-75, 109, 118, 120, 167, 175, 188, 189, 190, 215
Olympics-16, 176, 177
Organization of American States (OAS)-160-161, 224
Ottoman Empire-102, 186
Outer Space Treaty-227
Pact of Paris-70
Pakistan-147-156, 177, 198, 200, 206, 207, 214-216, 224
Palestine-102, 104, 118, 155, 189, 200, 221, 223
Palestine Liberation Organization (PLO)-118-120, 200, 204, 223
Panikkar-95
Papin, von-61, 62, 79
Partial Test Ban Treaty-227
Pasic-30-47
Pearl Harbor-16, 71, 73-76, 84, 199, 205, 207, 211, 214
Pentagon (See U.S. Defense Department)
Pentagon Papers-135, 146
People's Liberation Army-112, 143
Percham-171-176
Peres, Shimon-106
Persian Gulf-186, 215
Peru-104
Philippines-94, 134, 213, 214
Phuoc Long Province-143, 145
Pleiku-138
PLO (See Palestine Liberation Organization)
Poincare-34, 37

Pol Pot-181-185
Poland-16, 59, 63, 67, 68, 69, 152, 168-169, 176, 177
Poole, Peter-146
Porter, G-194
Pourtales-42
Power Politics (See also Realpolitik)-22, 50, 196, 201, 206, 209
Prange, G.-84
Princip-30-34
Propaganda-50, 80
Pusan-95
Pusanov-174
Quarantine-160, 164
Race and Racism-72, 79, 81
RAND Corporation-128
Rann of Kutch-148
Rauschnig, H.-86
Reagan, Ronald-192-193, 204
Realpolitik-184-185, 193
Reichstag-60-63
Religion-12, 19, 119, 196, 198, 206
Remak, Joachim-52
Reparations-63
Rhee, Syngman-88-90
Rhineland-63, 64, 68
Richardson, Louis P.-13
Ridgeway-96
Roosevelt, Franklin D.-18, 58, 68, 73-76, 82, 209
Rostow, W. W.-132, 133, 135, 146
Rothschild-101
Row-10
Ruhr-56,57
Rumania-67, 170
Rusk-135, 166
Russia (See Soviet Union)
Russo-German Alliance-211
Ryukyus-94
Sadat, Anwar-112, 113, 115-118, 119, 122, 189, 200, 205, 207
SALT (Strategic Arms Limitation Talks)-176, 226-227, 232
Samrin, Heng-182
Sarajevo-2, 27-34
Saudi Arabia-111, 120, 188, 190

Sazonov-34-42
Scandinavia-12
Schleicher, von-61, 79
Schlieffen Plan-41
Schuman Plan-82
Schuschnigg-65
Seabed Treaty-227
SEATO-99, 131, 132, 137
Selassie, Haili-70
Self-Determination-58,59, 176
Serbia-27-34, 46-47, 80
Seymour, Charles-25,53
Shah of Iran-188
Sharm-el Sheikh-106, 109, 114
Shatt-al Arab-186
Sheeham, E.-122
Shiite Moslems-188
Shiner, W.-84
Siegried Line-67
Simon, S-194
Sinai-109, 115, 117, 120, 205
Singer, J. David-10, 12, 24
Sivard, Ruth Leger
SLBM (Sea-Launched Ballistic Missile)
Small, Melvin-10, 12, 24
Social Democrats-61, 79
Socialism and Socialists-17, 60, 62, 125
Solidarity-16, 177
Sophie-30-34
Sorenson, T.-166
South Vietnam (See Vietnam)
Soviet Union-16, 23, 29, 30, 33, 34-42, 49, 57, 58, 59, 67, 69, 71, 73-74, 88, 96, 97, 98, 106, 107, 109, 110, 113, 116, 117, 125, 127, 148, 150, 154, 157-166, 167-179, 183-185, 190, 192, 196-198, 200, 201, 206-208, 210-212, 216, 217, 219-221, 224, 227
Spencer-15
Stalin, Joseph-68, 88-90, 99
Standing Consultative Commission-227
State Department-18, 91, 154, 160, 179, 232
Statistical Analysis-2, 23
Stevenson, Adlai-160
Stimson, Henry-72

Stoessinger, John-14, 24, 156, 228, 232
Strasser, Otto-58
Strategies-9, 22
Submarine Warfare-9, 43-46
Suez Canal-105, 106-110, 114, 117, 120, 215, 222
Suez War-106, 110, 168, 200
Sunni Moslems-188
Svoboda-170-171
Sweden-46, 96, 104, 221
Sweet, W. H.-24
Switzerland-12
Syria-105, 111, 114, 115, 117, 119, 120-121, 223
Taiwan-77, 93, 97, 98, 99, 134, 213, 214
Tankosic-30
Taraki-171
Tautologies-11, 15, 228
Taylor, A. J. P.-84
Taylor, M.-132, 135, 138
Technology-5
Territoriality-15
Terrorism-9, 27-33, 50, 208
Thailand-181, 214, 215
Thatcher, M.-192-193
Thiessen, D. D.-24
Thieu-141
Tiran, Straits of-106, 109, 110, 112, 114
Tisza-34, 37, 38
Tojo-75, 78, 79, 81
Toland,-84
Tonkin Gulf-136-137
Torah-102
Totalitarianism-13, 51, 79, 197, 198, 201, 204, 208
Toul-40, 42
Toyoda-75
Trans-Jordan (See Jordan)
Treaty to Prevent Emplacement of Nuclear Weapons on the Seabed-227
Tripartite Pact-76
Triple Alliance-33, 210
Truman, Harry S-18, 51, 90-92, 96, 98, 100, 130, 144, 209, 217, 228
Tuchman, Barbara-52
Turkey-27, 160, 161, 164

U-2 Affair
U.N. Disengagement Force
  (UNDOF)-223
U.N. Emergency Force (UNEF)-222
U.N. Forces in Cyprus
  (UNFICYP)-185
U.N. High Commissioner for
  Refugees-186
UNIFIL (United Nations Forces in
  Lebanon)-116-119
United Kingdom-2, 33, 38, 39,
  41, 42-46, 48, 55, 57, 58, 59,
  61, 64, 65, 68, 69, 70-71, 73,
  81, 83, 95, 101, 102, 104,
  105-108, 110, 119, 120, 125,
  131, 147-148, 169, 185,
  191-193, 198, 200, 211, 214,
  215, 219, 221-223
United Nations-6, 16, 23, 24,
  51, 82, 87-100, 104-119, 137,
  148, 150, 151, 152, 153, 154,
  155, 160, 169, 170, 175, 177,
  179, 185-186, 188, 189,
  191-193, 203, 204, 205-208,
  214, 220, 223, 224, 227, 229,
  231
United States-9, 23, 32, 42-46,
  55, 57-59, 71-83, 87-100, 206,
  223, 123-146, 151, 154,
  157-166, 181, 190, 192-193,
  203, 204, 205, 208, 219, 220,
  223, 224, 227, 229, 231
Uruguay-104
U.S. Congress-43, 46, 55, 61,
  74, 90, 91, 131, 136-137, 140,
  141, 142, 144, 158, 160, 176,
  193, 204, 217
U.S. Defense Department-91, 133,
  138
U.S. Department of State (See
  State Department)

U-Thant-113, 151, 221
Verdun-40, 42
Versailles Treaty-46, 51-52, 58,
  59, 60, 63, 64
Viet Cong-123, 146
Vietnam and Vietnam War-20,
  114, 123-146, 181-185, 186,
  200, 201, 203-208, 214, 215,
  221
Vinh-136
Volkischer Beobachter-56
Waldheim, Kurt-150, 221
War Powers Resolution-141
War Profiteers (See Greed)
Wars (See Individual Wars)-5,6
Warsaw Pact-170, 176, 211, 215
Welles, S.-74
West Bank-114, 115, 118, 120,
  204, 205, 222
West Pakistan-147-156, 196
Wilson, Woodrow-9, 16, 18,
  42-46, 91, 217, 228, 232
World Policeman -22, 23, 185
World War I-27-53, 5, 6, 7,
  16, 18, 55, 102, 196, 198,
  203, 204, 206, 207, 208, 210
World War II-55-85, 5, 6, 9,
  92, 196, 198, 199, 204, 206,
  207, 208 ,210, 217
Wright, Quincy-15, 25
Yahya Khan-148, 150, 151, 153
Yemen-121
Yom Kippur-117
Young Plan-60
Yugoslavia-29, 208, 221, 229
Zasloff-146
Zimmerman, and Zimmerman
  Telegram-44, 46, 52
Zinnes, Dana-10
Zionists-101

ABOUT THE AUTHOR

Amos Yoder has been Borah Distinguished Professor of Political Science at the University of Idaho since 1974, teaching courses on international relations. Before then he was in the diplomatic service of the United States for 25 years. He was assigned to U.N. affairs, Chinese affairs, and German affairs in Washington, D.C. He served abroad in the U.S. embassies in Thailand and Israel, and he was a delegate to international conferences. He also taught a year at the University of California, Davis, and part-time at George Washington University. He has published a text, INTERNATIONAL POLITICS AND POLICYMAKERS' IDEAS and articles on the Far East, the Sino-Soviet dispute, the news media, U.N. issues, the Ruhr Authority, and Soviet economic growth. His book entitled THE CONDUCT OF AMERICAN FOREIGN POLICY SINCE WORLD WAR II will be published at the end of 1985 by Pergamon Press.

He has a Ph.D. in International Relations from the University of Chicago (1949) and a B.A. from Ohio Wesleyan University. He served in the U.S. Army Air Corps and the U.S. Strategic Bombing Survey in World War II. He was born in Falls City, Nebraska. He married Janet Tatman of Cleveland, Ohio, and they have three children, who are now married.